Little Girl Lost

Johnnie Wise: In The Line OF Fire

D1225458

KEITH LEE JOHNSON

**DARE TO
IMAGINE**
PUBLISHING

Little Girl Lost:
Johnnie Wise: In The Line Of Fire

Keith Lee Johnson

Dare to Imagine Publishing
PO Box 935
Maumee, OH 43537

ISBN 13: 978-1-935825-01-2

Library of Congress Control Number: 2010938106

First Printing: October 2010

Printed in the United States of America

10 9 8 7 6 5 4 3 2 1

This is a work of fiction. Any references or similarities to actual events, real people, living, or dead, or to real locals are intended to give the novel a sense of reality. Any similarity in other names, characters, places, and incidents is entirely coincidental

Acknowledgements

Big, big thank you to Elodie Tavares, press manager, and Hanna Gliksman, communications assistant of Hôtel de Crillon in Paris, who graciously helped with much of the research I did on the hotel, the shopping area, museums, and thanks so much for your time and effort to help make my description accurate. Nevertheless, I embellish a bit to my liking.

Special thanks to my man, Phillip Thomas Duck, who took time from his own novels to edit mine.

Big thank you goes out to my girl, Miri Maxon for her editing expertise and further cleaning up the manuscript.

Special thanks to my good friend, Alisha Yvonne, who edited The Return of Johnnie Wise.

Special thanks to my good friend, Kendra Norman Bellamy, who also took time from her writing schedule to help too.

Special thanks to Fletcher Word, my man in Toledo, Ohio, who supported me from the beginning and has never wavered.

Special thanks to the fans of the Little Girl Lost series. You make it happen. And by the way, Little Girl Lost was the original title before Urban Books bought the rights to publish it. Now that I'm publishing the series, I've changed the title back to my original vision. I hope you all don't mind. To enhance your reading pleasure, I've added the faces of the characters on my facebook profile page! Check them out and see if you agree or disagree with my choices!

KLJ

Chapter 1

Nervous

Johnnie Wise knew she had made a lot of mistakes in her young life, but letting Earl Shamus into her room a little more than an hour ago was the absolute worst decision so far, she thought, as she nervously paced the living room floor of her hotel room. She tried to force the reoccurring images of Earl grasping for his heart while gasping for air from entering her mind, but she couldn't stop thinking about what had happened earlier that night. Her anxiety was such that she found herself constantly looking at the clock, trying to calculate how far Paul Masterson was from the outskirts of New Orleans. She hoped God had answered her prayer when she asked Him to give Paul peace in the face of impending danger. But still, she couldn't help wondering if he would have the necessary poise he would need if he got pulled over by the Highway Patrol.

In the hour that she had been in Gloria's office, she kept seeing images of being handcuffed by the police, fingerprinted, tried, and then hauled off to prison. She had put on the acting performance of her life, pretending to barter with Gloria for a reduction in price of her stock broker services if she typed up four copies of the portfolio she would dictate. Johnnie's performance was so convincing that Gloria thought she was the best negotiator in Jackson because she was able to get Johnnie to take her on as a client for six hundred and fifty dollars instead of her previously nonnegotiable eleven hundred dollar fee.

Gloria didn't take into account that she had to give Johnnie free room and board for the duration because she had been burned out of her home and even though she hadn't told Johnnie before the negotiations began, she wasn't going to charge anything; not one dollar. She was planning to surprise her. Free room and board was going to be a parting farewell gift. With the bartering out of the way, they had another slice of sweet potato pie and coffee at her kitchen table and discussed what stocks Johnnie was investing in. A half an hour later, Gloria, quite the typist, gave Johnnie three copies of the investment portfolio; a copy for Johnnie, and a copy each for Hank and Lucille.

As far as Johnnie could tell, Gloria had no idea that she was being kept away from the front desk so as not to see Paul carrying Earl's body to his Cadillac. Nevertheless, she continued pacing the floor, worried sick that Paul would somehow get caught. And if that happened, he would probably have to tell on her to keep himself out of jail. She liked Paul, but she didn't know him that well and her faith in God waned more with each passing minute. Although Paul seemed like a stand up kind of guy, she knew that pressure was the real barometer for character. She continued pacing the floor, telling herself how stupid she'd been for letting Earl in, wishing she could do it all over again, knowing she couldn't, which added to her growing frustration.

The conversation she had with Earl surfaced again. Earl told her that Tony Hatcher had been following her since she left Ashland Estates. That's when a frightening thought entered her mind. It was highly possible that Tony Hatcher had been in her room. And if he had, he probably planted more recording devices. Assuming that was the case, she realized that everything that happened that night had been recorded. Her only saving grace was the fact that Hatcher and his fellow detectives were currently in Houston, checking into Paul Masterson's background. As her fear mushroomed and threatened to devour her, she frantically searched both rooms, and found five recording devices.

Her heart started pounding when she found the first one under the sink in the kitchenette. Her anxiety went into overdrive when she found the second device under the dining table and a third in the crevice of the sofa. Driven by immeasurable fear, she then went into the bedroom and found another device under the bed and a fifth under the sink in the bathroom. She set all five devices on the dining table and stared at them for over an hour before she found the courage to listen. Most of what she heard was innocuous, but when she heard the entire conversation she'd had with Earl, her heart nearly went into cardiac arrest. The best thing about the recording was that it exonerated her of any future charges of Earl's murder. It proved that Earl had followed her to Jackson, had illegally bugged her dwelling a second time, and had blackmailed her into having sex with him and becoming his permanent lover.

She now knew that she didn't have to get rid of the body. She could have simply called the police and let them hear what happened in that hotel room. The recording in the bedroom proved that she had tried to revive him for twenty minutes, shaking him and screaming his name. All of that would lend weight to her innocence. But the recording of her talking to God would make her look like a crazy person. Only her voice was recorded. She realized that if the police heard that, she would look like she was losing her mind.

Then she heard a knock at the door and the conversation she'd had with Paul and she knew that recording would seal both their dooms. The police would know that they plotted to get rid of Earl's body, and marry to conceal their crime. Johnnie wished there was some way to call Paul to tell him to bring the body back, but there wasn't. The die had been cast and now she had to play it all out just as they had planned, otherwise, she was looking at doing some serious time behind bars. She was fully persuaded that her sentence would be much harsher because of what had been said about her in the newspapers.

She believed the judicial system would give her the maximum sentence because they couldn't get her on other crimes they thought she committed but were unable to prove. And hearing about the abortion would only add to their "righteous" indignation. The way she saw it, a jury of her "peers" would pay little attention to the fact that Earl had gotten involved with her when she was only fifteen. The thing that would bother that particular jury would be her knack for miraculously getting out of seemingly impossible predicaments with ease. And for that reason, she would be executed for killing her unborn child—at least that's what she feared.

She toyed with the idea of keeping the tapes that exonerated her, thinking that at least people would know that she never killed a soul, but the idea of the tapes somehow falling into vengeful, hate-filled hands, helped decide what would become of them. She hit the rewind button on all five devices and recorded over the incriminating conversations and the sexual interlude with the sound of radio and television and silence. In the coming weeks, she would pretend to call her father and confirm that she was going to East St. Louis. That way, when Hatcher returned for his recordings, there wouldn't be anything leading him to suspect that she had anything to do with Earl's death.

She didn't realize it, but finding the recordings offered an amazing sense of calm because she knew that she was free of them. The only thing she had to worry about now was whether or not Paul Masterson was able to handle his end. The more she thought about it, the more comfortable she became with the idea that Paul was more than capable of handling himself. If the Highway Patrol pulled him over for speeding or a lane change violation, he would let them know he was an evangelist and the authorities would probably give him a pass. He probably wouldn't even get a ticket. She looked at her watch again. Two more hours had passed. Finally able to relax a little, she sat down on the couch and made a list of the things she had to do the following day so that it would appear that everything was as it should be. Then she drifted off to sleep.

Chapter 2

"Don't ever say that. Don't even think it."

The sound of a brass knocker colliding with a fixed plate woke Janet Shamus up from a sound sleep. It was the first night she'd slept completely through since her mother was killed while testifying in a court of law three days earlier. The shock of seeing her mother, dead on a slab with a bullet hole in her forehead was nearly impossible to shake. She heard the knocking again and looked at the clock. 6:30 am. She closed her eyes again, thinking that her father would answer the door as usual, but again, she heard the knocking and wondered why her father hadn't gone downstairs to see who had awakened them.

Normally she and her sisters would have been up by now, preparing to go to school. But they hadn't been to school since their mother was killed. Yawning, she got out of bed, put on her white flannel robe, and left her bedroom. She went down to her parent's room to see if her father was up too. She knocked on the door and listened. Hearing nothing, she opened the door. When she saw that he wasn't there and his bed hadn't been slept in, she left the door open and made her way down the staircase, wondering if her father had an emergency at work. At the front door, she looked through the peephole and saw the Sheriff. Frowning, she opened the door, wondering what was going on.

"Sorry to wake you so early, ma'am," the sheriff said. "My name is Paul Tate. Can I come in for a minute?"

"My father isn't home, Sheriff. We're not supposed to let anybody in when our parents aren't home. What can I do for you?"

"Well, ma'am, I don't think your parents meant the law, do you?"

Janet folded her arms, ready for a fight if he tried to come in without her permission. "I think they meant anybody, Sheriff. What's this all about?"

Sheriff Tate exhaled heavily and said, "I'm afraid I have bad news ma'am."

With that statement, Janet thought she knew why the sheriff was there. With her eyes filling with tears she said, "It's daddy, isn't it? It's my father, isn't it? Tell me he's not dead. Tell me he's alive."

Sheriff Tate just stood there looking at her as the realization of her father's death filled her mind. Tate had always hated having to tell a family member that their loved one was dead. He hated telling parents their child was dead, especially if the person he had to inform was the mother. The look of sheer horror generally covered their faces. Then they went straight to denial. And when it occurred to them that it was in fact their child, mothers often fainted. This was the first time the situation was reversed, where he had to tell a teenaged girl that the man she depended on was no longer among the living. What made this notification even worse was that a few days ago he had told Earl that Meredith had been killed. But at least the children were in school when he came to deliver the news. Over the years, he started letting the people he had to notify figure it out on their own. That way he wouldn't have to say the words and the survivors wouldn't have to hear them.

With tears streaming down her face, she looked Tate in the eyes and said, "What happened? How did he die?"

"It looks like he had a heart attack on the way home last night."

"A heart attack?"

"Yes, ma'am. I'm gonna need you to come with me and identify the body. I'll wait in the car while you dress."

Janet stood there watching as Sheriff Tate walked to his squad car. Then she gently closed the door and leaned her head against it as memories of her father flooded her mind. She sat on the couch for a few minutes and mourned her father's passing. She knew that this would be the only time she could. She quickly realized that she was now the head of the family and for that reason, she had to be strong. Ten minutes later, she made the long trek up the stairs, and went into Marjorie's room. She looked down at her, wondering how she was going to take the news. She knew she was going to be devastated because she was very close to their father, but she was even closer to their mother. She took a deep breath and shook her younger sister.

Marjorie opened her eyes. When she was able to focus, she immediately recognized that something was wrong. She could tell by the solemn look on Janet's face. "What's going on?"

"I have something to tell you and Stacy. But I only want to say it one time. Get up and come with me to Stacy's room."

"Can't you just give me a hint?"

Janet glared at her for a second, but didn't offer an answer. Then they went into Stacy's room. Janet shook Stacy's leg and then looked at Marjorie and said, "Sit down."

Nervously, Marjorie sat next to Stacy, who was now in a sitting position.

Looking back and forth at them, looking deeply into their eyes, she said, "Sheriff Tate is here."

"Why?" Stacy said. "What does he want?"

Janet took a deep breath again and said, "Daddy died of a heart attack last night. At first, silence filled the room as Marjorie and Stacy let what they'd heard sink in. A small groan from somewhere deep within came from Marjorie before she grabbed her stomach and doubled over as if she was about to vomit. For a few seconds, Stacy made no sound at all even though tears were running down her checks. Janet walked over to her sisters and held them as they mourned their father's passing. Marjorie and Stacy clung to Janet for strength as the pain they felt continued to mount and became loud wailing when it occurred to them that they had lost mother and father three days apart.

After about ten minutes, sixteen-year-old Marjorie wiped her eyes and said, "Is God punishing us for what we did to Little Buck?"

"No, Marjorie," Janet said. "Don't ever say that. Don't even think it. What happened to our brother was an accident. We didn't kill him. He fell out of the tree and broke his neck. We didn't make him fall."

"But Janet, you were the one who said we should take him up there," fourteen-year-old Stacy said. "You talked us into it. You wanted him to fall and hurt himself."

"We all did," Janet said. "It wasn't just me. We all hated that grandpa treated him better than he ever treated us."

"And that's why God is punishing us, Janet," Marjorie said.

A loud slap filled the air.

Marjorie gasped and her eyes bulged when she felt the sting of her older sister's anger. She held her vibrating jaw and stared into Janet's eyes, wondering what she was going to do next.

"I told you not to ever say that again," Janet said, putting her finger in Marjorie's face. "Our little brother fell. It was an accident." She paused for a beat, eyed them both to make sure her orders were going to be obeyed and said, "Get dressed. We have to go with the sheriff and identify daddy."

"I don't wanna see him," Stacy said, wiping her eyes. "Not like that."

"Me either," Marjorie said.

"Fine," Janet said. "I'll do it, but you two need to get dressed and get downstairs in twenty minutes."

Janet then took a five minute shower, brushed her teeth, brushed her shoulder length sandy brown mane, and went back into her parents' bedroom. Following her parents' instructions, she opened the drawer of the nightstand on her mother's side of the bed and grabbed Meredith's personal phonebook. She flipped through the pages and found Seymour Collins's name. There were several numbers listed, including his home in Miami, another in Aspen, and another in Malibu. She decided to call the New Orleans home first. His wife answered.

"Hi Mrs. Collins, this is Janet Shamus. I have an emergency and I need to speak with Mr. Collins right away."

A moment later Collins said, "Yes, Janet. What's going on? Is everything okay?"

"Mr. Collins, my father died of a heart attack on the way home last night. The Sheriff's here and he said we have to go to the morgue to identify his remains."

"I'll meet you there."

"Marjorie and Stacy don't want to go. Do they have to?"

"Have the Sheriff drop them off here. And you and I'll go, okay?"

"We'll be there in a few minutes, Mr. Collins."

An hour later, Janet and Seymour Collins were in the inadequately lit basement of the city morgue, standing over a presumably naked body covered by a white sheet.

Chapter 3

"We were supposed to have my mother's funeral tomorrow."

T he coroner had met with thousands of family members from nearly every parish in New Orleans and each time a family came to the morgue, he watched the faces of the people standing over a body. He often wondered if they were praying, earnestly hoping that the deceased was someone else's missing husband or wife or child. Without fail the families were always shaken when he lifted the sheet no matter who the person on the slab turned out to be. He didn't think the two people standing in his morgue would be any different than the rest. He knew there would be one of two reactions—weeping or relived rejoicing. The latter was a rarity. Over the years, he discovered that the police seldom brought in the wrong family and even when they did, they brought a specific family in because the person had been missing for weeks; sometimes for months or even years. Still watching them, anticipating their reaction, yet wondering if these two would be the exception, he pulled back the sheet.

A loud gasp found its way out of Janet's mouth when she recognized the corpse her father left behind when he entered the invisible world. Earl's face was twisted, like he died in extreme intolerable pain. Her grief was so overwhelming that even though her mouth was wide open, not a single sound exited her gapping orifice as her anguish was still seeking a vocal passage. Crying hard, but silently, she took a breath and then immediately buried her face in Collins's chest. That's when the sound of agony located her vocal chords and expressed itself without restraint. That's when the loss of love, the loss of being her father's favorite, expressed itself as the memories of yesterday flashed spontaneously before her eyes. While she wept, the memory of being pushed on a swing, learning to ride her first bike, and being behind the wheel of her father's Cadillac surfaced and remained in an unstoppable perpetual loop. She wept loudly as she held on to the lapels of Collins's suit, ruffling them, nearly ripping them away from the rest of the material to keep from fainting when her knees loss their strength and buckled.

Collins held Janet while simultaneously rubbing her back as her body shook violently, shushing her like she was a newborn in need of its mother's milk. He suspected that it wasn't Earl's death alone that had caused so much sorrow. With both sets of grandparents being dead, he thought he understood that Janet suddenly felt almost completely alone in the world. She had her sisters, sure, but they couldn't take care of her, nor could they comfort her because they, too, needed to be embraced as the knowledge of both deaths settled in and cemented. But unlike most children whose parents died suddenly, Janet and her sisters were not destitute, Collins knew, because he had drawn up Meredith's will when her father died two years earlier.

Meredith had left nearly everything to Earl at her death with three trusts going to her daughters so that they would never have to worry about finances the way she and Earl had early in their marriage, prior to Little Buck's arrival, which was when her father lifted them from poverty's despair. In addition to that, Meredith had specifically named Janet as the next president of Buchanan Mutual with Phil Seymour, who headed the Chicago Division, as her mentor. Marjorie and Stacy were left trusts that they couldn't touch until their twenty-fifth birthdays. It was also Meredith's desire that all three daughters occupy significant positions within the company's power structure so that her father's misogyny would be forever eradicated in the Shamus family tree. It was Meredith's hope that her daughters would be tangible examples for other young ambitious women.

"Excuse me, Mr. Collins," the coroner said. "May I speak with you alone?"

"Sure," Collins said. He looked down into Janet's face and said, "I'll only be a minute, okay?"

Janet nodded.

The men walked into the coroner's office and closed the door. The coroner looked through the glass at Janet, who was watching them closely, and then back at Collins and said, "We think he died of heart failure, but it's the strangest case I've ever seen in over thirty years."

"Go on," Collins said. "Out with it, man."

"Well, sir, when we undressed the deceased, for some unknown reason, there was semen in his shaft and in his underwear. While I'm sure it's probably happened before, in thirty years I've never heard of a man experiencing a coronary and orgasmic bliss at the same time."

Frowning, Collins asked, "Are you absolutely sure about your findings?"

"Quite sure. At first I thought he was with a woman when he had the heart attack, but they found him alone in his car."

"Is it possible that he had sex somewhere else before he had the attack?"

Hesitantly the coroner said, "Yes, but that would mean that this man was either having an affair, or he was with a prostitute earlier that evening. And on the way home his heart stopped beating."

"How long has he been dead?"

"Ten to twelve hours."

"Thank you," Collins said, and opened the door to leave.

"One other thing I found peculiar, sir."

Collins closed the door. "What would that be?"

"He washed his lower region. I found traces of soap in his pubic hair."

"Interesting."

"Indeed, sir."

As Collins was walking Janet out of the morgue, he said, "Listen Kiddo, you've got some big shoes to fill. A lot of people are going to be depending on you. You're eighteen now, right?"

"Yes, sir," she said, looking into his eyes for answers to all her unasked questions.

"You'll be graduating a few months from now in May, right?"

"Yes, but I can graduate now. I have more than enough credits, sir."

"Then maybe you should graduate and enter the business world. You're the president of the company now. I'll be contacting Phil Seymour and have him fly down here to groom you."

"But I'm not ready to take over, Mr. Collins."

"I'm sorry, Janet, but you don't have a choice. That's how your mother wanted it. She had such high hopes for you. She thought you had the strengths she never had. She told me you would be the perfect choice because you could make the hard decisions that most people are too weak to make."

"But I'm only eighteen, Mr. Collins. Can't this wait?"

"For a few days, sure, but after that, you have to take the helm. As a matter of fact, you're going to have to start making some decisions today. I'm going to take you over to the funeral parlor and you're going to have to pick a casket for your father."

With tears still streaming down her face, she said, "We were supposed to have my mother's funeral tomorrow."

"Maybe we can get the funeral director to handle both. I'll talk to him. My wife can handle the food for the reception. She'll hire a caterer. Everything will be fine." He stopped their forward momentum. Then he lifted her chin and said, "You need to be strong now for your sisters and for all the people who work for you. Otherwise all of you might end up losing everything."

Chapter 4

Innocent Deception

J ohnnie's eyes shot open when she heard her alarm clock ring. She took a deep breath and exhaled, feeling like she needed seventy-two more hours of sleep so that the nightmare she was living would be over. Even though her eyes were still closed, she could tell she had left the lamp on all night by the brightness that overshadowed the darkness. She swung her feet to the floor and saw her list on the coffee table. She picked up the note pad and started reading the list she'd made before falling asleep. The first two items on the list would be simple. The last three would require focus and determination if she was to pull it off.

First, she had to go to work. Keeping up appearances was very important. Second, she had to pick up her Wall Street Journal to stay current and also create another witness who would corroborate her habits and demeanor if asked by the authorities. Third, she had to smile as often as she could. This would prove that she was in a good mood—at least as far as customers could tell. Fourth, she had to be consistently friendly and complimentary throughout the day. Fifth, she had to think of small talk to keep her mind off what happened to Earl while she was having relations with him to ensure that she wouldn't unintentionally let something slip out of her mouth. Every part of her day had to be orchestrated so that when she left Jackson, if the authorities did show up asking questions, she wanted the people in Jackson to say what a wonderful sociable person she was because that's all she would ever show them, no matter how rude they were to her.

She went back into the bedroom for the first time since she helped Paul Masterson dress Earl. She had to make up her bed and make sure both rooms were spotless because she wanted Gloria to tell the police that she was a tidy person if they asked. As far as she was concerned, the more positive things the police heard about her, the better. Deserved or underserved, she knew she had a horrendous reputation to overcome. She looked at the bed and froze for a second or two as what happened there played out in her mind. She shook herself to stop the invasive images. As she made up her bed, she wondered if Paul had left the hotel already. She hoped he had because if she saw him, she would know everything went well the previous night in New Orleans. And with that knowledge, she just might instinctively fling herself into his arms.

Forty minutes later, she was standing in front of Franklin Hill's paper and magazine stand, buying a couple Wall Street Journals—one was for Hank and Lucille. She had successfully handled the easiest part of her list and now she was about to go into Lucille's and began phase two of the innocence deception.

Chapter 5

"Perhaps we should discuss this in private."

Three weeks had passed and Janet had received a crash course on what it meant to be the head of Buchanan Mutual from Phil Seymour, the head of the Chicago division. He taught her as much as he could in that time, but he knew she would still need his guidance. The first thing he taught her was self-respect. The second was the importance of information. He made it clear that the people who worked for her were going to challenge her because she didn't have any experience, no credentials, and she was still a budding teenager. And more important, they were going to challenge her because she was female. She was a girl whose face could breakout with acne at any moment—at least that's what the adults who worked for her would think and probably talk about behind her back. Phil Seymour let her know that a number of her employees had children who had doctorates and families of their own and so it would be difficult, but not impossible for them to respect her even though she was the president of the company. He taught her to be polite, but firm, and that nearly everyone on her payroll was expendable no matter how long they'd been with the company. He made sure she understood that it might be necessary to fire several of them to get the attention of less important employees. He also made sure she understood that her word above all others was final.

Having laid their mother and father to rest, Janet and her sisters were ready to hear the official reading of the will. Janet hadn't told Marjorie and Stacy that Seymour Collins had already told her what was in the will. She didn't want them to think she was greedy for power even though a part of her wanted full control of what was once the Buchanan fortune. While she hadn't asked what she and her sisters were worth, she knew it was substantial because her grandfather lived an incredibly extravagant lifestyle. As a matter of fact, they were living in his house, which boasted a ten car garage, a golf course, several tennis courts, indoor and outdoor Olympic swimming pools, a bowling alley, a movie theatre, an indoor shooting range complete with fifteen hunting rifles with scopes, an endless supply of bullets and targets, and a host of other goodies. In short, the Buchanan home was a rich man's paradise where their grandfather wanted for nothing.

She went into her parents' bedroom to get her mother's personal phonebook again. She opened the drawer and picked it up again. But this time, she noticed something shiny underneath her mother's bible and a notepad. She moved them and found a key that didn't look like any key she'd seen before. She picked it up and looked at it, examining it, trying to figure out what lock it might open. She decided to ask Seymour Collins, hoping he would know; after all, he was her mother's lawyer. If he didn't, he could probably help her find out. It was a curiosity for her, a mystery that clung to her, and demanded her attention. Suddenly, she wanted to know her mother's secrets. She sat on the bed and called Seymour Collins.

An hour later, Collins arrived and the girls ushered him into the parlor where their mother often entertained her friends. The maid served tea and sugar cookies on a silver platter. They were all wearing lavender dresses, white lace gloves that matched their pearl necklaces, and their pear-shaped earrings. They composed themselves and waited patiently for him to get all the papers together so that he could read the fine details of the will and how the estate would be split up. Twenty or so minutes later, he was finished and asked them if they had any questions, expecting Marjorie and Stacy to ask why their mother had left control of everything to their older sister.

Janet waited for her sisters to ask questions about the nearly eight hundred million dollar conglomerate that Buchanan Mutual had become over the years or at the very least, the hundred million each of her sisters had in trust, but neither of them said a word. They just sat there on the couch eating cookies, occasionally sipping their tea, stoically half listening, as if they were still mourning the loss of both parents. It was as if they thought they had been left a mere hundred dollars instead of the enormous sum they and their children's children would have to live on for the remainder of their lives.

When her sisters remained quiet, Janet said, "Marjorie, do you have any questions for Mr. Collins?"

She shook her head and sipped her tea again.

"What about you, Stacy? Do you have any questions for Mr. Collins?"

She shook her head.

"Well, maybe you'll think of something later," Collins said. "If you do, I'll be available, okay, girls?"

They nodded.

Collins looked at Janet and said, "What about you? Do you have any questions?"

"Yes, as a matter of fact, I do," Janet said. She pulled out the key she'd found and said, "What's this?"

Collins recoiled and bit down on his lower lip. He recognized the key and instinctively knew what her next questions would be. Reaching for the key, he said, "Oh, that's nothing. I'll take care of that for you."

"What is it, Mr. Collins?" Janet said, with authority, fully cognizant that his livelihood was now in her hands.

He forced himself to smile. Then he cautiously said, "Well, uh, well . . . you see . . . uh . . . it's a safety deposit key. Yes."

Sensing that he was holding something back, Janet leaned forward and said, "And what's that, Mr. Collins?" Again she spoke with authority, locking eyes with him, letting him feel the weight of her power, fully expecting him to be forthright with his responses.

Collins cut his eyes toward Marjorie and Stacy who seemed to be tolerating what they thought was an unbearable ordeal, barely listening to him, and then back to Janet. "Perhaps we should discuss this in private." He looked at her sisters again and then back to her.

"Marjorie and Stacy, why don't you two have Mildred fix you something to eat while I finish our parents' business, okay?"

Seconds later, Marjorie and Stacy obediently left Janet and Collins alone.

"Now, Mr. Collins—"

"Uh, call me Seymour."

"No. This is business—my business. I'll call you Mr. Collins and from this moment forward, you'll call me Miss Shamus."

Collins knew at that instant, the power in the room had permanently shifted to the young woman sitting before him. He wondered if it was a mistake to tell her to graduate early and take over the business. In just a few seconds, he thought it might have been smarter to have Phil Seymour run things while young Janet got a Harvard education. That way he could protect his deceased client's secrets. But it was too late for that now. Janet was firmly ensconced on the presidential throne. "Okay, Miss Shamus."

"And another thing, from this moment forward, you will treat me like I'm the president of Buchanan Mutual and all of its subsidiaries, not the eighteen-year-old girl that was crying in the morgue a few weeks ago. You said it yourself. I've got big shoes to fill." She held up the key and said, "Now . . . tell me what this key is."

"It belongs to your mother's safety deposit box."

"What's in it?"

Collins cut his eyes to the left and swallowed hard. "Things about your parents and certain other parties."

"Things like what?"

Chapter 6

"Is she my father's whore?"

Less than an hour later, Seymour Collins and Janet Shamus were standing in the vault where her mother kept a large safety deposit box. She opened it and found twelve jewelry boxes neatly stacked to the left of several stacks of cash wrapped in ten thousand dollar bank seals. Then she saw a large pouch made of burgundy stained cowhide resembling a saddlebag that seemed to be stuffed with something valuable. She picked it up, all under the watchful eyes of her legal representative, shook it and said, "What's this Mr. Collins?"

"Miss Shamus, as your attorney, I must caution you not to open that package. Once you've opened it, there will be no going back. You cannot unring the bell. I beg of you . . . let me handle this. Let me sort through your mother's things and I'll give you everything you need to know. But if you continue on this course, I will not be responsible for what you find."

Janet stared into his eyes for a long moment or two and said, "I'll take it with me and decide later."

Collins sighed heavily and said, "If you insist."

Looking for truth in his eyes, she said, "Do you know what's in here?"

"I do," he said without hesitation.

With her eyes firmly fixed on his, she said, "Care to share, Mr. Collins?"

He shook his head and said, "Attorney client privilege."

"Was my mother having an affair, Mr. Collins?"

Collins never even batted an eyelash. He just stood there like a wall of stone, looking into her eyes, letting her see his impermeable resolve.

"That's it, isn't it? My mother was running around on my father, wasn't she?"

Again, Collins didn't respond.

"Was it you, Mr. Collins? Were you bedding my mother?" She paused for a second and waited for an answer. When none came, she continued, "You were, weren't you? Behind her sweet demure exterior, my mother was an alley cat with real feelings and emotions wasn't she? And you were the sweet catnip she needed, weren't you?"

With that, Collins slapped Janet's face and said, "Fire me if you must, but I will not stand here and listen to you talk about your mother that way. If it were your father—" He stopped himself. "Your mother was one of the finest women I've ever known. To my knowledge she was true to your father for the duration of their marriage. She loved him deeply—more than he deserved."

Massaging her stinging cheek, a smirk emerged when she realized that Collins may not have had an affair with her mother, but it was clear that he was in love with her and had been for quite some time. She inhaled and thought about what she had just learned, believing that her mother may have loved him too. Or at the very least she was fond of him, and were it not for her high morals, she would have bedded her attorney. Keeping her thoughts to herself for the moment, she said, "Then it was my father, wasn't it? He was having an affair and the evidence of it is in this pouch, isn't it?"

"Miss Shamus, you have possession of the pouch. It is now your property. Do with it what you will, but for the last time, let me handle your mother's personal business. It was in a safety deposit box for a reason."

"Indeed it was," she said and eyed the pouch, letting her curiosity tempted her, letting it seduce her, having no idea what decisions she would make that would affect her future if she satisfied her inquisitiveness. "So this pouch contains my mother's *personal* business, huh?"

"It does."

She lifted the flap and looked inside. Then she looked at Collins. "What's all this?"

"As I said, Miss Shamus, it's your property and if you so choose, it may very well become your problem. I asked your mother to let me handle it and she refused. I've asked you to let me handle it three times now and you've refused. You're mother is dead because of what's in there. Your father may be dead because of it too. I fear you'll be signing your own death warrant if you do any more than what you've done."

"What *I've* done?"

"You've looked inside, but you haven't seen what's in there. Nor do you know what it all means. Stop now while you can. Neither your mother nor your father could stop themselves. Now they're both dead. Please . . . be smart. You're mother and father wouldn't want you mixed up in any of this. Listen to your attorney, I beg of you."

"So you're saying my mother and father were both murdered because of what's in this pouch?"

"Murder is improper. Let's just say their deaths, at least your mother's for sure, was hastened by what's in there. And I suspect your father's death, although it was due to natural causes, was probably brought on by what's in there."

Looking at Collins, she said, "And with an exordium like that, you expect me to stop now?"

Collins sighed heavily and shook his head. "At this point, I don't think you can stop, Miss Shamus. I think you have to open it now, but again, for the fourth time . . . my advice is that you fight your intense desire to see what I've seen and know what I know."

"Did my father look through the pouch?"

"I don't know."

"Besides you and my mother, does anybody else know about the contents of this pouch?"

"Yes."

"Who?"

"A man named Tony Hatcher."

"And who is he?"

"A private detective."

Janet swallowed hard, her curiosity ever growing, her mind considering what she'd learned so far and what it could all possibly mean. She placed the pouch on the table and sat down at one of the two available chairs, thinking about it all, wanting to listen to her attorney, but finding it impossible to ignore what little she knew so far.

She looked up into Collins's eyes and said, "So . . . you think the woman who killed my mother did it intentionally? And that my father was killed over what's in here?"

"That's not what I said, Miss Shamus."

"But that's what you think?"

"That's not what I think either."

"What do you think, Mr. Collins?"

"For the last time . . . I think you should do what your mother and father didn't do . . . *listen* to me. I'm looking out for your best interests not my own."

Janet shifted her eyes from Collins, back to the pouch, and to Collins several times, trying to stop herself from opening the pouch. But she couldn't. As much as she wanted to take his advice, curiosity was in control now. She picked up the pouch and was about to empty its contents on the table.

Collins said, "Better be sure, Miss Shamus. Final warning."

Janet hesitated for a few seconds and then turned the pouch upside down. Photos, newspaper articles, handwritten notes, and lots of reel tapes tumbled out and onto the table.

Collins inhaled deeply, sighed disapprovingly, and rolled his eyes. He knew then that once she looked at everything on the table, once she understood its meaning, she would have a host of other questions that would lead her to more decisions, which would invariably lead to certain conclusions and eventually ramifications she was too immature to fully comprehend. Collins knew what Meredith should have known and what Janet was too young to know; that once you make a decision, you set yourself on a collision course with an often unpredictable destiny and there was no escaping its eventual trappings. Meredith had lived long enough for her youthful foolishness to catch up with her, which was why Collins knew she should have listened to his advice. But Janet was only eighteen. She hadn't lived long enough for her foolishness to catch up with her, but he had the sinking suspicion that whatever dirt she did in the past was now about to come to the surface like a blade of corn. And like corn, its stalks were going to grow at an alarming rate.

Completely absorbed with curiosity, she looked through the photos, passively looking at each one until she came to one of a beautiful Negress wearing an expensive red and black skirt suit, a wide brimmed hat and dark sunglasses. She held it up so Collins could see it and said, "Who is this?"

"Johnnie Wise."

"Who is she?"

A waterfall of silence filled the vault.

"Is she my father's whore?"

Collins cut his eyes to the left. "No."

"Hmph," she muttered, suspecting that he was either lying or she hadn't asked the right question. Phil Seymour had told her that she had to be especially careful with lawyers because they lie as easily as they breathe. He told her that lawyers learn early on in their careers, perhaps in college, to hide the truth. He told her that lawyers lie by answering exact questions, knowing what the person was seeking, but didn't know how to ask. With that knowledge, she realized that the woman in the picture could not be her father's mistress because he was dead. So she said, "*Was* she my father's whore, Mr. Collins?"

More silence bounced off the vault walls.

"Hmph. So . . . she *was* my father's whore. I guess I'm not surprised. I've heard of this sort of thing many times from the girls at school. They talk about their fathers having pickaninnies who look just like them and their live-in maids."

Collins picked up the pouch, put the contents back in it, and said, "Let's continue this in my office where we'll have privacy to get into the minutiae of these emotional complexities."

Janet stood up and said, "Mr. Collins, I'll go with you to your office to discuss this further, but you will tell me everything. You will leave nothing out even if it does hurt me, understand?"

"Miss Shamus, I will tell you everything and then some, but I will not tell you anything in the vault of a bank. Do *you* understand?"

"I do. But before we go, don't you *ever* strike me again. Both my parents are dead. Only they had the right to discipline me. This moment forth, I'm a woman and a paying client—you will respect me as such. Now . . . acknowledge that you've clearly understood *me*."

"I so acknowledge."

Loving the new power she suddenly had over everyone, including the most powerful attorney in New Orleans, a euphoric feeling was washing over her, giving her a sexual glow without having ever engaged in the act. "Now . . . we can go to your office."

Chapter 7

S uspicious that Earl Shamus had been found one day after he and his team of private detectives had gone to Houston to thoroughly investigate Paul Masterson, Tony Hatcher went to the morgue to talk to the coroner and learned that Earl had died of natural causes. The coroner also told him that he had found evidence suggesting that Earl had a sexual encounter prior to his death. While the coroner couldn't explain for an absolute certainty how Earl ended up dead under peculiar circumstances, and found it befuddling, it wasn't a big enough deal to do an autopsy. The coroner signed the death certificate and released the body to the Shamus family so they could lay their dead to rest.

Hatcher figured that Earl had paid for a full investigation of Johnnie and his unanticipated death wouldn't derail it. Besides, he was curious as to what happened between the time that he and his team went to Houston to investigate Paul Masterson, and Earl's coronary. He had also left valuable surveillance equipment in Johnnie's hotel room that he needed to retrieve. Hatcher immediately went to Jackson to see if Johnnie was still there, figuring that if she left before her car was fixed, that would have been a clear indicator that Earl had been with her when he died—at least that's what he thought. But she was still there, still working at Lucille's, acting as if she was the happiest woman on earth. He thought the tapes, if they hadn't been discovered, would tell him if Earl was in her room the night before his death, but found nothing incriminating on them.

Sitting at his desk, Hatcher was looking at some recently developed pictures of the wife of his current client going into a hotel when his phone buzzed. He pushed a button while still looking at the photo and said, "Yes."

"Your two o'clock is here, Mr. Hatcher," a woman said.

"Send him in," Hatcher said, and quickly put the photographs in his drawer.

A few seconds later, his door opened and Seymour Collins, who he recognized immediately but had never met, walked in. He was familiar with him because of his business with Meredith Shamus. He often checked out his clients because many of them couldn't be trusted to tell the truth. Sometimes they came to his office impersonating other people. Collins was wearing a pinstriped gray suit and carrying a large leather pouch. Hatcher stood up and waited for Collins to come to him, admiring his impeccable manner of dress, wondering how far the outfit set him back, if at all. He thought the whole ensemble would have cost him a month's salary. There was no way he could spend that kind of money for one suit. And even if he could, he wouldn't.

"Mr. Hatcher, I'm Seymour Collins, attorney for the Shamus family."

They shook hands and Hatcher gestured for Collins to sit. When he did, Hatcher sat too. "I always get you and the other Seymour mixed up. He's—"

"You must mean Phil Seymour. He's the head of the Chicago division of Buchanan Mutual."

"Yes, of course, that's him."

"You probably know the name because he's been mentoring Janet Shamus to take over as President since her father's death. And I must say she's quite precocious and has firmly taken hold of the Buchanan reins. She's going to make a wonderful executive."

"Actually I'm familiar with your name and other names within Buchanan Mutual because I make it my business to know who important people are and who they associate with. Now . . . what can I do for you, Mr. Collins?"

"Yes. Yes. I understand that you did some work for my deceased client, Meredith Shamus some time ago, and I have reason to believe that you also worked for her husband, Earl, for a week or so immediately after her death."

Hatcher didn't respond. Who he worked for was confidential.

When Collins realized that Hatcher wasn't going to divulge the information he wanted, he tossed the pouch on the desk and looked at Hatcher, but again Hatcher didn't respond. He just looked at Collins, waiting for him to ask a question.

"Did you take those pictures, Mr. Hatcher?"

"What can I do for you, Mr. Collins?" Hatcher said without bothering to open the pouch to see the pictures.

Collins reached for the pouch, opened it, and placed several black and white photographs on Hatcher's desk, facing him.

Hatcher glanced at the pictures briefly and said, "What can I do for you, Mr. Collins?"

Exasperated, Collins exhaled hard and said, "You can tell me if you took those pictures."

They were the snapshots that he'd taken for Meredith Shamus when she hired him to follow Earl. One of the pictures was of Johnnie meeting Earl at the Savoy Hotel. Another one was of Benny punching Earl in the stomach. There was a picture of San Francisco license plates and much more.

"And if I did? Then what?"

"Meredith showed me these about six months ago when she got them from you. She thought Earl had killed the girl's mother, a Creole prostitute named Marguerite Wise. As you know, Earl was having relations with her daughter and Meredith wanted to put a stop to it. I offered to talk to the girl and to offer her a few dollars to keep the Shamus name out of whatever happened to her mother, but Meredith insisted on handling the girl herself."

Hatcher looked at his watch and said, "Is this going somewhere, Mr. Collins?"

Collins exhaled again, growing weary of Hatcher's reluctance to cooperate. "I've got Janet waiting in your secretary's office. I don't want her to hear the things I'm going to tell you."

"Which are?"

"According to the coroner, semen was found inside Earl's shorts among other places if you follow what I mean. There were traces of soap on his leg and pubic hair. Someone had obviously cleaned the area, but they didn't think about the semen in his shaft that would eventually come out and end up in his shorts."

"And?"

"And?" Collins said, incredulously. "The man died of a heart attack, Mr. Hatcher."

"I'm aware of that, Mr. Collins. Listen . . . I'm busy. Please get to the point. I have other business I need to attend to."

"Does it make sense to you that a man dying of a heart attack would have semen dripping out of his shaft at the time of his death?"

"Stranger things have happened. What's your point?"

"I think Earl was with this Johnnie girl when he died, and she somehow got him to his car and ran it into a ditch near Moisant Field."

"And she did that from Jackson, Mississippi, where she's currently working?"

"So . . . you admit Earl hired you to track her down? That means that he may have met with her."

"Let's say he did meet with her, and he did have relations with her. Are you suggesting that she rode all the way back to New Orleans with him and when he died unexpectedly, caught a bus back to Jackson and resumed her job at the restaurant?"

"I'm suggesting that it's possible."

Hatcher chuckled and said, "Mr. Collins, Johnnie Wise would have needed a ride back to Jackson if that happened. She's a good-looking dame. Someone would have remembered her, don't you think, Mr. Collins?"

"What if Earl died in her bed?"

"So what if he did? He had a heart attack, Mr. Collins. He wasn't murdered."

"What if he had relations with her and died on the way back to New Orleans? That would account for the semen, would it not?"

"Let's assume for sake of argument that you're right. The girl is only guilty of tampering with evidence. Given the stated scenario and the fact that less than a month ago our illustrious prosecutor had her arrested on trumped up murder charges, charges he knew to be false before he even stepped into that courtroom, could you blame her for tampering with evidence? Besides, she would have needed help to get Earl in his car, wouldn't she?"

"What if she had help, Mr. Hatcher?"

"Tell me you have more than conjecture, Mr. Collins. As I've said, I'm a very busy man."

"Perhaps it is conjecture, but she's guilty of more than that, Mr. Hatcher."

"What else is she guilty of?"

"Abortion, Mr. Hatcher. And quite possibly the murder of a bellhop in Fort Lauderdale."

"She was acquitted of the murders, Mr. Collins."

"No, she was acquitted of Sharon Trudeau's murder. She was never tried for the bellhop."

"Are you sure?"

"I am. The district attorney didn't charge her with the bellhop's death. The papers only talked about Miss Trudeau's death, so that's what they indicted her for."

"So you admit that the charges were false from the beginning?"

Collins glared at Hatcher and said, "I admit nothing, sir."

"But her lawyers got her off because she couldn't have done that murder."

"Exactly."

Hatcher frowned and said, "What would be accomplished by hauling her into court again?"

"This time the district attorney will ask her where she was the night of the murders, and she'll have to say where she was. She'll have to say she was in Bayou Cane, Louisiana. And then, the prosecutor will ask her what she was doing there. And if she answers truthfully, we get her for murdering her child. If she doesn't answer, we get her for contempt of court. The judge will put her in jail until she talks. Either way, she pays for Meredith Shamus' death."

"You're forgetting she doesn't have to testify against herself."

"I've forgotten nothing, Mr. Hatcher. Let her plead the fifth. She'll be sealing her own doom."

"She can only plead the fifth if she takes the stand."

"She'll take the stand all right. She'll have to. I'll make sure of it."

"But she had nothing to do with Meredith's death."

"Sure, she did, Mr. Hatcher."

"I was there. I saw the whole thing. Ethel Beauregard killed Meredith."

"Miss Wise made a deal with Meredith not to bring her family into this. And she broke that deal. Earl was planning to reunite with her against my advice. He told me he loved her and that he was going to try to reestablish something with her. He told me that if it didn't work out, he was going to pursue this course of action."

"So, you think he met with this girl the night he died?"

"I believe he did, yes. Did you or anybody on your team of detectives see him go into her room?"

"No. We were all in Houston investigating Paul Masterson, the man Johnnie had been spending time with."

"Hmm. So he sent you and your team to Houston, so he wouldn't be seen going to her hotel room. He planned to make an outrageous offer—again against my advice. I believe the girl took it. She would have been a fool not to."

"What was the deal?"

"He was going to offer her twenty thousand cash, a newly built home in Jackson, a new car every year, college tuition, several vacations every year and much more."

"And you want me to go to Jackson and bring her back to New Orleans to stand trial for murdering the bellhop?"

"Yes."

"Why would I do that, Mr. Collins, when I know she isn't guilty of the crime?"

"How do you know she's not guilty?"

"I've listened to the tapes. Have you?"

"No. I haven't. I only learned of their existence today."

"Then how do you know about the abortion?"

"Meredith alluded to all sorts of things that she had no way of knowing."

"But I thought you said you didn't know of their existence."

"What I meant was that I suspected, but I had never seen them before today."

Hatcher looked at Collins for a long minute and said, "Okay, but you still haven't given me reason to continue this case. Mr. and Mrs. Shamus are dead. What's the point?"

"Reason, Mr. Hatcher? You're in the business of finding people, are you not?"

"I am, but—"

"Then find Miss Wise and collect your pay."

"I've already collected my pay. Besides, you no longer need me. I told you she's in Jackson. This is a job for the police, not me."

"We've been to the police and they are content that Earl died of a heart attack. They laughingly said they have better things to do than to chase down a seventeen-year-old black girl whose only crime is that she didn't kill her mother for selling her to Earl in the first place."

Hatcher smiled and said, "TJ Biller told you that, right?"

"Right. How did you know?"

"I know TJ pretty good. We go way back. Speaking of "we", a moment ago you said, 'we've been to the police'. Who's the other person?"

"Janet Shamus."

"The girl waiting in my secretary's office?"

Collins nodded. "What if Miss Wise is gone? It's been three weeks. Her car could be fixed and then she'd be on her merry way."

"Again . . . what would be the point, Mr. Collins?"

"Mr. Hatcher, at the very least, she's tampered with evidence. We could get her for that."

"So just get her for something, huh?" Hatcher said, smiling. "Surely you can find another more eager private detective to do this for you. Why me?"

"Mr. Hatcher, Janet Shamus chose you because Meredith trusted you. She said you were an honorable man. And aren't you the least bit curious as to what happened when Earl Shamus left his home that night? Aren't you the least bit curious as to how Miss Wise was able to pull it off?"

"I admit I am curious as to what happened, but . . . if I take the case, it's going to be really expensive."

"How much do you need as a retainer?"

"Depends on if she's still in Jackson. She should be gone by now. It's been nearly a month. Her car should be fixed, and she should be on her way to East Saint Louis."

"How much?"

"Assuming she's gone, I'll need at least five thousand. And that's just to start."

"Can you have your secretary send Janet in? She has the checkbook. With Phil Seymour's guidance, I think she'll be a lot like her grandfather—ruthless as hell. In many ways, she already is. I think that's why Meredith wanted her to run the conglomerate."

"So the girl knows about her father and Miss Wise?"

"She found the pictures among her mother's things in a safety deposit box, Mr. Hatcher. She wants to pursue this, too."

Hatcher pushed a button on his phone and said, "Mrs. Manheim?"

"Yes, Mr. Hatcher."

"Could you send in Miss Shamus please?"

Chapter 8

"What about Lucas Matthews?"

Tony Hatcher expected Janet Shamus to look pretty much like her mother, who was the poster child for what a plain Jane looks like, but either Meredith was stunning in her teen years or Janet had been adopted because she was drop dead gorgeous. Hatcher had to concentrate to get his mouth to close before a spider web of saliva inched its way down his chin. He stood up, but he felt like he should bow before her because the aura she projected was majestic. She was wearing a black skirt suit with a golden turtleneck, and black pearls with matching earrings. She had the longest legs he'd ever seen and offered a more than ample bust line that forced him to keep looking into her magnificent blue eyes so as not to give away the fact that he wanted to see so much more. He watched her walk up to his desk, stick out her hand, and say, "Hello, Mr. Hatcher. I'm Janet Shamus."

Hatcher took her hand into his, expecting a soft genteel feminine handshake, but Janet offered him a firm grip and added a little power to let him know that this wasn't a first grader's game of show and tell. The squeeze was supposed to decipher whatever cryptic message her face and body sent. She wanted him to know that this was the big leagues and that she was about business.

"That's some grip you've got there, Miss Shamus."

"Thank you Mr. Hatcher. I've been practicing for three weeks now."

"I see . . . well . . . it's paid off. Practice makes perfect as they say. Now, what can I do for you, Miss Shamus?"

Janet looked at Collins and said, "I'd like to speak to Mr. Hatcher alone, if you don't mind." Then she looked into Hatcher's wanton eyes, absorbing his lust, planning to use it against him if she ever needed to.

Collins said, "I'll wait in the other office."

"No," Janet said without looking at him.

"No?"

"No," Janet repeated softly, dismissing him, still looking into Hatcher's eyes.

"How will you get home?"

Again she didn't look at Collins when she said, "Mr. Hatcher will drop me off if we can come to an agreement or I'll take a cab. If I have to, I'll walk. But I'll get home, Mr. Collins."

Glaring at the side of her head, feeling like a kindergartner who was just told it was nap time, Collins said, "I'm sure you will." As a parting shot, he added, "Well I must say, Miss Shamus, you're nothing like your mother."

She looked at Collins and said, "That's the idea. Thanks for the compliment."

Collins looked at Hatcher, nodded sharply and walked off in a huff. He wanted to slam the door on the way out, but dignified refinement demanded otherwise.

When Janet heard the door close, she said, "Is he gone?"

Frowning, Hatcher said, "Yes, he is."

"Good. Now . . . let's get down to business."

Hatcher raised his hand like a police officer directing traffic and said, "Hold it. Let's get something straight from the beginning. I understand that you want respect, being a woman, and inheriting so much money, but nobody dictates to me. And nobody owns me. This is my little corner of the world and I rule here. Do you understand that?"

Janet smiled to stifle a burgeoning laugh, thinking, *I could buy you and this building with the change in my purse, little man.* "Yes, Mr. Hatcher, I understand. But I want you to understand that while you can run the show, I pay the bills. And because I pay the bills, I do have some say as to what I want done. Do you understand?"

Tony intentionally dropped his eyes to her breasts, smiled, and said, "Yes, Miss Shamus, I do."

"And Mr. Hatcher, if you *think* you can insult me by looking at the outer glands that will one day feed my children, be my guest, but when you're on the clock, be on the clock, understand? Don't get sidetracked by milk. You might miss a crucial snapshot or something."

"I see Phil Seymour has schooled you well, but listen, deep down in places you don't wanna look, you and I know you're a frightened little girl who's all alone in a cold cruel world. You don't fool me, sister. But you're right about one thing."

"What's that Mr. Hatcher?"

"It is your money and you do pay the bills. So again, what can I do for you?"

"Do you have a tape player?"

"I do. Why?"

She picked up the pouch and dumped out all its contents. "I want to listen to these tapes."

"I would think a rich gal like your mother already had one."

"I'm sure we have one, but I have no idea where it is. Have you heard the tapes?"

"I have."

"And . . . you don't think I should listen to them, do you?"

"No, I don't. As you so astutely pointed out, it is your money, but unfortunately I'm not on the payroll yet. So let's talk money."

"Sure, just let me get my checkbook," Janet said. She reached into her purse, grabbed her checkbook, and a pen. She started writing out the check. "Let's see . . . shall we start with three thousand?"

"Seven."

Janet offered Hatcher her blue eyes and said, "Mr. Hatcher, I'm going to pay your *five* thousand dollar fee, but I expect a top notch investigation."

Hatcher smiled. He liked Janet, but he didn't like being attracted to her. She was a vibrant well put together young woman with a fortune at her disposal; the kind of woman that would turn a man like him into a marshmallow. The man that dated her had to have big money, he thought while looking at her like he wanted to take her right there in his office. He knew he was out of her league, but still, he wanted to sample the merchandise because she talked tough and he had always liked women who talked tough and had spunk. Sex with them was otherworldly and the relationship always ended badly, but still, if she ever offered him a shot, he'd take it in a heartbeat and deal with the aftermath. And he'd keep on taking it until one or both of them got tired of the intercourse and moved on to fresh terrain.

"Don't worry, Miss Hatcher, you'll get a top notch investigation."

"What did you call me?"

Frowning, Hatcher said, "I didn't call you anything."

"You called me Miss Hatcher."

"Did I? Sorry."

"A Freudian slip, Mr. Hatcher?"

He looked into her eyes and said, "Where did you learn that term, Miss Shamus. You're still in high school, aren't you?"

"I graduated three weeks ago. I had the credits and the company needed me at the helm, my attorney said. So I left, but as to where I learned the term, I read a lot, Mr. Hatcher. My grandfather had an extensive library and I practically lived in there when we moved into his mansion after his death. I know lots of words and theories. Shall I opine?"

"How did you know I would accept the five grand?"

"I've seen my father's checkbook. It was one of the first things I did. And one of the first things I want you to do is find out what he did with the twenty thousand he withdrew from our bank account. Collins says that if it wasn't in the car, and it wasn't, the girl has it."

"The girl?"

"This girl," she said, pushing a picture of a black woman forward that was on his desk, but hidden by other material that was in the leather pouch. "Johnnie Wise. My father's whore. Come now, Mr. Hatcher, do keep up. You should know all of this better than I. Or are you playing a silly little game because you think I'm not knowledgeable concerning this case? Or perhaps you think I'm woefully inept intellectually."

Hatcher was about to mince words with her and run the risk of being embarrassed by what appeared to be a superior mind. If they

kept going back and forth, sooner or later she was going to say
something he didn't understand. And he wasn't about to let that
happen so he focused on the subject he did know—the case. "So
Collins was telling the truth. You do know about your father and this
girl."

"Girl? If only she were, Mr. Hatcher. She's anything but a girl.
I've seen all our financial statements and bank records. I've even
read your notes and your conclusions. She bilked my mother out of
fifty thousand dollars and she had my father embezzling money
from the company to keep her arrayed like a princess. All of this
while she was sleeping with his stockbroker, a young man named
Lucas Matthews, and the notorious gangster, Napoleon Bentley.
Now . . . have I sufficiently proven that I'm up to speed on this, Mr.
Hatcher?"

He looked into her beguiling eyes, smirked, knowing he was
going to enjoy this next bit of conversation, and said, "And do you
understand that your father paid her mother a thousand dollars to
have sex with her when she was only fifteen, knowing full well that
she was still a virgin? And that he wanted her when she was only
twelve? Are you aware of that as well, Miss Shamus?"

"Twelve?" She said and recoiled while staring at him. "You
can't be serious, Mr. Hatcher. The girl would have only been a child
then."

Hatcher leaned back and laced his fingers behind his head,
rocked back and forth in his comfortable chair, and said, "You were
only sixteen when you led your little brother up that tree, were you
not?"

Stunned that he knew about that, she said, "My mother told you
about that?"

Hatcher leaned forward, placed his elbows on his desk. Then he
exhaled and said, "Well . . . now . . . we know you're not totally up
to speed on everything, are you?"

"Apparently not, but I am a fast learner."

"I'll tell you what, why don't I call you a cab and have him drive
you over to Macy's so you can buy yourself a nice expensive tape
player. That way I can get started on this case. How 'bout that?"

"Fair enough, Mr. Hatcher. But don't bother calling a cab. I think I'll walk. I could use the time to think. Besides, it's beautiful out today." She looked out the window and said, "A sun like that is meant to be enjoyed."

"I'm inclined to agree, Miss Shamus."

She started collecting her things and said, "Well . . . I should get going."

"Not so fast," he said, finally feeling like he had the young woman on her heels and retreating.

"Excuse me?"

"Not so fast. Your father already paid me for this information even though I wasn't able to deliver it to him." He opened a drawer, pulled out a packet, opened it, and retrieved a photo. "If you're certain you want to pursue this thing, I can brief you on this guy."

He pushed a picture over to her.

"Who's that?"

"His name's Paul Masterson. If anybody helped Johnnie that night, it was him. That's what I believe anyway."

"Who is he? What do you have on him?"

"Well first off, your father had us go to Houston to investigate him. Masterson's an evangelist. He graduated from Dallas Theological Seminary in 1946 with a Master's in Divinity. He was placed in a holiness church, but ended up getting involved with a prostitute. And get this . . . the church hierarchy set him up with this woman." He pushed another picture over. "Her name's Anita Wilde. Apparently Masterson was preaching against church corruption."

"A regular Martin Luther, huh?"

"Yes, until he met—"

"Anita Wilde," Janet said, finishing Hatcher's sentence. She picked up the photo and thoroughly scrutinized it. "She's a stunning woman. I understand how they trapped him."

"Do you?"

"You men can't resist a beautiful woman. You simply don't have the strength. All women know this to be true. It's a reality of life we learn early on. The evangelist did what every man but Joseph and Jesus Christ would have done in the same situation." She paused for a half a beat. "Nevertheless, tell me why you *think* the evangelist would aid and abet Miss Wise's felonious conduct? Has he not yet repented of his sexual escapade with Miss Wilde?"

"Well, he's doing one-night-only preaching engagements to Negro congregations. He's been offered several churches, but he doesn't want to be a pastor anymore."

She leaned back in the chair and crossed her legs. "What else do you have on him?"

Hatcher inhaled deeply when he saw her long slender legs. He forced himself to look into her enchanting eyes before saying, "He joined the Army a few months after he left his church in late 1947. In early 1948 he joined the Special Forces. Most of his military record is sealed, which means he was probably heavily involved with our covert overseas operations. By the way, 1947 was the year that The Office of Strategic Services disbanded. It is now called the Central Intelligence Agency and the Office of Navel Intelligence. He probably used his preaching license to do surveillance for the government overseas. If he did, that would mean he had to be able to speak at least two languages. The people who ran the OSS preferred their recruits speak more. Masterson speaks French, German, Spanish, and Portuguese."

"When did he leave the Army?"

"I don't know that yet."

"So it's possible he may still be working for or with our government? Is that what you're telling me, Mr. Hatcher?"

"That's exactly what I'm telling you. Are you sure you want to pursue this?"

"Quite sure. What else do you have on Mr. Masterson?"

"He comes from a wealthy oil family in Houston, but he didn't want anything to do with the business. His father practically disowned him when he went to seminary. Apparently he hasn't had an easy time of it with the ladies. During his senior year of high school, he got his girlfriend pregnant. Her father forced her to have an abortion. It shook the kid up. I suppose you should go after her too, Miss Shamus. I mean both women had abortions. Shouldn't they both do time. Together perhaps?"

"Sarcasm doesn't become you, Mr. Hatcher. Please try to stay focused."

"What are you going to do with all this information anyway?"

"You had a rather lengthy conversation with my attorney, did you not?"

"I did."

"Then you know that this is about revenge. Is that direct enough for you?"

Hatcher locked eyes with her. "Revenge, huh? For what?"

"She killed my mother and she destroyed my father. I had often wondered what happened to him six months or so ago. And now I know what happened to him. What happened to my father is an all too common thing. It was the same thing that happened to Mr. Masterson and to David and to Solomon and to Samson. A woman happened to all of them. And if you're not careful, Mr. Hatcher, a woman will happen to you too. I see the way you look at me. But I have only two things on my mind—running Buchanan Mutual and the total dismantlement of Johnnie Wise and her eventual destruction. So . . . don't let yourself fall in love with me. I won't be good for you, I assure you. Stay on task and I'm sure you'll be just fine. Mr. Seymour says that lust is powerful and alluring, but it dissipates as soon as another attractive creature comes into view."

Even though Hatcher had received excellent advice from the teenage upstart, he couldn't help himself. Unlike her mother, she was beautiful and like her mother, she was well-read, intelligent, and articulate. Hatcher realized that from now on, it would be best to give her his reports over the phone. Seeing her, listening to knowledge pour out of her would be too much for his loins to handle. And so he would listen to her wisdom and stay far away—that was the plan anyway.

"Well if that's all you have, Mr. Hatcher, I should go and pick up that tape player and listen to what's on these tapes. By the way, are there any others that I don't know about?"

"Yes. But there's nothing on them worth listening to."

"I'll be the judge of that, Mr. Hatcher. I assume you're referring to the tapes from her hotel room in Jackson, Mississippi?"

"Yes. How did you know about them?"

"You know how I know. I'm up to speed on you and this case. Now may I have them please? I believe they are my property since

you were working for my father when you planted the bugs. Everything he and my mother owned are now mine."

"What do you plan to do with them?"

"I'm not sure. Perhaps I'll take them to an expert and have them
analyzed. There may have been something of value on there,
something we could have used, something incriminating and she
simply taped over it."

"She didn't even know the bugs were there."

"According to a newspaper article in the Sentinel, her attorneys
found numerous bugs in her home . . . bugs you planted, Mr. Hatcher. You don't think she thought about that when my father died in
her arms? If not, I may have the wrong man for the job."

"I thought of that too, Miss Shamus, but like I told your attorney,
the heart attack killed your father. And even if the sex could have
killed him, which it didn't, he would have gladly chosen that
departure gate. I don't know any men who wouldn't choose that way
to go."

"For the last time, Mr. Hatcher . . . this is about revenge. Johnnie
Wise is a menace and must be properly dealt with. She's responsible
for the death of both my parents and she's going to have to answer
for that even if I have to dispense justice myself. Think of it this
way. Your investigation could exonerate her totally and completely.
That way you could live with yourself and the money you're going
to make if she's left Jackson and you have trouble locating her."

And with that, she handed Hatcher a check and headed for the
door.

"Uh, Miss Shamus . . ."

She stopped, turned her long delicate neck, and looked at him
over her shoulder. "Yes, Mr. Hatcher."

"The check's for ten thousand dollars. What's the other five
for?"

"Oh, it completely slipped my mind. The money's for another
investigation."

"Another investigation?"

"Yes. I want your detectives to do a thorough investigation of
the Beauregard and Bentley families, Seymour Collins, and my
mentor, Phillip Seymour."

"Why?"

Still looking over her shoulder, she said, "I want everything on all of them . . . sexual alliances past and present . . . everything. This case shouldn't require much travel. I think all of them are currently in New Orleans. Five thousand dollars should be sufficient. If you find that it isn't enough, bill me. Good day, Mr. Hatcher."

"What about Lucas Matthews?"

"He seems innocent in all of this, but, if something changes, I'll let you know." She held up the leather pouch and said, "The tapes will determine if I need to pursue him or not."

And with that, she left.

Chapter 9

Rhode Island

When Johnnie saw Paul Masterson and his Stetson waiting on the platform of the train depot, a sense of calm swept over her. She knew that everything was going to be all right because she believed he would protect her from all threats, even at the cost of his own life. Now worry and fear of what was going to happen to her melted like snow in the spring. For three weeks she had stuck to her plan, reading and rereading her list of things to do each night prior to going to bed and each subsequent morning before heading to Lucille's. Every free moment she had at the restaurant, she sat at a booth and read her Wall Street Journal, occasionally scrutinizing pedestrians as they walked along the street, wondering if one of them was a private detective. While she knew who Tony Hatcher was, she had no idea what he looked like.

When her shift was over, she went straight to the Clementine Hotel to see if the recording devices were still where they were planted. For a little over a week, the devices were still there, surreptitiously hidden throughout the rooms. In some small way, she hoped that one day she'd return to find them missing. At least that way she would know that Hatcher or one of his people had been in her room to retrieve the recording equipment. Until that happened, she knew she would be full of anxiety, uncertain if the detectives were back from Houston yet.

She had diligently searched the Jackson Newspapers, looking for an article confirming that Earl had been found, but there was nothing in any of the local papers. That meant that either Earl hadn't been found or that his death wasn't big enough news for the local papers to care. Then, one night after she'd gone to one of the Tiger's home basketball games, she returned to the Clementine and discovered that the recording devices were gone. At first her heart pounded hard when she thought about someone being in her room, going through her personal things, looking at her unmentionables. Touching them was analogous to touching her and that gave her an uneasy eerie feeling. Later though, she was able to relax, hoping that everything was okay since the police hadn't come to arrest her—she wasn't a suspect—at least not yet anyway.

During the three weeks since Earl's death, she had heard from Paul just once and that was yesterday during the going away party that Hank and Lucille had thrown for her. Before he called, she thought that Paul had come to his senses and changed his mind. She thought he had realized that marrying a Negro teenager wasn't in his best interests. She was having second thoughts of her own, wondering how it was all going to work out being married to a white man, even though they were planning to travel the world for a few years. In a way, she wished Paul had changed his mind because she was on the verge of calling the wedding off and taking her chances with the police, which was one of the reasons she had gone to Fort Jackson to see Lucas.

She believed that if she had seen Lucas and had gotten a chance to explain her actions face to face instead of leaving a letter she wasn't sure he'd ever get, let alone read, she could have persuaded him to change his mind about ending their relationship. If Lucas changed his mind and gave her one last chance to do right by him, there was no way she would have gone on to Rhode Island. She would have stayed with Lucas and took her chances because she didn't love Paul. But at the same time, she was conflicted. She was glad she didn't get a chance to talk to Lucas because she believed Paul had been right—the recording devices alone were all the proof she needed. Sooner or later, people might start looking for her. If they found her, she wasn't certain that she'd escape again.

The train stopped forward momentum. People were suddenly in a hurry to get off and greet their loved ones, but she anticipated that. Seeing what happened at previous stops, she stood up as soon as the train stopped, grabbed her two suitcases and started down the aisle. Before long she was walking down the stairs and over to her fiancée. She saw the twinkle in his eyes and knew then that there would be no surprises. Not only hadn't Paul changed his mind, the look in his eyes let her know he was looking forward to seeing her and going through with the ceremony.

But still, she couldn't help thinking about Lucas at that moment. She couldn't help wondering if he ever got her letter and if he did, had he read it. She remembered sitting in the train depot waiting for him, looking at the door every time it opened, hoping it would be him, but also hoping he wouldn't come. While she wanted to be with him, her instincts told her that it was better to stick to the plan. It was better to be safe than sorry. It was better to flee the country and live than stay with her one and only true love and die. She convinced herself that God had answered her prayer and had handpicked Paul Masterson specifically for her. Besides, she had been through enough. She had hit rock bottom and now she was ready to do what she knew was right, what she had been taught by the teachers at Mount Zion Holiness Church in Sable Parish.

Even though he had called the previous day, a mountain of trepidation was still anchored to her heart because she wasn't sure Paul would be there waiting for her. Due to her own ambiguity, she thought he probably felt the same way, but he was too much of a gentleman to be honest about his true feelings over the phone. It had all happened so fast. Neither of them had time to consider the consequences of an interracial marriage. But three weeks had passed and they both had more than enough time to weigh the pros and cons of entering that kind of legal relationship. On the way to Rhode Island, she started thinking that he had only called to see if she was still going to show up; that way he wouldn't have to let her down. Now that he was there, she told herself that she was going to be totally committed to him and the marriage.

She looked deep into his eyes, hoping to see whatever hidden truth he might try to hide from her and said, "Are you sure you want to marry me, Paul."

Without hesitation, he smiled and said, "Yes. I am."

"Good, because I think you were right."

"About?"

"I found five recording devices in my hotel room."

"What?"

"Yes. I think we're doing the right thing."

"Why didn't you tell me this over the phone?"

"I couldn't take that chance. I didn't know who might have been listening. Besides, what could you have done?"

"You'll have to tell me all about this when we get on the train. If someone figures out you came here, I don't want anybody to recall anything you said in our taxi."

Then he took her luggage and they walked to the cab he had waiting. An hour later, they were at the courthouse promising to love, honor, and cherish each other for the rest of their lives. After reciting their vows, Paul insisted that they get a bite to eat at Camille's restaurant on Historic Federal Hill. Two hours after having a fabulous meal, they were in a private car on a train heading to New York City, their Port of Call, where they would board the SS Independence, set sail for France, and spend two fabulous weeks at the Negresco Hotel in a suite overlooking the breathtaking French Riviera.

Chapter 10

Know Thy Enemy

J anet Shamus stayed up nearly all night, going through all the material in the pouch, examining each photo, listening to tape after tape, reading the newspaper articles about Johnnie, her mother, the Beauregards, Sharon Trudeau, and Klan leader, Richard Goode. She wanted to learn everything her mother had learned about her father and his beautiful courtesan. It was more like a study session, like she was preparing for a final oral exam with the most demanding teacher in her school. She had an insatiable desire to know the material and the subjects she had read and heard about as well or better than they knew themselves. This was her mission, the endeavor that she was wholly committed to for however long it took.

The main subject of interest was Johnnie Wise. She looked at Johnnie's pictures longer than any in the collection, hoping to get inside the mind of a woman as beautiful as she, trying to determine what she was capable of. Unlike her mother, if they ever met face to face, Janet would be well armed with the intimate details of her nemesis' life, her education, her stock portfolio, her tastes in food, clothing, shoes, jewelry, and the opposite sex. She would leave no stone unturned. No cave would be unexplored. As the tape of Bubbles delivering the two hundred and fifty thousand that the police never found played through the headphones she was wearing, she looked at photos of the lovers Johnnie had chosen.

Of the four she had been intimate with, three of them were tall white men. That's when she realized that even though Hatcher hadn't mentioned it in their initial interview Paul Masterson was white too, making him the fourth white man to enter Johnnie's life and sooner or later, her body. As far as Janet was concerned, Johnnie Wise had a bent for white men with money. It was starting to make more sense as to why Hatcher had said that if anybody helped her, it was Masterson. According to his photograph, Hank was probably strong enough to put her dead father in his Cadillac, but a black man would have had trouble getting all the way from Jackson driving an expensive car in the wee hours of the morning. Maybe Sammy Davis Jr. could drive one in Beverly Hills without being questioned by the police, but in the south, he would be pulled over in a heartbeat and asked lots of questions. Even if Davis could prove that the Cadillac belonged to him, he still may have had to spend the night in lock up to satisfy some good ol' boys' jealousy or his power lust—perhaps both. Then it occurred to Janet that Hatcher had given her a report on Masterson.

In her haste to read the newspaper articles and listen to the recordings, the report had completely slipped her mind. There was probably a photo in there too. She had left the package in the kitchen where she ate dinner and had a slice of Mildred's homemade coconut crème pie. She stopped the tape, pulled off her headphones and went into the kitchen. The package was in a chair right where she left it, which made it easy to forget—out of sight out of mind. She opened the package as she made her way back to the library.

There he was. Paul Masterson. She wondered if they were together in Jackson or East Saint Louis perhaps. She found him extremely attractive and let her mind ease into the realm of the forbidden—at least by her mother's standards. Meredith had taught her daughters that not only shouldn't a lady do lustful things, they shouldn't even think them, yet that was exactly what Janet was about to do—think about the forbidden and allow scandalous enticement to ensnare her. And in so doing, she could perhaps understand her father and men and women like him, which would make the pursuit of Johnnie all the more appealing. Still looking at Masterson's photograph, she fingered the black pearls that she hung around her neck, wondering what it would be like to have dinner with him, where she could question him, listen to his answers to determine if he was even worth the time to take him from Johnnie.

In an instant, she imagined having sex with him in Johnnie's bed at a time that they knew she could return to their den of wickedness. She pictured the look on Johnnie's face when she first heard their rhythmic sighs, and then saw her white paramour inside her, enjoy-ing her body, thrusting wildly like an unbroken colt, calling her name as his release drew near. God she would do anything to see Johnnie's face at that moment. Perhaps then she would have an inkling of what her mother felt when she saw pictures of her father and Johnnie together. Surrendering her virginity to Masterson might even be worth it.

Continuing her wanton gaze at Masterson's picture, she won-dered what her father could have been thinking to get involved with a girl a year younger than she. She also wondered if it was true that he would have gotten involved with her when she was twelve. At that instant, the memory of her father giving her a brand new red bicycle on her birthday surfaced. She remembered the birthday party and having all her friends over for the celebration. She remembered him hugging and kissing her several times that day. Now she was wondering if all the kisses and hugs were incestuously rooted. She wondered if she was somehow the blame for what happened with Johnnie. She wondered if he was so twisted inside that he wanted to bed his own daughter, but took his evil yearnings out on another vulnerable girl; one that nobody cared about, not even her own mother who profited off the illegal activity.

While she knew her father was the initiator of the libidinous re-lationship, she nevertheless blamed Johnnie almost exclusively for taking her father and all he had to offer away from her, procuring *her* time, stealing *her* hugs, *her* kisses. The words "grand larceny" came to mind. Because of the great love that she had for her father, she saw him high on a throne; he could do no wrong. She therefore excused his unfaithful behavior toward her mother and his complici-ty in the relationship because he was her hero—her knight in white satin, her man of the century—no man was greater in her eyes. Besides, what was the big deal anyway? Weren't all men guilty of doing those sorts of things to their wives and children? Wasn't it in their blood?

But Johnnie and her conniving mother knew better and had tak-en advantage of her father's weakness. Beside, all women knew that another woman's family was sacred ground, not to be trampled upon. All women knew they were home-wreckers if they got involved with a married man and would be labeled as such once the secret liaison was discovered. She picked up a picture of Marguerite, who was wearing a painted on white two-piece bathing suit, and examined it for the tenth time, mentally acknowledging her alarming beauty and the curves that men like Tony Hatcher would lose their minds over. She was so consumed with revenge that she almost hoped Marguerite was alive so she could take a measure of vengeance out on her as well for rearing her daughter to be the woman she became, following in her footsteps, thinking that such behavior was not only acceptable, but that it was righteous as well. But alas, Marguerite was dead. Therefore Johnnie would feel the full force of her fury one way or the other. The only question that remained was whether or not she would tell her sisters about the tapes and let them listen.

She decided she would, that way they could help her destroy the woman who had destroyed their family. Her eyelids were getting heavy as time moved forward with no regard for her desire to continue studying her enemy, preparing for the eventual showdown. She looked at the clock on the library wall. 3 am. She was listening to the sexually charged phone conversation Johnnie was having with Napoleon Bentley on Christmas Day, totally disgusted by everything she'd heard, yet found herself being aroused by it too. The thing that bothered her most was that Johnnie had just gotten home from visiting her boyfriend who was in prison. Yet she was making plans to see Napoleon that very night at the Bel Glades Hotel with every intention of doing the unmentionable things they openly talked about. She was about to take the headphones off when she heard Johnnie swearing at someone. Then she heard what sounded like the door being kicked in and lots of commotion. A man was threatening to rape Johnnie. Moments later, he was raping her. Then there was complete silence. As the silence lingered, Janet picked up an article and read about the brutal death of Billy Logan, the man in the kitchen raping Johnnie. Hearing a woman being raped made her feel sorry for Johnnie for a few minutes, but when the rape was over and her assailant left her home, the quiet made her eyelids heavy and she fell asleep.

Chapter 11

"Don't you think there's been enough death in our family, Janet?

"Miss Shamus. Miss Shamus," Janet heard Mildred, her Negro maid, say as she was coming out of the fog of deep satisfying sleep. She opened her eyes and wiped the saliva off her mouth. She was still in the library with the headphones on. The tape player was still spinning, having played the entire tape. Her head was resting on her right arm which was stretched out on the table. She raised her head and reflexively said, "What time is it?"

"It's six o'clock, Miss Shamus," Mildred said "Time to shower and get ready for work."

Janet looked at Mildred, who was standing right next to her. Hugging her she said, "What would we have done without you these past few weeks? You know me and my sisters love you with all our hearts, don't you, Mildred."

"Yes, ma'am, I know. You tell me that every day. Now . . . up and at 'em."

"Are my sisters up?"

"Yes. I woke them up first. You looked so peaceful that I didn't want to wake you. I wanted you to continue having peace for as long as you could. Peace of mind is such a precious thing, Miss Shamus. I wouldn't trade it for all the riches of this world."

"Really?"

"Really."

"I could use a good dose of serenity. What's the secret to lasting peace?"

"The good book says to love your enemies? That's what I do."

An arrow of conviction pierced Janet's heart. She looked at the floor for a moment and then into Mildred's eyes. "But what if your enemies severely wounded you?"

"Then they need more love," Mildred said, smiling. "Even my enemies don't know they're my enemies."

"So you're telling me you wouldn't want revenge for what they did to you?"

"No. I'm saying I would want revenge at first. It's human and natural to want to hurt the person that hurt you or someone close to you. But I wouldn't take revenge because then I would have to surrender peace of mind. You cannot seek revenge and have peace of mind. You can medicate yourself with entertainment, having friends and family over for a party, drinking, eating, or whatever, but you'll never find true peace that way. The secret to lasting peace is forgiveness. The more you forgive the more peace you'll have. The less you forgive the less peace you'll have. Now, get in the shower and by the time you're done, I'll have a delicious breakfast for you and your sisters."

"What are we having?"

"I think we'll have pancakes, sausage, eggs, biscuits, grits and cantaloupe."

"Sounds delicious. I'll be back down here in about thirty minutes."

On her way up the stairs, Janet thought about what Mildred had said and quickly dismissed it as unsound religious sophistry. She was going to take care of Johnnie Wise no matter what. All she needed to know now was whether or not her sisters wanted to be apart of it. She knocked on Marjorie's door.

"Come in."

Janet entered the room and said, "I need to talk to you and Stacy on the way to school."

"What about?"

"What happened to mom and dad and who's responsible. And what we're going to do about it."

"What *we're* going to do about it? What do you mean?"

"I'll talk to you about it after breakfast before I drop you and Stacy off for school, okay?"

Hesitantly, Marjorie said, "Okay."

"What's the matter? Don't you want the person responsible for their deaths to die too?"

Marjorie shrugged her shoulders.

"Answer me," Janet said, raising her voice a little.

"Don't you think there's been enough death in our family, Janet? Do you really want to spill more blood? I've had enough. I just wanna live and do what's right."

Janet rolled her eyes and said, "I think you'll change your mind once you know what I know."

"I doubt it."

Janet stared at her for a long minute without saying anything. Then she said, "Make sure Stacy's awake. Mildred's making pancakes." Then she left Stacy's room in a huff.

Chapter 12

<u>"And you're not going to hold any grudges?"</u>

"I don't understand you two," Janet said loudly later that evening. They were in the library, listening to the tapes and examining everything that was in the pouch. "Mom and dad are dead because of Johnnie Wise and you two want her to get away with it?"

Stacy said, "Mom was killed by Ethel Beauregard, Janet. The Sentinel article you asked us to read says so."

"Yeah, and dad died of a heart attack on the way home," Marjorie said.

"But why was mom in the courtroom in the first place, Stacy?" Janet asked angrily. "Wasn't she there testifying about the relationship dad was having with this Johnnie person?"

"Yes," Stacy said, nodding. "But if dad hadn't been involved with the girl, mom wouldn't have had to testify. She wouldn't have even been in that courtroom if it wasn't for dad."

"Did you hear the tapes, Stacy?" Janet shot back, furious now after hearing her baby sister defend the woman she had every intention of destroying.

Stacy nodded and said, "Did you?"

"Then you know mother gave her fifty thousand dollars to keep our family out of it. Did you hear that or what?"

"Of course I heard it, Janet," Stacy said. "You played the tape back three times. But the fifty thousand was to keep our family name out of her mother's murder. Mom must have thought that dad had killed the girl's mother."

"Yeah, Janet," Marjorie said. "There was nothing in the agreement about Johnnie being tried for Sharon Trudeau's murder. And from these tapes, we know Johnnie had nothing to do with Sharon's murder. If anybody killed her it was that George Grant person. I mean he was the person who gave her back the money. Johnnie wasn't even in Fort Lauderdale. If dad hadn't gotten involved with Johnnie in the first place, none of this would have happened. I've learned my lesson from what happened to our brother. I think we oughta leave it alone. I really do. Otherwise something terrible will happen if we don't."

"Something like what?" Janet shouted.

"Janet, you've read the papers. You know that anybody that gets involved with Johnnie Wise ends up dead one way or the other. The Beauregard family was pretty much wiped out in one day. They lost four men and one woman on Thanksgiving Day, but nothing happened to Johnnie. The papers say that Ethel was trying to kill Johnnie in court and hit just about everybody but Johnnie."

"She got lucky, Marjorie," Janet said angrily.

"Did she, Janet?" Marjorie asked. "Or was God looking out for her?"

"So you're saying God wasn't looking out for our mother and father?"

"Apparently not, Janet," Stacy said. "Mom and dad are in their graves. Johnnie Wise is still alive. What do you think?"

"You know what I think," Janet said, through clenched teeth. "And I'm going to see to it that justice is done. Mom and dad will be avenged one way or another. Now . . . are you two with me on this? Or do I have to take care of it on my own."

"I'm not with you on this, Janet," Stacy said, looking her eldest sister in the eyes. "It's wrong. I can't be a part of it."

"Fine, I'll count you out," Janet said. She looked at Marjorie. "Are you in or out?"

"The last time I did what you wanted, my little brother ended up accidentally dead," Marjorie said. "So . . . no, thank you."

"Fine," Janet said, glaring at her sisters, thoroughly disappointed by what appeared to be apathy. "Do you at least want to know anything about it?"

"No," Stacy said.

"No," Marjorie said.

Shaking her head, Janet said, "Did you two even love our parents? Or were you two just content to live off them?"

"The truth is we were all living off grandpa, even though he died," Marjorie said. "All the money was his. Mom and dad lived off him and then we lived off him through them. I still remember how we lived before our little brother came along. We lived like the Negroes in Sable Parish. Now what do we have, Janet? We've got a big house with lots of rooms, plenty of food, lots of green grass, horses, two swimming pools, cars, and all the money we'll ever need. We'll never want for anything ever again thanks to grandpa. I don't want to go back to the way we lived before."

"We won't," Janet said. "I promise."

"You promised that Little Buck wouldn't get hurt too," Stacy said. "Look at how that turned out."

Janet raised her hand to slap Stacy, but Stacy cowered back, protecting herself.

Marjorie said, "Is that your answer to everything, Janet. Are you going to beat or kill everyone who disagrees with you?"

"Yeah, Janet," Stacy said. "Now that you have control of grandpa's money, you're starting to act just like him."

"Yeah," Marjorie said. "It's a good thing mom left us trust funds. Otherwise Stacy and I might have to fend for ourselves."

"I could never be like grandpa. I could never treat my family the way he treated us. If you two don't want to help me do what I have to do, fine. I'll do it myself."

"And you're not going to hold any grudges?" Marjorie asked.

"No. No grudges," Janet said. "You're the only family I have left. I'm going to do everything in my power to see to it that you two have the very best of everything. And if I have to spend the rest of my life proving to you that I'm nothing like our grandfather, that's exactly what I'm going to do."

"Really, Janet?" Marjorie said. "So you're going to let me to go to the prom with Wilbur Mitchell if he asks me?"

"Dad didn't like him and neither did mom," Janet said. "I don't think it's a good idea. Who knows what he's capable of?"

"But you just said you were going to do everything in your power to prove that you're nothing like grandpa. Now you're not going to let me go out with a dreamboat like Wilbur Mitchell, the star of the football and basketball teams?"

"I'll tell you what, if he asks you to the prom like a gentleman, not only will I let you go, but I'll hire a seamstress that'll make sure you'll be the queen of the prom, okay?"

"Really Janet?"

"Really. Anything for my little sister."

Chapter 13

"Where are we having our first dinner in Nice?"

J ohnnie and Paul had spent eight wonderful days at sea, being totally pampered by dedicated stewards who wore white jackets, white gloves, and white bowties while waiting on them hand and foot, seeing to it that they wanted for nothing, which was to be expected for guests whose accommodations were the presidential suite of the SS Independence. Now they were in their honeymoon suite at the Negresco Hotel in Nice. So far, everything had gone marvelously well for them during the journey except for the sex—there wasn't any. When they left the courthouse, Johnnie thought Paul would rush her over to the nearest hotel so he could have his way with her, but he didn't and she found that extremely puzzling. Her experiences with Earl Shamus, Napoleon Bentley, and Martin Winters, all white men, had been altogether different, and gave her the impression that all men of Masterson's hue were of the same character.

After having eaten a scrumptious dinner at Camille's together, she thought for sure they would head over to a hotel and have the obligatory sex that was expected after the nuptials, but again it didn't happen. Then, after they boarded the Independence, she knew he would plunder her there. She thought Masterson had been savoring the moment because he didn't want to be in a rush. He wanted to take his time. As a matter of fact she was looking forward to it since he had made her wait. She couldn't wait to see what he looked like without his clothes on nor could she wait to be in bed with him to see if he could live up to her fantasies, but it didn't happen then either. While she appreciated his restraint, she also thought he was trying to prove that unlike the white men she had known before him, he had mastered his lust and despite her alarming beauty, he could wait to enter her indefinitely; all of which fed into her burgeoning desire to be naked with him in a quiet room where he could not escape her advances. So when he carried her over the threshold of their suite and entered one of the bedrooms, she immediately started undressing, but he stopped her and said, "Wait a minute, Johnnie."

Disappointed, she said, "Wait? For what? Don't you want to do it to me?"

Nodding, he said, "Yes, I do."

"Then what's the problem?" she said and put her hands on her hips, ready to have their first marital spat. "We're married. It's legal. God is okay with sex like this, isn't He?"

"Yes, but—"

"But what? Are you funny or something, Paul? Do you like men or what?"

He folded his arms, thinking, why do women always have to push the homosexual button when a man doesn't make sexual advances? But rather than get into that long debate, he simply answered her question. "No. I'm not."

"Then what's the problem? Am I not pretty enough for you? I bet if I was that woman you had the affair with, you would have done it to me by now."

That last sentence stung a bit because it was true. If his blushing bride were Anita Wilde, he would have taken her straight to the nearest hotel and plowed into her with no regard for whether she was ready to be plowed. In fact, he may have taken Anita straight to the hotel, and had his way with her. Then, after he had a measure of wicked physical satisfaction, he would have taken her to the courthouse, rushed through the vows, and then he would have taken her back to the hotel for another sizzling round of passionate pleasure. He wouldn't have cared about setting, mood, or romance. His lust for her would have driven him, forced him to take what he wanted especially since it would have no longer been wrong to do so. Looking at his bride, he exhaled softly and said, "Sit down, Johnnie." She locked eyes with him for a moment and then sat on the bed. "Listen to me for a second, okay?"

"Okay," she said, afraid of what he was going to say, hoping he wasn't going to confess that he was impotent.

"Johnnie . . . you're seventeen-years-old. You're just a kid. I know you don't feel that way, given all you've been through, but you are. Men have been disrespecting you for so long, using your body for their own base ends, you think that's its okay for me to treat you the same way, and you're disappointed that I haven't. So you question my sexuality because you don't know any better. You don't know any better because even though you've had a number of men, not one of them treated you the way a lady should be treated. I suspect that you've never even been courted by a man. It wouldn't surprise me if you've never been on a date. The men you've been with did what their lust told them to do. As a consequence of their twisted behavior, you no longer act like you did before they came along and devoured your innocence. And it doesn't help that most of the men that used you were white men."

"Yeah, but we're married, Paul. Although there's a lot of truth in what you say, you won't be using me. Even if you were using my body to fulfill your longings, we are legally bound. Besides, I want to be a good wife to you, Paul."

"And I plan to be a good husband to you. From this moment forth, I plan to do my best to reverse all that's happened to you, if you'll let me."

"If I'll let you? To be respected and treated right is all I ever wanted from anybody, including my own mother. I want you to know that from the moment we recited our vows, I was yours, mind, body, and soul. Now come on, let's consummate the marriage."

"No. That's your old mind trying to control you. You think because its legal, we should just plunge in, but that was never my plan and it isn't God's plan either. I know it's antiquated today, given the world you were raised in, but God made woman to complete man. And yes, we are married, but what kind of marriage is it? It's a marriage of convenience at this point, nothing more. The truth is we are not in love, right?"

Nodding, she said, "Right."

"I've seen similar marriages when I was in the service. As quiet as it's kept there are a number of homosexuals and lesbians married to each other to hide their deviant lifestyle. But because they're married to each other, no one suspects."

"You're joking, right?"

"Not at all. Every weekend they go out with another couple living the same lifestyle. They go on camping trips, vacations, and movies together so they can spend time with each other openly. Only a few people know this is going on. Those are marriages of convenience too."

"You've seen this, Paul?"

"As a matter of fact I have while it was going on."

"Were you in the room or something?"

"No. I was the base chaplain. A number of them came to me and told me all about it and who was involved. Some of them were high ranking officers and their wives."

"I guess they had a loveless empty marriage, huh?"

"They probably had to have relations with each other if they couldn't find another couple doing the same thing, but what kind of sex would it be? It would probably be empty, wouldn't it? I'm not content to have that kind of going-through-the-motions marriage. And when you're ready for a divorce, I'll sign the papers. But until that day, I'm going to do my best to get to know you and share a life with you the way God intended. Isn't that worth waiting for?"

"Honestly, Paul, I don't know. I've never been in a relationship where we waited. Not one. I suppose we could count my relationship with Lucas, but we only waited a couple weeks, if you want to classify that as waiting."

"See, that's exactly what I'm talking about, Johnnie. You don't know what it is to have a real relationship with a man because you've been led to believe that even the relationship with your boyfriend was a good one. Getting involved in that kind of lifestyle at fifteen has undoubtedly affected every part of your life and you don't even know it. For example, if your mother and Earl Shamus hadn't done what they did to you, you would be graduating from high school in a few months, wouldn't you?"

Johnnie lowered her eyes to the floor, thinking about all the girls she knew who would be walking across the stage to get their diplomas. She hadn't thought about school in a long time. Now, though, she could see the faces of the girls who were not as bright as she was, but they would probably be getting their diplomas and she wouldn't. They would be starting their lives, getting an education at one of the Negro colleges, or getting jobs, making choices she no longer had because she was on the run. She fought it, but her eyes welled as the tidal wave of emotions threatened to become a tsunami. She took a deep breath and said, "Yes, I would be graduating. And I have no doubt that I would have been valedictorian. I was a good student, Paul."

"Of that I have no doubt. So don't you see why I'm reluctant to do to you what other evil reckless white men have done?"

She nodded. "I guess I do."

"You need to be shown love, true love in all of its forms."

"What do you mean true love in all of its forms?"

"Johnnie, I've traveled the world and I've learned quite a bit from other cultures. For example, the Greeks have at least five different words for love whereas we only have one word and we use it in all of our relationships, including parent-child love, which adds to the confusion in many relationships. Do you understand?"

"Not really."

"I think you will in time," he said, while looking into her eyes. "When we were in Jackson, we only spent a few hours together. Don't get me wrong, Johnnie, I enjoyed spending those hours with you. It was all I thought about the last few weeks, but the truth is, we don't know each other and I don't think we should have relations until we do. I think it will be so much better if we wait. You still don't know if you did the right thing by marrying me. You only married me to protect yourself from legal consequences in the future. I know that and I understand that. But in time, you may come to regret that decision. You'll remember everything that happened and if I give into my passion now, you'll end up resenting me because you'll think I only married you to have relations with you. You may not understand that now, but as a man more than ten years older than you, I have lived long enough, been through enough, to know that right now you think you owe me something because I helped you when you needed it most. Were it not for your past, those feelings of gratitude you are now experiencing would be met with a gracious thank you, not obligatory sex. As a man, I have to take responsibility for what happens to you now because your relationship to me will help shape your future with men in general and your children. Somebody has to show you something different than what you've seen so that you can become whole again. Let's get to know each other first. Let me court you awhile. Let me take you on dates. Let me show you the world. And while I show it to you, let me take you out and wine and dine you every night so that you can experience what you should have a experienced a long time ago. Let me try to create an atmosphere that would make us fall madly in love with each other. And then perhaps our marriage could be all that it could and should be."

"You know what, Paul?"

"What?"

"You've got to be the strangest white man I've ever met, but right now, I wouldn't trade you in for nothing in the world. So this is what respect is? This is what it feels like?"

"I guess. I don't know what you're feeling, Johnnie. Talk to me about it. Explain your feelings to me if you can. I need to know what's going on inside you."

"Well, to be honest, it almost feels like being unblemished again. It feels like I deserved to wear white at our wedding. For the second time in my life it feels like a man, a real man actually cares for me and not the satisfaction my body offers him. It feels good to be respected, Paul. It really does. It feels good to know what it really means too. What did I ever do to deserve such a caring man?"

"Wait a minute," he said. "Just hold on there now." He sat on the bed next to her. "Did you forget what I told you in Jackson? That I had gotten involved with a woman and ended up leaving my church?"

"Yes. So what? That's the past, Paul."

"Yes it is. But it's been my experience that the past tends to visit the present when least expected."

"What are you saying? You expect to see this woman again or something?"

"No, but who knows. What if I impregnated her like I did with my high school sweetheart and I have a child or even twins and don't even know it? What if we return to the States and she shows up at our doorstep with junior? What then?"

Johnnie reached out and took hold of his hand, lacing her fingers between his. Then she looked him in the eyes and said, "We'll have to deal with it if and when it happens. Just like we'll have to deal with my past if people come looking for me. It's going to be fun running around for a few years and seeing the world, but you and I both know that eventually we'll have to go back home and try and build a life together."

"I know."

"Do you really? By the way you talk, I wonder if you understand."

"Trust me. I know what we're up against back home in the States."

"I just hope you were right about all those white folks in all those states that legalized marriages between coloreds and whites. We can't run away from race hatred forever, Paul. You know that, don't you?"

He nodded. "But we can do it for a nice long while."

"How, Paul? We're in Europe. I've seen plenty of white folk so far. I'm sure they'll hate me just as much as the whites in the United States."

"That's why it's good to travel, Johnnie. We're going to have a marvelous time. I promise. With the exception of a few, I doubt that we'll have any trouble at all. And the few will probably be racist Americans traveling abroad. Whatever trouble we have, we probably won't even notice. People with money can usually buy all the respect they want, even in the States. And if not respect, fear. Most people either respect or fear those who have money."

"Most people? I thought all people respected money."

"Poor white trash in the States, don't. They can be as broke or even more destitute than the Negro, yet they think they're better."

She exhaled softly and rested her head on his shoulder and said, "Promise me you'll put my life above your own if we happen to see Americans who hate me because I'm colored."

"I promise," he said and kissed her forehead. "Now . . . are you hungry? I'm starved."

"Me too," she said, smiling. "Where are we having our first dinner in Nice?"

"I thought we might take a short walk down Promenade des Anglais and head over to Abrielle Darci's for some of her delicious grub."

"What do they serve?"

Taking opportunity to impress her with his French he rattled off a portion of the menu. "Abrielle has a wonderful selection of foods I think you'll enjoy the Steak Frites, Poulet Frites, Blanquette de Veau, Coq au Feu, Bouillabaisse, Boudin Blanc, Foie de Veau, and Foie Gras. And for dessert you may want to try the Mousse au Chocolat, Crème Brulee, Religieuse, Madeleine, Tarte Tatin, Éclairs, or the Profiteroles."

She smiled and said, "I'll bet you're having the steak and fries, right?"

Paul returned her smile and said, "That was probably easy for you to figure out? But what about the rest of what I said? Do you have any idea?"

"Hmm, let's see, I believe you also said, chicken and fries, veal, rooster in red wine, beef stew with mixed vegetables, fish soup, flavored sausage, calf's liver, and fatty duck. Do I need to translate the dessert menu too?"

Smiling he said, "No. I guess not. But you've proven my point. You realize that, don't you?"

"Which was what, Paul?"

"We don't know each other all that well. I had no idea you spoke French so fluently, although I shouldn't be surprise with you being from New Orleans and all. Tell me, do you speak any other languages?"

Shaking her head, she said, "Just English and French. What about you?"

"I speak French, German, Spanish, and a little Portuguese, Hindi, Burmese, and Mandarin."

"Really?"

He nodded, proudly. "I'm still trying to absorb those languages. I'd like to learn more. I think they'll come in handy with all the places we're visiting."

"Will you teach me those languages? That way we can have secret conversations if we want to discuss people where we're traveling."

"Sounds like fun," he said. "Why don't you take this bedroom and I'll take the other."

"You mean we're not even going to sleep in the same bed?"

"Honestly, I don't think I could stand being in the same bed with you night after night without losing control. I don't think any man on the planet could. So, why don't you unpack, freshen up, and meet me in the living room in twenty minutes or so."

"I'll see you then."

Chapter 14

It was a couple minutes after 9 pm and Janet Shamus was at home, in her office, firmly ensconced in the comfortable chair that was first her grandfather's, then her mother's, and finally, her father's, meticulously going through information Tony Hatcher had given her earlier that day. According to the dossier, Paul Masterson was the youngest of four boys and three girls born to Bryce and Johann Masterson. Bryce, the son of a surgeon, was a developer who met and married the daughter and sole heir of sugar cane magnate, Conrad Wagner, and his wife Carly, in 1910 against her parents' wishes. The Wagners, natives of Queensland, Australia, immediately disinherited Johann, hoping she would leave the struggling developer and return to the comforts of home, where they were planning to fix her up with a more suitable beau who had old money. But when the deal Bryce had struck to turn the land he had been bequeathed by his grandfather into a luxurious suburb for the affluent twenty-five miles outside Houston was mysteriously pulled off the table, a vast vein of oil was discovered on the land and turned Bryce into an instant millionaire. Soon afterward, Bryce was ceremoniously welcomed to the Wagner family with open arms. Bryce later discovered that his father-in-law ruthlessly used his influence to get the bank to withdraw their finances at the last minute to ruin him.

Paul Masterson was born August 1, 1924. He graduated from St. Johns high school in 1942 and was the first student athlete to graduate class valedictorian. His speech was titled: The Continuing Need for Truth and Justice. Paul was an all around athlete. He lettered in football, basketball, baseball, and track. While it was kept under wraps, he had gotten Wendy Malstrom, his high school sweetheart, with child. Wendy's father, being a doctor, had a colleague dispense with the child, thus freeing his daughter of unwanted parental and marital obligation. Paul had taken the abortion hard and entered Dallas Theological Seminary during the summer of 1942, where he graduated in 1946 with a Master of Theology degree and became the assistant pastor of Trinity Holiness Church, a smallish house of worship in the Greater Houston area.

The head pastor died unexpectedly a month later but Paul, who was only twenty-two, had made an immediate impact on the congregation and was asked to lead. He humbly accepted the responsibility and in less than three months, the membership had outgrown its building and they bought another; it too was growing at an astounding rate. His parishioners couldn't get enough of his emotionally charged expository sermons that compelled Christians to turn away from their sins and back to their God. After being the lone voice crying for reform in what had become a religious wilderness, openly demanding accountability among church leadership, Masterson met vivacious Anita Wilde September 18, 1947, a little over a year after accepting the position of head pastor.

Hatcher found Anita Wilde in Scottsdale, Arizona, where she was living with her husband, a well-established Pentecostal preacher named Judah Jacobson. Janet looked at Jacobson's photo which instantly reminded her of Paul Masterson. She placed both photos on the desk side-by-side and examined them. Janet thought the two men could be brothers or at least distant cousins with one major difference. Jacobson looked older than Paul by about twenty years. She shuffled the papers until she came to the information on Jacobson. He was born January 2, 1903, making him fifty-one-years-old. Janet assumed that Anita had found herself another Paul Masterson and married him, which led her to believe that even though she had taken money from the church elders to bring Masterson to his knees, she had apparently fallen deeply in love with her supposed victim.

Janet further assumed that when Masterson joined the service, Anita, longing for him, or perhaps feeling the pangs of what she had done, went in search of her long lost love and when she couldn't find him, replaced him with a suitable surrogate June 17, 1949. The Jacobsons had three boys during their five year marriage. Janet wondered if Anita was truly converted and had changed her street-walker ways. A number of questions came to mind. Was Anita's marriage a hoax? Had she truly fallen in love with another man who happened to be a preacher? Or was whoredom and greed in her blood? If it was, could she still be bought and sold at market value? Did her husband know of her decadent past? If not, could that fact be used to blackmail Anita into being one of her instruments of revenge?

She continued reading Hatcher's report and learned that Anita's pedigree was of the sort that one could understand why she accepted the bribe offered by the church elders. She was born November 21, 1929, in Tupelo, Mississippi, twenty-four days after "Black Tues-day" October 29, 1929, the most financially devastating day in U.S. history. Her parents were landowners, employing a hundred Ne-groes. They were living a lavish lifestyle, but the crash wiped them out and they found themselves working alongside their former Negro employees as dirt poor sharecroppers. Anita left home the day she graduated from high school, apparently seeking a better life in better surroundings, no doubt hoping for someone to rescue her and give her the life she dreamed of. The details as to how she became a prostitute were not in the file, but it wasn't hard to figure out. Janet assumed that young Anita left home with unrealistic fantasies and eventually ended up selling the only thing of value she had. How she became what she became didn't matter though. What mattered most to Janet was what Anita would do if she faced the pressures of losing everything and starvation. If she used her considerable wealth to apply the necessary pressure would Anita allow herself to be used again?

Janet examined Jacobson's finances and saw a glaring weakness. While he was doing well for a man of the cloth, all of his money was tied up in real estate. Owning land was normally a good and safe investment. However, for an ambitious, bent on revenge executive like Janet, it was a huge opening. A broad smile crept across her lips when an idea for pressure came to mind. She believed that a man twenty-six years older than his spirited twenty-four-year-old wife probably couldn't keep up with her. Janet started to wonder if Anita had any extramarital affairs during the course of their marriage. She shuffled through the papers again and found that Mrs. Jacobson had indeed had affairs with three different men so far, and was still currently seeing the third man on Wednesday nights when her husband was teaching midweek bible study at the church. After learning of Mrs. Jacobson's extracurricular indiscretions, Janet wondered if the sons she had were her husband's. It didn't matter if they were or not. The fact that she could use the knowledge of the affairs was all she needed to have sway over her prey. No mother wants her sons to know that she had been a whore in her past life and was still practicing the wicked vocation in the present.

The phone rang. She removed her right earring, picked up the receiver, placed it to her ear, and said, "Janet Shamus."

"Tony Hatcher here."

She looked at her watch. It was 9:30. "Yes, Mr. Hatcher. I take it you have something to report."

Chapter 15

Whatever Happened to Marla Bentley?

Tony Hatcher had married his high school sweetheart and they had five beautiful children together. They had been very happy until his private eye business blossomed and made it possible for them to live at a much higher standard. However, success demanded that he work lots of hours. There didn't seem to be any end to the clients. But he made the mistake of getting involved with a client who initially wanted him to investigate her husband's activities. As usual, the wife was right. Her husband was having an affair with his secretary and Hatcher had gotten the goods. When he showed his client the pictures, she fell completely apart.

Attempting to console her, he ended up having sex with her on his desk with the sordid pictures of her husband and his secret beneath them, watching her flesh vigorously receive Hatcher's. It was a onetime thing with her, and he was very sorry for what he had done and vowed never to do it again since he had gotten away with it. His wife didn't know and never suspected that the love of her live had been in the orchard of not only another woman, but a married woman. As time progressed, Hatcher ended up having numerous affairs with his clients. Some of the affairs were short and others were long and hot. After awhile, he got careless and soon, a private detective had gotten the goods on him. His wife's heart was completely shattered.

There was no fixing the marriage. She left him that very day and he'd been paying alimony and child support for the last five years. Nevertheless, his business continued to grow. He had more clients than he could take on and so he moved downtown and hired a staff. He even bought himself a bachelor's pad where he could bring hot wives for quick meaningless romps. Then, when he thought things couldn't get any better for him, the bottom fell out and now he was in debt up to his ears. Were it not for Meredith Shamus' generosity, he would have gone under six months ago.

In the meantime, he had to work for people he didn't particularly like to try and get out from under. Were it not for the hefty payday he could get from Janet Shamus, he wouldn't even consider taking her on as a client. Even though he had become a philanderer over the years, he still had a code of honor that he didn't violate. Part of the code was that he didn't bed wives if their husbands were faithful to them. He wasn't a home wrecker—at least that's what he told himself. He convinced himself that the husbands brought what he did to their wives on themselves. The way he saw it, they got what was coming to them. Hatcher on the other hand got hot sex without the headache of having to be in a relationship that required lots of work to keep it going in a positive romantic direction.

Hatcher's eyes were tired and watery after making the eleven hour drive from East St. Louis to New Orleans. He parked his car and entered the home he had purchased four years ago when business was going well. He was in a hurry to get back home so he didn't bother stopping the last two hundred miles. Now it was urgent that he relieve himself. He fast-walked to the bathroom and emptied his bladder. Even though he was tired, he went into the kitchen, turned on his Westinghouse radio, and listened while he made himself a sandwich. He grabbed a cold beer, sat at the kitchen table, and was about to start eating when Janet Shamus' image invaded his mind.

A sexual struggle ensued for a moment or two when he thought about calling to let her know he was back and what he had learned, but he figured it could wait until morning. Besides he was just too tired to deal with her if she wasn't satisfied with his report and he didn't want any further incursions of her image when he was in the dream world. While he ate the last conversation he'd had with her replayed itself. She had told him not to fall in love with her. He smiled when he thought about her arrogance and then envy made an appearance when he thought about all the money she had at her disposal; money she hadn't earned but had gotten for being born at the right time in the right family. He wished he had a rich grandfather who thought enough of him to leave him a fortune too.

Feeling the full weight of dissatisfaction, he then looked around his kitchen and realized that his life hadn't improved over the years. He realized that being a good private detective wasn't good enough to make it big. He realized that his vision of having the best private detective agency in New Orleans was never going to happen unless someone like Janet Shamus used her money and influence to make it happen. But he had too much pride to let some teenage girl put a ring in his nose and lead him around like an elephant in a Barnum & Bailey Circus act. But still, he knew he wasn't getting any younger and while he could afford to have principles when he was twenty-two, he was now thirty-six, and rapidly approaching forty. As he listened to a radio announcer deliver world news events, he opened his beer and gulped down several swallows.

"This is Sherman Johns and welcome to the Sherman Johns Associated Press report brought to you by Maxwell House coffee. In just a minute, I'll get you caught up on what's been happening around the world for the past two weeks, but first, a word from our sponsor."

The Maxwell House coffee jingle began. "For coffee that's good to the very last drop, reach for the coffee with the stars on top. Try instant Maxwell House coffee today."

"And now back to the news. On March 1st Earl Warren was confirmed as Chief Justice of the Supreme Court. The United States tested a hydrogen bomb with the force of 1000 Hiroshima bombs on Marshall Islands located in the central Pacific Ocean north of the equator. On the sporting front, baseball great, Ted Williams flew 39 combat missions in the Korean War without a scratch. But on March 1st, he fractured his collar bone playing a game of baseball. In more serious news, five congressmen were wounded by Puerto Rican nationalists in the U.S. House of Representatives. A woman identified as Marla Bentley was found in her Cadillac in Red River, Louisiana. Her neck had been broken."

Hatcher looked at the radio and frowned.

"She checked into the Red River Motel, the proprietor said, but she didn't bother returning the key to the front desk when she left the following day."

Hatcher took a couple more swallows of his beer. Then grabbed a map of Louisiana off the refrigerator and unfolded it on the table.

"The Cadillac had Chicago plates," Sherman Johns was saying. "Her mother told the police she was living with her in Chicago and that she had filed for divorce. The police have tried contacting her husband in New Orleans, but he hasn't been seen in as many weeks as Mrs. Bentley has been missing, his neighbors say."

At first Hatcher thought that perhaps Napoleon had killed Marla, but that didn't make any sense. A broken neck was an act of passion. Why would Napoleon kill her? It couldn't have been because she was divorcing him. She had already moved to Chicago. And even if he did, why would he kill her in Red River? Why not have one of his associates in Chicago take care of her in the Windy City. Besides, he'd heard the sexually explicit phone conversation between Napoleon and Johnnie. According to what he heard during the course of that conversation, Napoleon didn't miss Marla at all. In fact he seemed to be glad she was gone. Then Hatcher remembered that Lucas had been at the courthouse the day Meredith Shamus was killed and wondered if he had done the deed. Looking at the map, he realized that Marla Bentley would have had to drive almost nine hundred miles to Red River.

A woman in love would make the drive, Hatcher reasoned, especially if she knew her lover wouldn't make the drive up to Chicago. He had heard the tapes of Johnnie and Lucas talking in her bathroom and he knew that Marla and Lucas were having a sizzling affair. Lucas on the other hand would have to drive about two hundred miles from Angola. That was doable, especially since he hadn't had any sex in over a month. The trouble was he didn't have a car in prison. If he went to Red River, it was in all likelihood by bus. Hatcher further reasoned that if Lucas did take the bus there, it was probably at night so that no one could see him with a white woman in a motel. Did he go there to kill her or to have sex? Or did he go there to have sex and then kill her? Was her death an accident? How

could it have been an accident if her neck was broken? He would
have to have had his hands around her neck.

Hatcher wondered if Lucas knew where Johnnie was. If he did,
he could use the news flash as leverage. But first he had to confirm
that Lucas knew that Marla was going to be in Red River. Then he
would have to find the bus driver and confirm that he had picked up
a Negro male fitting Lucas's description that night. That would be
difficult enough because bus drivers pick up people all the time. To
positively identify one man, even if he was a Negro would be
difficult to do. The other problem was that he would have to depend
on the Angola Prison guards to remember if Lucas was getting mail
from Chicago. The guards at Angola were known for not cooperat-
ing with private detectives over the phone. They needed to see ID,
which meant he'd have to go to the prison. He wasn't about to make
that drive. He figured he could bluff his way through. Lucas didn't
know what he knew or didn't know. If Lucas killed Marla, he would
be scared and might just tell on himself if he applied enough pressure.

Chapter 16

"Find Johnnie Wise no matter the cost."

H atcher looked at the phone again, contemplating whether or not he wanted to call Janet Shamus. He didn't, but she was a paying client so he picked up the phone. While the phone rang, he decided to hold back his thoughts on whether or not Lucas killed Marla. He didn't have any tangible evidence and he didn't want Janet to get overly optimistic and end up disappointed. He figured he'd investigate the lead and determine later if she should know about it or not. He heard the receiver pick up on the other end and then Janet's soft voice. "Miss Shamus, Tony Hatcher here. I just got back to New Orleans."

"Yes, Mr. Hatcher. I take it you have something to report."

"I do, but it's not good."

"Gone on," she said. "Let's hear what you've learned so far."

"The trail's gone cold. Apparently Johnnie duped us all."

With her face twisting into a scowl, Janet screamed, "What do you mean she duped us all, Mr. Hatcher?"

"According to Lucille, the restaurateur, Johnnie told everyone at her going away party that she had finally found her father in East St. Louis and that she was moving there to live with him. But when I found her father, he said he hadn't heard from her since her mother's funeral six months ago."

"Any chance he could be deceiving you, Mr. Hatcher?"

"Is there a chance? Sure, but I don't think so."

"And why is that?"

Hatcher exhaled softly before saying, "Miss Shamus I've been doing this for a long time. I can usually tell when someone is lying to me. He seemed to be genuinely surprised that she had told people in Jackson that she had called."

"So then you think she found the recording devices in her room and simply recorded over them?"

"That's exactly what I think. If she did that, Miss Shamus, there must have been something on those tapes she didn't want me to hear. It could have been intimacy with Paul Masterson, but I don't think so."

"Why is that?"

"Johnnie's a smart girl. If she was involved with Masterson, there would be no need to erase the tapes. She could have easily told me or the police something like that and it would have been an alibi that couldn't be denied. However, that would also mean that she knew she needed an alibi. But if she's innocent, if she doesn't know that your father is dead and she hadn't seen or talked to him in her hotel room, why would she think about an alibi?" He paused for a beat. "She wouldn't, Miss Shamus. She would only need an alibi if she knew of a crime that implicated her or . . ."

"Or if she knew my father was dead and they had been together in her hotel room the night of his death."

"Exactly," Hatcher said. "My guess is that your father did see her the night of his death, but that doesn't mean she killed him."

"Oh she killed him all right, Mr. Hatcher. At this point I'm not comprehending why you think anything else could have happened in that hotel room. What's it going to take to get you fully on board with this?"

"I understand you're still grieving, Miss Shamus, but let's not forget that the coroner said your father died of a heart attack. There's no way that Johnnie Wise could induce a heart attack even if they were involved in salacious activity."

"While your conclusions may be valid, it doesn't change the fact that my father was there, in her hotel room, engaging in carnal activity with a girl younger than me, does it? Nor does it change the fact that she ruined my parent's marriage in the first place and they are in their final resting places because of her, does it?"

Hatcher exhaled again. He had a retort, but he didn't think it would do any good to repeat what he and others had already told her. Instead, he said, "What do you want to do now?"

"Pursue her, Mr. Hatcher," Janet said with conviction. "Pursue her to the ends of the earth. Find Johnnie Wise no matter the cost."

After a long pause, Hatcher said, "She could be anywhere, Miss Shamus."

"No. Miss Wise could not be anywhere. Come now, Mr. Hatcher. You're an experienced detective. She's in a specific place. Find that place. She's afraid and she doesn't have much money. Where would she go?"

"What about the twenty thousand you told me your father withdrew from the bank that hasn't been found? If we assume that your father was in her hotel room the night he died, we have to assume that she has the money. Add the five thousand she inherited from her grandfather and she could hide for a while."

"But is she hiding? Perhaps she thinks she's duped us all as you've suggested. If that's the case, she'll come out of hiding when she's comfortable that no one's looking for her."

"If that's the case, she'll probably go to San Francisco or South Carolina. If I had to choose one over the other, I'd say she went to live with her brother, hoping she'd thrown anybody looking for her off her trail. After what her boyfriend heard in the courtroom about her relationship with Martin Winters, I don't think she'd go to see him. But you never know."

"I'd like you to come to the mansion, Mr. Hatcher."

"Now? Tonight?"

"Yes. I have something for you."

"Can't it wait until tomorrow? I just drove eleven straight hours and I'm tired. I wasn't even going to call you tonight, but I thought you should know what I have."

"Fine, then meet me here at eight o'clock tomorrow morning. By then you should have sufficient sleep to continue the investigation. Don't bother getting breakfast. I'll have Mildred put something together for you."

"That's kind of you, Miss Shamus."

"I'll also have my chauffeur pick you up at 7:30."

"Uh, chauffeur, huh? When we spoke in my office, your attorney brought you and you didn't know how you were going to get home. Now you have a chauffeur?"

"Yes, Mr. Hatcher. I'm very busy these days and a driver became necessary. He'll be there at 7:30 sharp."

"Um, Miss Shamus, if it's all the same with you, I prefer to drive my own car."

"Please don't be late, Mr. Hatcher."

"I'll see you at eight."

Hatcher hung up the phone and packed a bag. That way he wouldn't have to do it in the morning.

Chapter 17

Another Revelation from Paul Masterson

I t was a little after two in the morning and they were sitting in the living room of their suite, enjoying the heat the roaring fireplace provided. It was thirty-five degrees in Nice at that hour in March. Johnnie couldn't sleep. She put some clothes on and decided to take a walk on the Rivera, but when she went into the living room she saw Paul sitting on the sofa with a quilt pulled up to his chin. She stood there and watched him for awhile. He looked troubled about something. She wanted to sit with him under the cover, but she thought he wanted to be alone and she didn't want to disturb him. So she stood there for a few seconds, trying to decide if she wanted to return to her bedroom or interrupt his solitude.

"Couldn't sleep, huh?" Paul said.

"Sorry, Paul, I didn't mean to disturb you. I was just about to take a walk."

"It's chilly out there. And I'm pretty sure you didn't bring a coat. You sure you wanna go out there? If you do, I'll put some clothes on and go with you."

"Do you have any other alternatives at two o'clock in the morning?"

"I know what you mean. It's only nine in Rhode Island. I think it's going to take a while for our bodies to get in synch with the time here. Are you hungry?"

"Yes."

"We could get room service. I'm pretty sure all the diners are closed. What do you have a taste for?"

"Believe it or not, as cold as it is, I would love to have apple pie ala mode."

"Why don't you order some for both of us?"

"Isn't the kitchen closed?"

"I doubt it. I'm sure the hotel is full of Americans and other tourists that can't sleep. After you've ordered, I've got something to tell you, Johnnie."

"Okay."

After she ordered the desert, she went back over to the couch and sat next to her husband. They pulled the quilt up to their necks and let their body heat warm them.

"So what did you have to tell me?"

"How do you feel about kids? Do you want any?"

"Yes, I want about five or six of them. I have an older brother, but he got married and left home. It was just my mother and me. Why do ask? You want kids, too, don't you Paul?"

Quiet filled the living room.

Johnnie looked at her husband and said, "What's wrong, Paul?"

He exhaled and said, "I can't give you any children, Johnnie. And now, since I know that's what you want, when you're ready to divorce me, I'll sign the papers."

"Why can't you have children, Paul? You told me you had gotten your high school sweetheart pregnant. You even mentioned that there might be a kid out there with the woman you had a relationship with. What's going on?"

"It's a little complicated."

"I understand complications. Trust me."

"Do you remember when I told you I joined the Army a little while after I left my church?"

"Yes."

"Well, I guess after what I had done, I had a bit of a death wish. Looking back at it, I think that's why I joined. But prior to leaving for boot camp, I went to my doctor and had a vasectomy. I hadn't seen Anita in months, but I was only about twenty-five at the time and I was still struggling with lust issues."

"So that's why you don't want to have sex with me?"

"I'm still able to perform, Johnnie. I just can't get you pregnant."

"Are you sure you can perform?"

"I'm quite sure. Anyway, during boot camp, the Army administered language tests. They weren't mandatory, but if you wanted to get out of kitchen detail, all you had to do was take the tests. Well, I had a couple years of high school French so I took the test and I passed. I didn't think much of it at the time, but later, after graduation, my commanding officer told me a couple guys from the newly formed Central Intelligence Agency wanted to talk to me. So I went over to the church. For reasons they never explained, that's where they wanted to meet me. They told me that I had scored very high on all my tests not just the French test. I don't know how they knew, but they knew my father had hired a Japanese man named Yamamoto, an Aikido expert, to teach me the art because I used to get beat up for standing up to some of the race bullies that picked on Negroes and other minorities."

She looked at him and kissed him on the cheek. "And you're still defending us, aren't you, Paul?"

Masterson smiled and continued, "When I learned how to use the art, I put a stop to injustice wherever I saw it. It didn't matter what color a person was. I was always against injustice and I still am. I think the Central Intelligence guys knew that about me. Anyway they told me they had a position in Paris opening up in a few months and they thought I would make a great operative."

Johnnie looked at him and said, "What are you saying, Paul?"

"I'm saying I was a spy for our government. I'm also saying that once I knew I was leaving America, I knew I would leave whatever moral code I had in the United States on those shores. I was going to France and I spoke French. I knew I wouldn't be alone long and I wasn't. So before I left the country, I had my doctor make it so I wouldn't be able to give another woman a child and then have that woman kill my child without me having anything to say about it. I thought it best that I didn't get another woman with child to prevent the hurt I felt when my first child was taken from me. But what I didn't know was that once I had left the scrutiny of the church and had real freedom here in France, I would lose my moral foundation and my strength of character. The price I've had to pay is incalculable. As I traveled from country to country, I picked up other languages along the way."

"Room service."

"I'll take care of it," Masterson said.

A few minutes later, they were eating their apple pie ala mode, while Paul regaled Johnnie with tales of his travels. Shortly after eating, they fell asleep in each others arms.

Chapter 18

"I was just trying to rattle your cage a bit."

Tony Hatcher's alarm rang out loudly at 6:00. He opened his eyes, found the clock, and shut it off. He inhaled deeply, like getting out of bed was a job he hated, but had to go to or starve. A full length view of Janet Shamus' image immediately entered his mind against his will. The last thing he wanted to think about was an egotistical teenager whose beauty and curves seriously stimulated his loins, but think about her he did. He took another exasperated breath, swung his feet to the floor, and exhaled. Then he hopped in and out of the shower, put on a pair of black slacks, added a sports jacket and tie, and then headed out the door. He stopped by his office a few minutes before seven to see if his people had left any information on Seymour Collins, Phil Seymour, and the Beauregards in his absence. The information was sitting on his desk along with a pile of overdue bills. He sat down and read what they had gathered and then headed over to the Shamus mansion. As punctual as ever, he looked at his watch and waited until it was precisely eight o'clock and rang the doorbell.

A Negro maid opened the door, smiled, and said, "You must be Mr. Hatcher. I'm Mildred. Miss Shamus will meet you on the north terrace. If you'll follow me I'll take you there."

Hatcher was thinking, "North terrace? How many terraces do you have to have before you have to separate them by direction?" As he followed Mildred through the mansion, he couldn't help noticing how immaculate the place was. The ceiling stretched towards the heavens, tall centuries-old oil paintings of men wearing white wigs, women with tiny waists wearing dresses that flared out like a bell covered the walls along with thoroughbred horses near a bright red barn. The sheer size of the place and the elegant furniture it housed gave it the feel of a museum with roped off rooms rather than a home where people lived. The décor of the mansion notwithstanding, Hatcher found himself preoccupied with one aspect of his conversation with Janet Shamus that kept coming to mind. She was now being driven around by a chauffeur. He shook his head and thought, "It must be nice to have all that dough."

"By the way, Mr. Hatcher, you ever do any skeet shooting?" Mildred asked.

"Skeet shooting? Once or twice, I guess. But I'm no expert by any stretch of the imagination."

"Miss Shamus has been shooting clay pigeons for about a month. Hired herself an expert to teach her how and now she's gotten the hang of it. She rarely misses."

"That good, huh?" Hatcher asked sarcastically. "And only a month of training too?"

"About a month, yes. I think she wants you to give it a try. There's a vest draped across your chair on the terrace. Try it on for size. I think it'll fit you nicely."

As they stepped out onto the terrace, Hatcher couldn't help wondering why Janet Shamus all of a sudden had taken up skeet shooting. He didn't like where his mind was going. Nor where it appeared hers was going for that matter. Did she want him to find Johnnie so she could kill her? Was she that obsessed?

"Try the vest on, Mr. Hatcher," Mildred said, "While I fix you something to eat."

Hatcher took off his jacket and hung it around the chair on the right of where he would sit and have his breakfast. He saw Janet Shamus standing on an upstairs terrace looking down at him, but he pretended he didn't see her. She was wearing an off-white cotton nightgown. The way it clung to her, he could tell she wasn't wearing support by the way her thick breasts hung and freely separated. Without intending to, his mind imagined that she wasn't wearing panties either. Her arms were folded, like she was trying to determine something about him that could only be seen when the subject wasn't aware he was being watched. He put the vest on while keeping an inconspicuous eye on Janet, wondering why she was watching him surreptitiously and if she had hired someone to investigate him. Still watching her from his periphery, he noticed that she went back inside, which was somewhat of a relief. He didn't like being watched even though that was what he did for a living.

Mildred pushed a cart over to the table and removed two silver lids. Steam rose from the hot food underneath of one while the other housed fresh fruit. She picked up his plate, piled it high with food and fruit and said, "Dig in."

Hatcher looked at the food still on the silver plates and saw an assortment of eggs, ham, croissants, grits, sausages, smoked salmon, steak, French toast, pineapples, red grapes, pears, oranges, peaches, and melon. His mouth watered. He couldn't remember the last time he'd seen a spread like that, if ever. He shook out his napkin and tucked it inside his collar. "Will Miss Shamus be joining me? She told me to be here at eight."

"She's already eaten, Mr. Hatcher. Her days start at about four in the morning. Sometimes I wonder if the poor child sleeps at all these days." Mildred picked up his glass and poured orange juice into it. Then she poured milk into another glass. "This is all for you. Now is there anything else I can get you?"

With a mouth full of food Hatcher couldn't speak, so he shook his head and continued eating like a man who hadn't had a good meal in years.

"If you need anything, just call," Mildred said. "I'll be in the kitchen."

Hatcher nodded and continued eating.

Twenty minutes later Janet Shamus walked onto the terrace. She was carrying a couple shotguns, one in each hand. "Good morning, Mr. Hatcher. I see you're enjoying Mildred's wonderful cooking."

Hatcher nodded a couple times and continued eating.

Janet said, "Do you shoot?"

Hatcher kept eating and shrugged his shoulders.

She leaned one of the shotguns against the chair on his right, where his jacket was and said, "It's not loaded. When you're finished," she tilted her head to the right, "I'll be over there practicing."

Hatcher swallowed and said, "Practicing for what, Miss Shamus?"

Janet smiled and said, "You never know when target shooting will come in handy, Mr. Hatcher. I suppose it's like any other skill. Take changing a tire for instance. What does a woman do if she has a flat? I'll tell you what she does. She has to wait for some man to come and fix it like any other problem. But . . . what if she could fix the flat or the problem herself? What then? She can save herself a whole lot of time, couldn't she?"

Frowning, Hatcher said, "What exactly are you saying, Miss Shamus?"

"I think I was quite clear Mr. Hatcher." She stared at him without blinking for a few seconds and said, "If you're finished, come with me. It's time to practice."

Hatcher put the last of his food into his mouth, guzzled the orange juice and milk before grabbing the weapon she brought him, and followed Janet over to the cement balustrade where a Negro wearing gray tails and a gray vest was waiting.

Janet put two shells into her shotgun and yelled, "Pull!" A clay pigeon flew through the air. She aimed and fired. The pigeon shattered. "Pull!" Again she aimed and fired. Again, the pigeon shattered. Then she looked at Hatcher, smiling as she reloaded. "You ready to give it a go, Mr. Hatcher?"

"What's in it for me?"

"What do you want?"

Hatcher's eyes dropped to the mounds of flesh on her chest and back to her eyes in a microsecond. He didn't mean to, but his libido made him do it. Knowing she had watched his eyes, he stared into hers, wishing the moment just prior to his failure could begin again, knowing it couldn't, he said, "I don't think I have anything to gain."

"I'm sure I have something you want, Mr. Hatcher," Janet said, still watching his every move, calculating his responses and her own.

"You do indeed."

"So what are we shooting for . . . a peek down my blouse? Or do I have to get completely naked and let you do a mural in oil so you can look at me whenever you want for as long as you want?"

Again Hatcher's eyes found her bust without permission. He looked into her eyes again. Given his experiences with Meredith, who was refined, well-spoken, and modest, he couldn't believe Janet had given him an invitation to discuss such things.

"Yes," Janet continued, "I could tell you were looking at me while I was on my bedroom terrace. And I know you want me, but that's not on the table. If you want more money I can do that. Or I can make sure my grandfather's friends hire you. Isn't that what you want most, Mr. Hatcher? Don't you want to expand your business and make lots of money? I can make that happen with just a few phone calls and you'll be on easy street within six months." Looking deeply into his eyes she added, "Perhaps you'd like that more than bedding me."

Hatcher realized that what he saw on her bedroom terrace was a show of the inhibited burlesque variety. Still looking into her eyes, he wanted to smile when he heard her proposition, but his pride wouldn't let him because he knew that with each passing day, Janet Shamus was growing, becoming a goddess of sorts; a mixture of a beautiful Hollywood Starlet and Greek mythology intertwined, with men of all walks of life answering to her, doing her bidding as she became aware of just how much power her money and good-looks wielded over mere mortals. With that power, she would own him if he accepted the kind of help she was offering. She could easily throw him all the business he wanted, but she could also withdraw her favor in an instant and leave him destitute, both wanting and needing her, lapping at her soiled heels like a witless animal. He inhaled deeply when he smelled her alluring perfume, then while looking into her magnetic eyes, he loaded his shotgun and said, "Nonsense. Janet, you and I both know everything's on the table including your virtue."

Keenly aware of his desire to provoke her by deliberately being crass, baiting her by using her first name when he knew she expected to be addressed in a more dignified and professional manner. She ignored the bait, knowing he wanted her to lose control, and throw a tantrum like teenagers were prone to do. Instead she decided to go along and said, "What makes you think that?"

Hatcher smiled, knowing his sexual shot in the dark was on target and had landed in the center of the bull's-eye. He now knew that young Janet Shamus was attempting to play a grown-up game that she neither had the skill nor the experience to play. He knew that not only was she obsessed enough to kill Johnnie Wise, but if she thought giving up her virtue in exchange for his silence, or perhaps even becoming her accomplice, she would do even that. In fact, from the way she looked at him, he could tell that letting him into her private orchard would be a miniscule sacrifice at best, given what the stakes were and the satisfaction she thought she'd gain. But she had to pretend that she would only sacrifice her body for a just cause, which was the requited blood of her unsuspecting rival. "How about we just shoot for fun? Pull!" A second later, a clay pigeon shattered. He looked at her and said, "Can you have your man release two at a time."

Skeptical, she stared at Hatcher, examining him, trying to ascertain if he was being serious. When she realized he was, without looking at the Negro man in gray tails, she said, "Wilson!"

"Yes, ma'am," Wilson called back.

"Release two from now on."

"Very good, ma'am."

Hatcher reloaded and said, "Pull!" A clay pigeon flew to the right and the other to the left. He fired twice and hit both clay pigeons.

"Nice shooting, but can you do it again?"

Hatcher reloaded and said, "Pull!" He hit one and intentionally missed the other. "Hmm, I think the sights are a little off."

"There's nothing wrong with the sights, Mr. Hatcher," Janet said, smiling. She reloaded and said, "Here, try mine."

Hatcher exchanged weapons with her and said, "Pull!" Again, he hit the first target and intentionally missed the second.

Janet reloaded the shotgun Hatcher had given her, and said, "Pull!" She fired twice, hitting the first target, but missing the second. She reloaded and tried again. This time she missed both targets. She tried ten more times and could never hit both targets on one pull.

While she reloaded for an eleventh try, Hatcher said, "I thought you said you had something for me. Surely you didn't have me come all the way out here to watch you practice shooting."

"I do have something for you," she said. "It's in your vest pocket. Pull!"

Hatcher patted his pocket and felt something hard. He reached inside and pulled out a Diner's Club card with his name on it."

"With that you can eat just about anywhere. It'll be part of the expense account I'm establishing for you. Soon you'll be able to board a plane, check into a hotel, and eat without cash. That way you won't have to carry so much money with you."

"Yeah, and you can keep track of every penny I spend, right?"

Janet laughed and said, "You're a smart man, Mr. Hatcher. I want you on a plane to San Francisco as soon as we finish our chat. If you learn that Johnnie Wise hasn't been there, get on a plane to South Carolina. If the boyfriend doesn't know anything, go back to Jackson and talk to the woman who owns the Hotel. She may know something. If that fails, find Paul Masterson. He might know something. Exhaust all avenues, Mr. Hatcher. Johnnie Wise is in a specific place. Find her."

"I'm going to need another advance to do all of that."

"There's an open ended plane ticket waiting for you at the airport. Another five thousand will be wired to Western Union. If you need more, let me know. Now, are you sure you don't want something from me? It looks like we're evenly matched."

"You're right, Miss Shamus. There is something I want from you."

"Miss Shamus again, is it? A moment ago it was Janet, like we were old school chums."

"I can call you Janet again if you prefer."

"If you win, not only can you call me Janet, but I'll let you have your way with me one time. But—"

"If I win, you keep your virtue. While I'm sure bedding you would be a delectable delight, it would also make me a fool. My price is that you give up this foolish notion of killing Miss Wise.

"Fine," Janet said. "But if I win, you put forth your best efforts to find her and once you have, you forget you did and leave the rest to me."

"Deal," Hatcher said, confident that he would win, but also suspicious that she had something else up her sleeve even after he won the shooting contest. "You go first. Ladies before gentlemen and all that jazz. And don't let the pressure of missing get to you."

"Pull!" Janet said, and fired, hitting both targets. She smiled and said, "Now . . . what was that about the pressures of missing?"

Hatcher huffed. "So . . . you're a flimflam artist to boot, huh? You set me up with the maid and everything didn't you?"

"Don't take it so hard, Mr. Hatcher. Just know you never stood a chance of winning. There's no way I'd put my virtue on the line so easily. What kind of girl do you think I am? And by the way, while you're shooting, just know that you could never win me without great effort."

"Well, then there's no point in me shooting if I have nothing to gain. I'll just head over to the airport and do the job you paid me to do since it wasn't a real bet."

"Oh it's a real bet alright. I would have gladly let you have your way with me if you agreed to help me do what I have to do. Now though, you're going to have to find Johnnie and think about what you could've had because there's no way you can beat me. I've been shooting for two years now. I'm a marksman."

"Since you have nothing to lose, let's sweeten the deal. If I do get lucky and win, you send me all the business I can handle like you said earlier."

"And if I win, you find Johnnie Wise and you walk away."

"Pull!" Hatcher shouted and hit both targets. Then he looked at her, smiled and said, "We can still put your virtue on the table, such that it is."

Janet reloaded. "Pull!" Again, she hit both targets. I can do this all day, Mr. Hatcher. Can you?"

"Well, see. Pull!" He hit both clay pigeons again. He looked at Janet and said, "Looks like we both can do this all day. Let's add another target each round."

"What's on the table?"

"Your virtue and you leave this thing with Johnnie Wise alone."

"If I lose, Mr. Hatcher, not only will I give you my virtue, but I will give you everything you've ever wanted. Having my revenge against Johnnie Wise is not negotiable. If you lose, you'll not only find Miss Wise, but you'll stop trying to talk me out of what must be done and you won't say a word about what you know." She paused for a second and said, "Is it a deal?"

"If I win, I collect immediately." He titled his head to the right and said, "Up there . . . in your bedroom right now."

"Deal. But you go first this time."

Hatcher reloaded and said, "Pull!" He hit the first, but missed the second. Missing the second target made him nervous and when he grabbed her shotgun, his aim was a little off and he missed the third."

Smiling, Janet said, "Tsk, tsk, tsk. Looks like the thought of bedding me threw you off just a tad, huh? You must think about having me every day to miss so terribly."

Reloading the gun, he said, "You still have to hit two targets to win, Miss Shamus. And before you shoot, I think you should know that I have the information you wanted on Seymour Collins, Phil Seymour, and the Beauregards."

Janet leaned her shotgun against the balustrade, folded her arms and said, "Let's have it now if you think it'll help you, Mr. Hatcher."

"I'll just give you the highlights. First, your attorney, Mr. Collins is as clean as a whistle, at least around New Orleans. But he's had as many affairs as he has houses."

Janet locked eyes with him, tightened her folded arms and said, "Was my mother one of his conquests?"

"I'll tell you what, why don't we come back to that one." He smiled triumphantly. "Now on to Mr. Seymour, your illustrious mentor. He's a husband of twenty years, has five children, three of them in Ivy League colleges, two still in high school, a beautiful wife and a great home in the Chicago suburbs."

"But . . . Mr. Hatcher? I feel a "but" coming."

"But he's a flaming homosexual. He and Mr. Williams, another married man with a wife and children, meet in his office every other Tuesday and Thursday to engage in deviant carnal knowledge." He paused and waited for a response that never came, and then he continued. "As for the Beauregards, what you read in the newspaper clippings your mother saved is true. They are related to Johnnie, but they covered it up like many of the families around these parts. Rumor has it that Katherine, Ethel Beauregard's maid, leaked that

Johnnie and her brother are entitled to a million dollars each, but she denies saying it to anyone. Ethel left her the Beauregard mansion. I guess that was Ethel's way of making sure Johnnie and her brother never heard about the million dollar bonanza they had coming their way."

"If it's true you mean," Janet quickly pointed out.

"Yeah, if it's true," Hatcher repeated sarcastically. "God knows a faithful Negress like Katherine wouldn't lie about a minute detail like that. The trouble with the "lie" is that it would make more sense if she'd said that Ethel left her a million dollars in addition to the mansion."

"So you think it's true, Mr. Hatcher? Johnnie Wise is rich and she doesn't even know it?"

"I most certainly do think it's true."

"So there's a chance she might come back here then?"

"I sincerely doubt that, Miss Shamus. I think Johnnie is gone for good. And that's all the more reason to let her go."

"I thought we agreed you wouldn't bring letting her go up again?"

"We did. But that was only if you won. You haven't won yet. You still have to hit at least two targets or I get another crack at three."

Janet picked up her shotgun and looked through the sights. "Now, what's this about my mother and Mr. Collins?"

"You mean the affair he was having with her when she found out that your father was bedding the woman you want to destroy when in fact Johnnie's the victim in all of this? Is that what you wanted to know, Miss Shamus?"

"Pull!" Janet shouted angrily. She hit the first two targets and then grabbed his weapon and hit the third. She looked at him and said, "The third one was so you would know it wasn't luck. Since my virtue is as safe as I knew it would be, we don't have to worry about you missing your flight, do we? But don't worry, Mr. Hatcher. You find Johnnie for me, walk away and keep your mouth shut, and I'll keep my bargain and make you wealthy."

"I guess my report gave you focus, huh?"

"I guess it did."

"Just so you know . . . your mother didn't have an affair with Collins. I was just trying to rattle your cage a bit. It was just a little gamesmanship."

"Duly noted," Janet said while reloading. "Now, please leave before I get you confused with a target."

Chapter 19

"I don't know how. I feel so stupid."

Wondering how he let a young upstart like Janet Shamus and a Negro maid dupe him into believing he had a chance to win a skeet shooting contest and stop a needless murder had Hatcher baffled all the way to the airport. He thought that if he could be outsmarted by a teenager, he must be getting too old for the business. His thoughts shifted to how Janet found out that he was a marksman. While she made no mention of his stint in the Army, she clearly knew he was a crack shot. Then he realized that if she knew that much, she must have had him investigated, which meant she knew a whole lot more about him than she let on. Assuming Janet knew certain things about him, he wondered what she planned to do with the information. So far she hadn't held or used any of it against him. In fact, she had done everything she could to not only keep him working for her, but she had tried to make him an accomplice to what he thought was her cold calculated plan to murder Johnnie Wise.

As he waited in line to get his ticket, he seriously considered accepting her beguiling proposal for the first time. He thought about the debt he'd accumulated, which included his alimony and child support payments. He still loved his ex-wife even though they had been divorced for four years, but there was no chance of getting back together with her. He had hoped she would get married so he could get out from under the strenuous weight of taking care of a woman another man was getting sexual fulfillment from, but she was too smart and too angry to marry someone else and let him off the hook. No. She was going to punish him for the rest of his life. She had loved him with all her heart and the injury she sustained would not heal. He even considered killing her for a few moments, but he loved his children too much. Besides, no woman would ever love them as much as their mother did and he didn't have time to care for them the way she could. So he quickly nixed the idea and then told himself that he wasn't serious about killing her anyway.

As the idea of throwing in with Janet Shamus started to appeal to him, he asked himself, "Who is Johnnie Wise anyway? Why was her life any more valuable than any other life?" Then he answered his own questions. "Johnnie Wise was an insignificant human being like most of the people in the world. Who was going to miss her besides her brother? Her father wouldn't miss her because he didn't really know her and hadn't even heard from her in six months after their so-called reunion." Hatcher further reasoned that her father had a beautiful wife and children he had to be concerned about. As for her brother, Hatcher thought, he could be easily taken care of as well.

In fact both father and brother could easily be handled the same way—with money. Janet Shamus had a lot of it and she had the power to control the unforeseen variables to cover their tracks if someone learned of their clandestine plans to finally and permanently end the life of Meredith Shamus's nemesis. Then the visual of Janet in her nightgown came to mind. He could see her nipples trying to break through the fabric and roam, pointing the way to the Pacific and Atlantic oceans. He stiffened. After two meetings, she had grown on him. Her power and diabolical cunning only added to her physical allure. Just before it was his turn to step up to the United Airlines counter, he smiled and told himself that part of the deal would be bedding young Janet, not just once, but for as long as Johnnie was alive. To ensure his perpetual pleasure, he would see to it that Johnnie lived at least six months, perhaps a year or two, depending on Janet's persistence.

"May I help you please?" the woman at the counter asked?

Hatcher stepped up to the counter and said, "You have a ticket for Tony Hatcher leaving this morning for San Francisco?"

"Yes sir, I do," the woman said.

"Isn't that an open ended ticket?"

"Yes sir," she said. "According to your account, you can change it to wherever you like. Basically you can get a ticket to go anywhere within the continental United States."

"Great!" Hatcher said. Is there a flight leaving for Columbia, South Carolina later on this evening?"

"Let me check." A few seconds later she said, "Yes sir. There's one leaving at four this evening. Would you like me to book you on that flight?"

"Yes."

"No problem Mr. Hatcher," she said. "When you return, just come to this counter and you'll be all set."

Hatcher fast-walked to the nearest payphone, dreaming of what it was going to be like bedding Janet Shamus, while at the same time wondering what her response was going to be when he countered her original proposal with one of his own. He dialed her number and listened while the phone rang. His heart was pounding feverishly.

"Janet Shamus."

"Hatcher here."

"Yes, Mr. Hatcher. Is there a problem with your flight?"

"Yes, Miss Shamus there is. And we need to discuss it right now."

"Aren't you supposed to be boarding a plane to San Francisco? Did the airline not have your ticket or what? If not, a simple phone call from me will suffice, I'm sure."

"Meet me at my home in a half an hour and we'll discuss it."

"Discuss what, Mr. Hatcher. I'm very busy."

"Not over the phone."

Hatcher rattled off his address and hung up, knowing curiosity would compel her to come to his home and see what he wanted. He wasn't sure if he could get her to go along with his new plan, but he knew that having his way with her was essential to controlling Janet. He wasn't going to be her puppet. She was going to be his, at least until Johnnie Wise was dead. But he needed to secure his own future, which he fully understood did not include marrying into the Shamus fortune.

As he was coming down the street a half hour later, Hatcher saw Earl Shamus' Cadillac parked in front of his house. Janet was sitting behind the wheel. Hatcher thought, "No Chauffeur." He could see her eyes watching him through her rearview mirror. Hatcher pulled into his driveway and got out of his 1952 New Yorker Convertible

Coupe. Janet got out of her car and walked up the sidewalk to the front door, watching Hatcher the entire time. They met each other at his front door. He looked into her eyes and instantly knew that no matter how difficult she made the terrain they were about to embark upon, she had already made up her mind to give him what he wanted just as she said when they were at the mansion. Knowing he had the upper hand made him stiffen again, but he had to remain fully engaged in the scene until the end like a seasoned thespian.

The stage had been set and now the script had to be played out as it was written because Janet wasn't a whore and she would not allow herself to be treated like one. She had to at least pretend that she was being coerced by an older more experienced man so she could blame him later for the loss of her virtue. Hatcher understood how the female psyche worked; that it had to twist the truth into something palatable that a woman could live with and still do that which has been ordained as an unsavory pleasure. Hatcher knew all too well that later, when Janet realized that she had played the harlot and that he was the catalyst for her shame, she would hate him for taking advantage of her, but it was a burden he was more than willing to shoulder. After all, he was expecting to be well compensated for being an accessory to first degree murder.

Janet started the foreplay by pretending to be angry as she walked up to him in haste and said, "What's going on, Mr. Hatcher? I thought we had a deal."

Looking around like someone could be watching them, he said, "Not out here. Come into the house and we can discuss it."

"Fine," Janet said. "But we need to make this quick. I'm quite busy."

Hatcher whispered, "It's dangerous to be quick when you're planning to kill someone . . . even if that someone is a Negro."

Janet's mouth fell wide open. She looked around much like he had done seconds ago. She was about to say something when Hatcher said, "Not out here."

He opened the door and they went inside. He closed the door, keeping his eyes on her ample hind parts, following her, watching as his mind imagined doing nasty things to her. As she was walking toward the living room, unable to stop himself, he reached out and grabbed her, forcefully turned her around and kissed her hard on the lips. She pulled her head back, but his lips advanced as hers retreated. His arousal gained momentum, demanding that he press his lips against hers even harder. He grabbed a thick hunk of both her rear cheeks and they staggered into the center of the living room with her hands on his chest in a vain attempt to get his lips off hers.

Janet finally snatched away from him and fired off a vicious slap across the face that was designed and delivered to wake him up from the sexual trance he was in. "Have you lost your mind?" she yelled.

Breathing heavily, he said, "Yes. I most certainly have lost my mind. My soul too. And so have you."

"What are you talking about?"

"Murder, Janet," he said, still panting. "I'm talking about cold-blooded murder."

"And that's why you think you can take unsolicited liberties with me? Because you *think* I'm going to kill Johnnie Wise?"

"Come now, Janet. You're a smart girl. The problem though is that murder is a very monstrous thing and one must handle these machinations with the utmost care. It's good that you can handle a firearm with the best of them. I'm sure when you have Johnnie in your sights you won't miss. The problem with your little scheme is how do you get away with it? And for that you need me because all you have is your anger and your skill with a shotgun. Unfortunately, your anger is a liability because it has blinded you to reason and it has limited your imagination, both of which are necessary to murder someone and get away with it."

"If I *we're* going to kill Miss Wise, why would I need you?"

"First you need me because I already know about it. Otherwise you'd have to kill me to be sure you weren't found out. The problem with that is you don't know if I've told others, leaving yourself open to blackmail for the remainder of your life. If I did tell someone and they wanted money, you'd have to resort to tracking your blackmailer down to kill him or *her* too. But the problem with that is they may have told others and so on and so forth. You therefore need someone who can help you plan and execute your operation with flawless precision."

"And that someone is you, Mr. Hatcher?"

"Yes," he said. "Now let's sit down and talk this thing through thoroughly and intelligently. We dare not figure out all the variables otherwise we'll get caught. You need to be absolutely sure you want to do this because the penalty for murder is the electric chair. With Johnnie being Negro and the circumstances surrounding the murder, you probably wouldn't get the chair. But it's possible you could get life behind bars." She sat on the sofa and he in the matching chair. "Can I offer you something to drink? A cold beer perhaps?"

She shook her head. "Tell me, Mr. Hatcher, what do you expect to get out of this plan of *yours*?"

"Let's be clear about one thing, Janet. You plan to murder Johnnie Wise, not me. I'm just saying that if that's what you want to do, you're going to need help."

"For a price?"

"Of course. Nothing's free in this world."

"And your price, Mr. Hatcher?"

"Everything you promised for starters. I'd also like you to take care of all my creditors, including what I owe on this house. The bank is threatening to foreclose. I think a fully paid for New Yorker is in order along with a financial nest egg for a rainy day."

"Is that all, Mr. Hatcher?"

"Yes. And this goes without saying. I want the privilege of bedding you."

"You want a lot, Mr. Hatcher."

"As do you, Janet. Murder is no walk in the park."

"Are you certain you want nothing else?"

"Unless you can think of something I missed. No." He smiled. "I admit I may have forgotten something. This was a spur of the moment decision."

"Spawn by your mounting debt, no doubt."

Hatcher shrugged his shoulders. "What can I say? I've made some mistakes. Now I need relief from it all. I'm going to kill a girl who has done nothing worthy of death. The money will go a long way in soothing my conscience."

"Yes. I was wondering what happened to it. Yesterday and today, in fact a few hours ago, not only didn't you want anything to do with *supposed* murder, but you tried to stop me from committing it. Why the change of heart?"

"Two reasons. Debt is first and foremost. There's nothing like being in need to make one compromise a principle. I'm no different than any other man or woman when it comes to debts and the need to survive. I'm not getting any younger."

"And the second reason?"

"Despite my behavior a few minutes ago, to a much lesser degree, sexual greed demands it."

"What was the one thing that made you compromise?"

"You and your maid. I knew that if you two could fool me, I was getting old and I should get out of the business or leave it up to the people who work for me."

Janet let a victorious grin surface and said, "So I take care of your debts, purchase a new car in your name, establish a nest egg, and surrender my virtue. Is that about right?"

"About right, yes."

"So there's something else?"

"Well, you'd need to do more than give up your virtue."

Janet frowned. "You mean I'd have to marry you?"

"Not exactly."

"What then?"

"You'd have to let me bed you as much as I like until the deed is done."

Janet leaped to her feet and screamed, "What?"

"That's a deal breaker, Janet. Murder is a full partnership. Just like a marriage. I just want the conjugal rights that come with a marriage without having to actually marry you. The decision's yours."

"And you wanted me to come here to consummate the marriage right now? Is that it?"

Nodding, Hatcher said, "You *are such* a smart girl."

Janet walked over to the fireplace and leaned up against it, contemplating the deal. She wanted Johnnie Wise dead. She knew that all bargains have to meet the need of both parties. That was how business worked according to Phil Seymour, her mentor.

While she was still thinking, Hatcher said, "You don't have to do this, Janet. Like I said earlier, only do it if you're absolutely sure. There are other alternatives, but it could get complicated."

"What alternatives?"

"Well there's always blackmail."

"But she doesn't have anything I want."

"Not Johnnie. I gave you the goods on Collins and Seymour. You could perhaps use that leverage to get them to do some work for you. If you read the information I gave you, you know that a Chicago based mobster provides Mr. Seymour with young men when Mr. Williams is unavailable. Some of them are just boys, younger than you."

"But if I do that, more people will know and you just pointed out the fallacy of doing business that way."

"I did indeed."

"What about Collins? How can I use his adultery against him?"

"I'm sure he has clients that can get what you need done. But again . . ."

"I know. More people are involved, increasing the risk of being caught and going to prison."

Hatcher silenced himself and watched her closely as he knew she would come to the only viable solution to murder. He looked at her backside with an intensity that only a jeweler could appreciate. His mouth watered as he anticipated his inevitable triumph. He felt the weight of being in debt rising from his shoulders, floating upward through his roof, continuing to the sky, and eventually the stratosphere. Unable to control his inner feelings of conquest, evil glee crept across his face and lingered there while he enjoyed the precious moments prior to complete and unconditional surrender. The image of her standing on her bedroom terrace filled his mind again. She had looked so lovely up there, and so vulnerable. Now she was his to do with as he pleased. By the time he finished with her, she would have the skills of a professional lover and her future husband would owe it all to him.

Without looking at him, she said, "Will you be gentle? This is my first time."

When Hatcher heard that, his heart raced and nearly exploded. He swallowed hard, breathed deeply and said, "I'll be very gentle."

She turned around and said, "Okay then. I guess we should go to your bedroom."

"Not so fast," Hatcher said, trying to hide just how incredibly desperate he was to enter her folds of flesh and give her the unspeakable pleasure necessary to ensure that she looked forward to future sessions. He knew that in order to have her on demand, she had to get the same pleasure he was getting. Otherwise, she would eventually renege on the deal and compensate him some other way. He knew that sex with her now would be rather pedestrian and unfulfilling. "First we have to make plans."

"What did you have in mind?"

"I have a lead. One that I didn't tell you about this morning."

"So you're ready to tell me now?"

"I am. I heard that Marla Bentley's body was found in Red River."

"Napoleon Bentley's wife?"

"Yes. They were getting a divorce."

"What was she doing in Red River?"

"She was staying at a hotel. I have reason to believe she was there with Lucas Matthews."

"So you think he may have killed her? And you want to use that information to get him to tell you where Johnnie is?"

"Bingo!"

"Do you think it'll work?"

"It will if he knows something?"

"Do you think he killed her?"

"I do. The news report said that Marla's neck was broken. I don't believe Napoleon did it because I don't believe she would meet him there. She was a mobster's wife for twenty years. She had to know that the mob kills people in remote locations, far from their own lair. Plus, for Napoleon to know where she was, she would have had to tell him. No. She was there with Lucas Matthews. He's the only man in Louisiana that she would make a fourteen hour drive from Chicago for. I think Lucas told her he was getting out of prison early and they planned a rendezvous of sorts far away from New

Orleans so as not to be seen by whites who might lynch and castrate him for having relations with her."

Excited about finding Johnnie, she said, "When do you plan to leave?"

"My flight leaves for Columbia, South Carolina at four this evening."

"And you came back here for me?"

"I did."

He walked over to the fireplace where she was still standing. Gently, he pulled her close, found her eyes with his own, and stared into them until he couldn't stand it any longer. Then he moved his head forward a bit and waited until her lips gave him permission to forge ahead without caution. Her kiss was sterile and dispassionate.

"Don't worry," he said, still looking into her magnificent eyes. "We have time."

"I've never kissed anybody but daddy. I don't know how. I feel so stupid."

"You'll get the hang of it, but you have to relax."

"I think I'll have that beer now. Perhaps then I can relax."

Fifteen minutes later, he could taste the beer on her breath. She was far more relaxed and returning his kisses with her own. She was a fast learner. As they gave into their carnality, Hatcher realized his suspicions were right. She was her father's daughter, which meant that Janet Shamus was the ravenous wolf that her father was only she didn't know it. He was planning to fertilize the seed of whoredom her father planted in her genes, albeit unintentionally. He knew that it wouldn't take long for her to become all that her father was and he would greatly benefit from the pleasure she would give him as the seed grew and matured.

As Hatcher slowly undressed her, methodically taking her clothing off piece by piece, she accepted his touch and the stimulation that accompanied it offered her a sensation that she had never known, but she wanted to go on feeling it, giving into it as each thrill promised another. When he removed his mouth from hers and moved them to her neck, a guttural sigh echoed in the room. The unparalleled ecstasy was mounting and she felt herself losing control, wanting the invasion to commence and be explored for the very first time. Hatcher explored her uncharted territory for more than an hour. When he left, Janet's eyes were closed, her mouth was open, and she was breathing deeply. He chuckled when he remembered that Mildred had said that she wondered if Janet had been sleeping at all.

Chapter 20

"I want to know everything about you," Paul said as he and Johnnie ate a hearty breakfast together on the veranda overlooking the scenic French Riviera and the rippling blue water of the Mediterranean.

"Everything?"

"Yes. Everything."

"If you want to know everything about me, you're going to tell me everything to know about you, right?"

"Right."

A smirk rose before Johnnie said, "Does everything include your top secret dealings with the Central Intelligence Agency?"

"Johnnie, I told you I can't go into that."

"Sure you can, Paul. Who would know? Besides, I think you just want to know about the men in my life. Isn't that right?"

"I do, but not just the men. As I said, I want to know everything about everyone who had an impact on your life."

"So the Central Intelligence Agency didn't have an impact on *your* life?"

He smiled and said, "You're sharp. I like that about you."

"Thank you, but you didn't answer the question, Paul. You skillfully avoided it."

"No I didn't answer it. How about we start off with something innocuous? Instead of starting off with the men you've known, let's start with girls or women you've met and had relationships with."

"Why do you want to know about that?"

"It was something you said the first night we met. You said that you don't get along with white Christian women. I simply want to know what women you've gotten along with because you're mother was Negro and from what you've told me so far, you didn't get along with her either. I want to know how you came to the conclusions that have shaped your life. I want to know what experiences you've had with white Christian women."

Johnnie sipped her orange juice and said, "So you want to do a book on me, huh?"

"I don't want to write a book about you, no. I want to read the book that's already been written about you. Will you let me read you? Will you let me get a thorough understanding of who you are and how you came to be the person you are today?"

"I'm not sure I can, Paul."

"What do you mean? Why can't you?"

"Paul, you think so much of me. The last man that thought the way you think was my boyfriend, Lucas Matthews. And when he found out the honest to goodness truth about his angel, he walked out of my life without as much as a good-bye. I'm so hurt by that—even now. I loved him so much, Paul. Do you understand what it means for a woman to love a man like that, where she would do absolutely anything for him?"

"I wish I could say yes, but unfortunately I can't. Can you help me understand?"

"I could tell you about him and why I fell in love with him. That's about it. But telling you about him and how we met and what he did for me doesn't mean you'll understand my uncompromising devotion to him. I'm married to you, but the truth is Paul, I went to Fort Jackson. Lucas is in boot camp there and had I gotten a chance to see him and talk to him and explain everything . . . if he had taken me back, I would never have come to Rhode Island. That's the truth. Now . . . what do you have to say about that truth, Mr. Masterson?"

Paul swallowed his food and said, "I say that's a great beginning."

"So it doesn't bother you that I still have affection for Lucas?"

"No. Not now. If after we've gotten to know each other and fall in love and your feelings about him do not diminish, that would be a problem. Right now, as I've said, we don't know each other. Right now, we're just acquaintances with conjugal rights if we so choose.

Now let's discuss your trip to Fort Jackson. I had my basic training there too. So I know the guards wouldn't let you through the gate without a sponsor, right?"

"Right."

"So what did you do then?"

"I had written him a letter in case I couldn't see him. I left it with the guards to give to him."

"But you never saw Lucas, right?"

"No. Why?"

"What did the letter say?"

"It was personal, Paul."

"Did you mention anything about getting married or where we were going?"

"I said nothing about getting married, but I did tell him I was going to be traveling the world for a few years."

Paul exhaled and his back fell against the chair. "Now *that's* a problem."

"What? Why? I didn't tell him where we're going or anything."

"I realized that, Johnnie, but the fact that you told him that much makes us vulnerable now because if someone came looking for you, they might try and find him. And we know they might be looking because you found the recordings—five of them. That means they're serious people. And didn't Earl tell you that he had spoken with his attorney already and had given him instructions to scour the earth for you after he died?"

"Yes, but I don't think he was serious about that. I think he was bluffing. I think he would have gone to the police about the abortion as long as he was alive, but I don't think he would have gone as far as having his attorney search the world for me."

"But what if he did? Can we take that chance? No. We can't. We're gonna have to check out of here today. I had hoped to show you the sights in Marseille, Monaco, and Genova, but we can't risk it."

"Even if Earl did set his lawyer on me, Lucas would never tell the police where I went. He may never speak to me as long as he lives, but he'll never hurt me or let anyone hurt me."

"I know you believe that, Johnnie, but pressure has a way of making people think about themselves first."

"What kind of pressure?"

"His life for one. If they threaten his life, do you honestly think he won't tell them everything they want to know? Also, you gave him too much information."

"What do you mean? I didn't tell him much of anything."

"It's what you didn't say, Johnnie. For example, you said that you would be traveling the world for a few years. How could you do that without any money? You can't, can you? So what then does that tell the people looking for you? It tells them that you're with a man. . . a man of means. Not only that, it tells them that in all likelihood, you're with a white man. Now consider this. If the people the attorney hired are really good, they're going to talk to Hank, Lucille, Gloria, and Scotty over at the Flamingo Den. You remember Scotty, don't you?"

"Yes."

"You remember I had to force him to let you eat there?"

Johnnie closed her eyes and nodded.

"What do you think they're going to say? There'll only be one common name and one common description—mine. And guess what else? I was registered at the same hotel as you. And of course good ol' Scotty would love to tell them my name and what I do for a living. And let's not forget that Earl had my name and had already sent a team of detectives to Houston to find me. When they can't find either of us, they'll assume we're together, which is why I told you not to say anything to anyone."

"I'm so sorry, Paul. I didn't think of all that. I just thought I could trust Lucas with anything, even now."

"I don't doubt you can, Johnnie. But if white men threaten him with castration, I get the feeling he'll tell them what they want to know, don't you? Be honest."

Johnnie lowered her eyes to the table and nodded.

"That's why we have to get outta here right now. I might be paranoid, but paranoia is a reasonable strategy, given what you've told me. They may not have figured it all out. Nevertheless, we'll make them spend every penny they have to find us. That's the plan anyway."

"Where are we going?"

Paul smiled and said, "Can I trust you not to tell anyone?"

Smiling, she said, "Yes, you can."

"Listen, Johnnie, don't worry about Lucas and what he may have told someone. It may not even come to that. But we have to leave now. We're going to take the train to Paris and we're going to have a picnic under the Eiffel Tower. Paris has all the latest fashions so we'll let you shop like never before. Then we'll check out a jazz club called, Caveau de la Huchette. We'll also see Notre Dame, go to the Louvre, and have the best ice cream in the world at Berthillon."

Johnnie leaned over and kissed Paul on the cheek. "Thanks for not being angry with me. I know I messed up, but it won't happen again."

"I know it won't, Johnnie. But, I have good news."

"What?"

"I know you'd like to let your brother know where you are. So from time to time, we can fly back to the States, get a hotel and send him a letter. If he's being watched they'll have to look in the state where we sent the letter from, but we won't send the letter until we leave the state. There's a lot to see in the United States too. For example, we could go to South Dakota and see Mount Rushmore. From there we could go to Arizona and see the Grand Canyon. And then we could go to Las Vegas if your brother has a fight. After that, we'll have to get outta the country again. What do you think?"

"It sounds great, Paul. You sure know how to get into a girl's heart."

"I'm trying."

"Okay, I'll get dressed and we can check out," Johnnie said and left the veranda.

Paul waited until she was out of earshot and picked up the phone. "United States, Langley, Virginia." And then he recited the number. When a female voice answered, he gave her his control number.

"Connecting," the woman said.

"Masterson, great to hear from you?" a male voice said a few moments later. "What are you doing in Nice?"

"I need a favor."

"I thought you were out of this dirty business."

"I am out. I'm just collecting on favors that are overdue."

"Well, you understand policy. One favor deserves another."

"Understood. I'm heading to Paris within the hour."

"With that gorgeous Negro wife of yours, I presume."

A sea of silence stood between them.

"Do you have anything in Paris or not?" Paul said through clenched teeth.

"There's always something to do, Paul. You know that. Now . . . what do you need?"

"Have someone check out a PI in New Orleans named Tony Hatcher. I need to know what he's doing and who he's working for."

"Done. How will you be traveling? By train, I trust."

"Yes. By train."

"You'll be contacted somewhere on the way to Paris. You'll need to pass the package to a contact in Cairo."

"Is that it?"

"That's it, unless you need another favor."

"Got it."

"So . . . how are things at the Negresco? I'm told that you two—
"

Masterson hung up the phone.

Chapter 21

A Shadow Warrior's Redemption

Masterson remained in his chair, thinking about the cryptic conversation he'd just had with Marcus Yarborough, his handler, who he loathed for taking advantage of him when he was psychologically unfit to make decisions that would affect him for the rest of his life. Yarborough was one of the men who had administered the language test he'd taken years earlier when he was in the Army. Yarborough then recruited the impressionable young man who was full of self-hatred for his moral failure with Anita Wilde. Masterson was so full of remorse that he wanted to die. He would have killed himself, but his faith taught that if a Christian commits suicide, he forfeits heaven and he wasn't about to accept a one way ticket to the fiery flames of hell no matter how sorry he was for what he had done.

Later, after accepting Yarborough's invitation to join the Central Intelligence Agency while it was still in its infancy, he reasoned that his friendly recruiter must have sensed that he was suicidal and could be used on foreign soil with his authentic pastoral credentials as cover. The two had become fast friends—at least that's what Masterson thought since he was a constant fixture at Yarborough's home in Langley, Virginia. Yarborough's wife treated him like a member of the family and he had even become friends and a big brother of sorts with their son, Marcus junior who he called MJ. For a moment or two, MJ flashed in his mind. He was eighteen now and was probably starting his freshman year at Yale. It wouldn't be long before MJ followed in his father's footsteps and joined a secret society called, Skull & Bones, affectionately know as, The Order.

Masterson's secret desire to die made him the perfect weapon because he would take many chances with his life and he would never allow himself to be taken alive, which made him even more of an asset. With each dangerous mission, Masterson lost another piece of his soul in his quest to be killed on a classified mission. His life slowly spiraled out of control and he started drinking to anesthetize the pain that haunted him day and night. After that, he developed a relationship with a famous Hollywood actress who reminded him of Anita Wilde. Before long, they became intimate. Masterson later found out that she was a CIA operative too and that Yarborough had set them up. He thought he was doing Masterson a favor. He didn't expect him to get involved. Her cover was perfect because as an actress, country borders were invisible since movies were shot all over the world. The famous actress wasn't the only one in Hollywood working for the agency. There were directors, actors, writers, set designers, and wardrobe operatives involved in clandestine operations all over the world.

After Masterson took a bullet that nicked his heart from the gun of an enemy agent who had discovered he was a spy, he found the desire to live again and extricated himself from the Agency. Now though, he needed his old chums. And they wanted him back in the fold. If he had to complete another mission for the Agency, which meant he would be completing a mission for his country, he would do it to keep his bride safe, but he didn't want to be ensnared by the excitement of uncertainty and the adrenaline rush it gave him. He didn't want to kill again either, but he would if it was necessary to protect Johnnie from the people he knew were pursuing them.

Masterson was keenly aware that Johnnie possessed an inner innocence despite her wayward actions. In many ways, she reminded him of himself and his high school sweetheart before they were swept up in the cyclone of their hormones. He had made a decision to go all the way with the girl he thought he loved and they produced a child. He and his girlfriend had played Russian roulette and lost. Johnnie, on the other hand, made no such choice. She was forced into the situation which led her to him. It was like his God was giving him a second chance to get it right. He had every intention of getting it right and this time there would be no abortion to put a wall between them because he would never get Johnnie pregnant.

He knew his seventeen-year-old wife thought she knew what she was doing, but he knew she didn't. She was damaged goods and if someone didn't step in and do for her what he wished someone had done for him when he was lost and stumbling around in the wilderness of psychological uncertainty, she might never recover. He understood what it was like because he had lived it. There had been an endless string of women he had been involved with when he was an operative, yet not one of them was able to provide the cure he sought. He knew Johnnie was on the same path and she too needed direction. In a way, by saving Johnnie, he was saving himself and getting the redemption he needed for all the things he'd done.

He took a sip of his coffee and shifted his thoughts to Marcus Yarborough. Making a deal with him was like making a deal with the devil. He understood now that no matter what the devil gave you in exchange for doing his bidding, he was going to get so much more from you than you ever got from him. The thought of having to kill again surged through his mind. He still knew how to do it and do it quietly. But if he did kill again, would the blood thirst return? Would its clutches be even more powerful now that he had been away from it for so long?

"Hey, what are you still doing out here?" Johnnie said.

"I was just thinking about our plans and how to make sure we're not found."

"I thought we were in a hurry."

"We are. But I still have to think things through just in case I'm right and your enemies are pursuing us."

Johnnie smiled. "Thank you, Paul."

"For what?"

"For being a real man. The kind of man who can control himself. The kind of man who thinks of others before he thinks of himself. Before I met you, I would have bet all my earnings that there wasn't a man on this planet that wouldn't jump at the chance to do it to me. I thought you were strange the night you refused to come into my hotel room. I wouldn't have given you any, but it's nice to know a man wants you. You're the only man that refused to do it to me and you're my husband. I'll never forget you for that and everything you're doing for me. It's a miracle as far as I'm concerned. After awhile, I don't think we women realize how easily we prostitute ourselves for gain, even if it isn't financial gain. Sometimes we do it just because we think the man cares, but he doesn't. He just wants to get inside us as often as he can."

When Masterson heard that, he reached out for her, beckoning her and she went to him. Her words soothed his soul and he wept silently. It was then that he realized he'd do whatever it took to keep her alive. If that meant he would have to kill again, so be it. He wasn't about to let this delicate flower fall into the hands of ravenous wolves that prowled the streets at night nor the vultures that patrolled the skies by day. He took her hand and kissed it.

Johnnie felt him trembling and looked down at him. "What's wrong, Paul?"

"Nothing," he said quickly, trying to hide his emotional state.

She reached out and lifted his chin. "Are you crying?"

Masterson wiped his eyes and said, "No. It's the onions in my omelet."

Johnnie knew he was lying, but she didn't care. She respected him because he was at least trying to do the right thing by her. "You still want to know about my friends?"

"Yes," he said, looking into her eyes.

"On the way to Paris, I'm going to tell you all about my best friend, Sadie Lane."

Chapter 22

"You promised to tell me all about your family."

"Sadie was pretty, dark, and shapely. She had dreams of being a choreographer," Johnnie was saying to Paul in their private car in the first class section of the train as it sped down the tracks on the way to Paris. "But she, like lots of women, made the mistake of getting involved with the wrong man. This particular wrong man went by the name Santino Mancini. Now she's stuck in New Orleans and she'll probably end up being his bed wench for the rest of her days or until she's too old to please him as she does now. I wonder if Santino is making her have sex with his other friends now that she's probably living in the apartment over the garage."

"Wait a minute," Paul said. "You're telling me that she moved in with her lover?"

"I don't know what she did. I left, remember? But she didn't have anywhere to go and she had less money than I did. Her money burned up in the fire too. Sadie told me that Mrs. Mancini knew about the affair and laughed in her face. She called her a black bitch and then said bitch was too good for her. Can you imagine the humiliation she must have felt to let some slimy looking police detective stick his thing in her? And he made her suck it too. The whole thing is so messed up, Paul. We had planned to leave New Orleans together and then it all fell apart."

"How do you know he made her do that?"

"I heard him say it when he dragged her out of my house. When she came back to get her kids, I gave her fifty thousand dollars so she could get away from Santino for good. That way she would no longer have to depend on him."

"And Mancini is Italian?"

"Yes. And don't think for a second that I don't know you're trying to avoid asking if he was white. You know he's white, Paul."

"I know and it upsets me when white men do things like that."

"You must be the only white man it upsets—at least in the United States. The rest seem to wish they could get their brown sugar, as
my mother used to say before that cracker killed her."

"You're referring to Richard Goode, the Klansman, right?"

"Yes, and he got his too! Goode is part of the reason I ended up
getting involved with Napoleon Bentley. He wanted his brown sugar
and tricked me into doing it with him."

"I can certainly see why you have so much angst against white
men, but I don't see why you feel that way about white Christian
women."

"I can't think of one Christian white woman that didn't think she
was superior to me. Not one of them behaved civilly and treated me
like a human being. They were just a bunch of jealous women who
were upset with me because I'm beautiful and they couldn't keep
their wayward men from wanting me."

"You're forgetting two?"

"Who am I forgetting?"

"What about Gloria, the woman who owned the Clementine Hotel?"

"Gloria was a nice woman. She doesn't count."

"What about Sharon Trudeau your stockbroker?"

"She doesn't count either and neither woman was a Christian."

"Wait a minute. Are you telling me they don't count because
they weren't Christians?"

"That and they both treated me like a human being."

"But Sharon Trudeau stole all your money, didn't she?"

"Yeah, but I got it all back. She didn't steal my money because
she was a good-for-nothing cracker bitch, Paul! She stole my money
because she was a greedy bitch."

"And for that, she gets a pass?"

"In my book, yes. If she had stolen my money because she
thought that a black woman shouldn't be rich, that would be one
thing. I couldn't give her a pass. But she stole over a million dollars.
Most of the money she stole was white money. So she wasn't a

cracker bitch. Like I said, she was a greedy bitch. She saw an opportunity to live the easy life and she took it. I won't hold that against her. What she did to me had nothing to do with race. Being a criminal and being a racist don't necessarily go hand-in-hand."

"I see. Now, what have your experiences been so far here in France?"

"They've been great, I'm surprised to say. But what does that say about the country I was born in? It says that I have to leave the shores of my birth and sail across the Atlantic to get the kind of respect I should have gotten by being an American citizen. That's what it says. And if I find that white folks all over Europe treat me with the same respect, I might just make this my home. I mean why go back to the United States when they don't want me there and make sure I know they don't want me there every day?"

"Well, now, I'm sure you'll experience racism here too to some degree."

"If it's only to a degree, Paul, I can live with that. You've got simpleminded folks everywhere. Nothing you can do about that. But if the majority of my experiences with Europeans are as good as they've been so far, we really ought to consider staying here. What do you think?"

"So you think you can stay in the marriage to death?"

"With a man like you, I'd give it my best shot. You care from the heart, Paul. I remember my pastor preaching about something Jesus taught. Jesus said Christians are to give not expecting anything in return. That's you, Paul. That's so you. That's why I trust you. And that's why I've made up my mind to do right by you."

"What if you see Lucas Matthews again? Will you still do right by me?"

"Paul, now you know that's not a fair question. I still love him and I told you already that if he had given me another chance, we wouldn't be together. I can't swear to you that I wouldn't be with him again. I can't. Can't you understand that?"

"I do."

"He's at Fort Jackson anyway. You don't have to be jealous of him."

"I know, but I am. Isn't that strange? I hardly know you and yet I feel so connected to you."

"It is strange, but I told you that I prayed to God when Earl died and I believe he answered me. I heard him. It was as clear as a bell. He told me that he had sent me angels at the cemetery and that he had sent me someone else. And then you knocked on the door."

Masterson kind of laughed and said, "You're being serious?"

"I am. When I look back on everything that's happened to me in the last two years or so, I know God has protected me. Don't you remember when I told you my Aunt Ethel pointed a loaded gun in my face and fired?"

"Maybe the gun wasn't loaded, Johnnie."

"If the gun was unloaded, why did it fire? If there was an empty chamber, I would've heard the gun click, wouldn't I?"

"Yes."

"Paul, you don't have to believe me. I know what happened. I've denied it many times because I wanted to keep living the way I was living. Given all that's happened, I can't keep denying what I saw and heard. Frankly, I'm surprised at your attitude. You're a preacher and you don't believe in miracles?"

The train was slowing down as they pulled into Lyon.

Paul wondered if his contact was there waiting for him. He looked out the window at the people on the loading ramp and said, "I do believe in miracles, but I also know with surety that we are His instruments. I just needed to know if you were sure you believed."

"I do believe. It just took calamity to remind me of the truth."

"Let's get off here. We've got twenty minutes before the train leaves."

"Okay," Johnnie said. "I'll meet you back here in a few minutes."

On the way to the men's room, a woman bumped into Masterson.

"Excuse me," she said in French.

He felt her hand slip something into his inside breast pocket and knew she was his contact, but he played it off, knowing someone could have been watching her, or Johnnie may have seen too. The last thing he wanted to do was get Johnnie involved. He went into the men's room and found an empty stall. He reached into his pocket and pulled out two envelopes. One had the letters "P" and "M" on it. He opened it and read the following:

There's been a change in plans. In three days time, you'll need to be in Rome. I'm sure you'll be able to pull this off and your black beauty won't suspect a thing. You'll need to be in the lobby of the Excelsior Hotel by noon to hand off the package to a schoolteacher from Tulsa, Oklahoma. She'll contact you and give you further instructions. By the time you arrive, I should have the information you wanted.

Best of luck old friend,

Marcus

Masterson put the note back into the envelope and returned it to his inside breast pocket. Then he relieved himself and headed back to the train. He stepped into his private car.

"I saw that woman bump into you. Did she slip you anything?"

"Did she slip me anything?" Paul said nervously, like he was afraid she had sniffed him out.

"Yeah, like her phone number or something?"

"Oh. No. Not at all. We were both preoccupied with other things, I think."

"Uh-huh. I'm keeping my eye on you," she said playfully and hit him on the arm. "I've told you about Sadie. You promised to tell me all about your family. Let's hear it."

"Well, my grandfather was a surgeon. And my father was a developer before he found oil on the land my grandfather left him . . ."

Chapter 23

"Oh . . . why didn't you say so, Mr. Hatcher?"

Hatcher boarded United Airlines flight 420 with time to spare. The DC-6 took off on time and landed at Lexington County Airport two hours later. After bedding Janet Shamus for over an hour, he was sleepy and had planned to sleep on the plane. But he was seated next to a loquacious fifty-eight-year-old woman whose husband of thirty-eight years had died a few days earlier. He had fought and been wounded during World War I and his body was being flown to Arlington Cemetery. Being a fellow serviceman, Hatcher felt it was his duty to stay awake and listen to the love story that poured out of her when she spoke of the only lover and hero she had ever known.

By the time he deplaned and picked up his overnight bag at luggage claim, it was after seven. He considered checking into a hotel and calling it a night, but with it being a Saturday, he thought the recruits would be on liberty. That's how it was when he served. He grabbed a cup of coffee and took a cab to Fort Jackson. He told the MPs he had served as a grunt in the Army. As a favor to a fellow serviceman, they gave him a lift to Lucas's barracks. He recognized Marguerite's car and smiled, thinking he had hit the jackpot by playing a hunch he'd had. Initially, he didn't think Johnnie and Lucas had a prayer of ever getting back together. He was glad he was wrong.

Johnnie was with Lucas which meant his work for Janet Shamus was over before it even started. It also meant that if she kept her end of the bargain, he'd finally live his dream and be on easy street. On the other hand, they still had to kill Johnnie and that was going to take time. Plus another unforeseen complication had occurred, he realized. Images of the American Airlines clerk, the cabbie, the MPs he'd met, and Lucas Matthews all came to mind. There were lots of people who could tell the police he had been to Fort Jackson if Johnnie's body was ever discovered. The plan had gotten complicated already and he felt his conscience creeping up on his conscious again. Nevertheless, he was undeterred. He told himself that Johnnie was responsible for a riot where lots of people had been killed. She had pretty much wiped out the Beauregard family. He also reminded himself that she had orchestrated the death of Klan leader, Richard Goode. But what finally silenced his conscience was the fact that she had also killed her unborn child. He told himself he was doing the public a favor by getting rid of her.

The rewards of killing Johnnie Wise were too great to let the inconvenience of killing her get in the way of being financially free for the first time in years. A licentious smile surfaced when he realized that if he played his cards right, he could prolong Johnnie's execution for months so he could continue collecting unmentionable favors from gorgeous Janet Shamus. For the first time, he fully understood why his ex-wife refused to remarry. Keeping him on a financial string had its rewards. Love took a backseat to money. In other words, why should she be encumbered with another marriage when the first one failed? Remaining single and having a boyfriend kept a steady check coming in from him. In addition to being rid of the headache that marriage often turned out to be, she was being properly bedded regularly without the legal entanglements of holy matrimony.

Hatcher realized that she was getting all the benefits of marriage without the documentation and the hassle—money and honey. Why would she ever give that up? She wouldn't and neither would he. He figured that if a woman could take advantage him, he could take advantage of women—never mind that he had ruined his marriage by committing adultery in the first place. He would drag the search out for as long as he wanted the fresh flesh that Janet's body offered. He'd keep giving her updates on how the search was going, but he wouldn't give her much detail, otherwise she'd get impatient and demand that he take action before he was ready. He smiled within, thanked the MP for the lift, grabbed his bag, and headed for the barracks.

A sergeant was coming out of the barracks. Hatcher figured it must have been the sergeant one of the MPs had called to get permission to come on the post and said, "Excuse me, sergeant, I'm Tony Hatcher and I'm looking for Lucas Matthews. One of your MPs dropped me off here. Am I'm in the right place?"

"Depends," the sergeant said. "Where you from, Tony? With an accent like that you definitely ain't from around these parts."

"I'm from New Orleans."

"That's what I thought," the sergeant said. "I have a recruit with the same twang. Are you a cop?"

"No, sir. I'm a private detective."

"Uh-huh. And you want to talk to Private Matthews about what exactly?"

"Excuse me sergeant, but who are you exactly?"

"I'm his drill sergeant. The name's Limitless Cornsilk and I'ma full-blooded Apache—a descendent of Geronimo, which means, I don't like you pale-faced son of a bitches comin' around here botherin' my best recruit for any reason."

"Well Sergeant Cornsilk, I only have a few questions. I was in the Army myself during WWII so I understand your position."

"I bet pale-faced bastards like you think that little item somehow gives you some sway. Let me be very clear, Tony. I don't give a damn if you were in the Army. It wasn't my Army and you were not my recruit. Private Matthews is my recruit and I don't want him bothered for any reason. Furthermore, this is a federal installation. That means that neither you nor the sheriff nor any police agency has any *authority* here."

"I see you're very fond of him."

Cornsilk snarled and with venom said, "Did you just interrupt me, *Tony*?"

"I was only—"

"I don't like being interrupted for any reason, Tony. Besides, Private Matthews served his time in Angola. He's paid his debt to society no matter what you think he's done in the past. He's doing things the Army way now and that's all that matters as far as I'm concerned. So I don't want a pale-face like you messing up his chances of becoming a fine officer in my Army. You got that, Tony?"

"I believe I do, but the trouble is, I'm not looking for him. He's not in any trouble whatsoever—none that I know of anyway. I'm actually looking for someone he knows and I'm hoping he can point me in the right direction."

"Oh . . . why didn't you say so, Mr. Hatcher?" Cornsilk said, smiling.

"You know, sergeant, I really don't know. My day has been a colossal failure."

"Sorry for giving you a hard time. We look after our own."

"No problem," Hatcher said, knowing he was about to lie to relax the sergeant who believed in protecting his own. "I fully understand your position. My day started with an irate old maid demanding that I find out who killed her dead husband. It didn't matter to her that when I looked into her case, I discovered that her husband was very much alive and actually living with her. Nevertheless she still came by my office this morning to tell me the most fantastic tale. She claimed that the man living with her is not her husband. I told her it was a job for the police, but she kept insisting that she had paid me and that I was obligated to look further into her case. From there it got worse and I don't have to tell you what it's like to make ends meet. So I have to take clients that I wouldn't even have considered taking five years ago when things were good for me. Now that I'm here, it doesn't look like its going to get any better either."

"It might, Mr. Hatcher, now that I know you're not after my boy."

"I'm sorry for the intrusion. It'll only take a few minutes, perhaps ten. So is he in the barracks? I promise you I won't keep him from his duties long."

"No. Private Matthews is the barracks chief. And he's a good one. Loves the Army. Loves the way we do things here. He's going to be an excellent officer, but if you tell him I said that, I'll deny it."

Hatcher laughed. "I understand. So where can I find him?"

"Being the barracks chief gives him certain privileges the other recruits don't get. He runs a tight ship so I give him time off on Saturday and Sunday evenings so he can spend time with his girl."

Hatcher fought the urge to smile, knowing he had found Johnnie rather easily.

"He's probably at a dive called The Blue Diamond," Cornsilk continued. "It's a restaurant on the Negro side of town. The Army no longer tolerates segregation, but the civilians haven't caught up yet. He's probably there with his girl, Lieutenant Perry. They're not supposed to be seeing each other, but they're both Negro and as long as they keep the relationship off post, well, nobody's gonna say anything."

A little deflated that he hadn't actually found his prey just yet, a number of questions invaded Hatcher's mind. The first question was, if Lucas was with Lieutenant Perry, where was Johnnie? Did she come here to reconcile, but learned that he was dating another woman or what? If that was the case, why would she leave her car here? It made no sense. If so, is she still here? He'd have to get those answers from Matthews. He said, "Do you think they're still at the restaurant?"

Cornsilk looked at his watch. "It's only a little after eight and there's not much to do around here except go to the movies, eat, and find a quiet spot to spend some time with your favorite girl. I'd be happy to drop you off there. Will you be staying the night? I see you brought an overnight bag. I can suggest a couple of nice hotels."

"I brought the bag just in case I couldn't speak with Private Matthews tonight. You never know how these things are going to go. Now that I know where he is, I doubt I'll be staying the night, but give me the names just in case I change my mind. If I can, I plan to catch the first plane to New Orleans after I've spoken with Private Matthews."

"Would you like me to hang around and then take you to a hotel or back to the airport? It's no trouble."

"Thank you, no. You've done quite enough. I'll probably get something to eat at the Blue Diamond and then call a cab to take me to the airport."

Chapter 24

"Let your ego decide."

A half hour later, Hatcher walked into the Blue Diamond. It was far from what he expected. From what he knew of Negroes, Saturday nights was their time to cut loose and live it up. Not only wasn't the Blue Diamond a lively eatery to dine in, the place was a ghost town. There were only five people in the restaurant. Two of them were women. Of the three men patrons, he was sure that Lucas Matthews wasn't one of them. He figured that if Cornsilk knew where he was, Lucas must be a regular at the restaurant. If that was the case, the proprietor would probably know who Lucas was and quite possibly where he was. Hatcher walked up to the counter where a heavyset Negro woman was ringing up one of the men. When she finished Hatcher offered her a friendly smile, knowing that she probably thought a white man in a black joint was trouble for business. He knew she probably thought he was a detective and at first he was going to play it that way. But when he opened his mouth, "FBI, ma'am," came out. He waited for the response he hoped to get; one that said the woman was scared to death and would cooperate even though he hadn't shown her his federal credentials. "I'm agent Hatcher and I'm looking for Lucas Matthews. His drill sergeant thought you might know him."

"I know Lucas, sure. He's a regular here."

"Has he been in here tonight?"

"Yes sir. He'll probably be back in a couple hours."

"What makes you think that?"

"There's a big dance down the street at the Coconut Grove Ballroom. This place will be packed with people when it's over. Would you like something to eat while you wait?"

"Sure, I'll take a burger and fries."

"Anything to drink, sir?"

"A cold beer."

"We don't serve beer here, sir. We don't have a license."

"A Coke then. Do you have a payphone I can use?"

"Yes sir. We've got a couple in the back. Can I ask you a question, sir?"

"You wanna know what Lucas did to bring heat from the FBI, right?"

She nodded.

"Nothing actually. I'm on a missing person case. Mr. Matthews could probably help me."

"Who you lookin' for, sir? I might know where she at."

"That's confidential, ma'am. FBI stuff. I'm sure you understand. I have a phone call or two to make. Could you bring my order to the booth please?"

"Yes sir."

A minute later, Hatcher entered the booth and called Janet Shamus's home office phone. She didn't answer. He hung up the phone and thought for a second, wondering where she was, even though she could be in a hundred different places in New Orleans. Then it occurred to him that she could still be at his place sound asleep. An egotistical smile emerged. He called his home hoping she was there, and would answer his phone. If she was there, he assumed she was still sleeping or she was thoroughly going through his things, trying to find out more about him. Either way, if she answered, he would know that she was checking to see if any women were calling him. And that tidbit of information would let him know that their earlier escapade had left an indelible impression, which meant she was looking forward to the next session.

Hatcher's curiosity waned considerably when he heard the phone rang seven times. He was about to hang up when he heard someone pick up the receiver. Hopeful excitement returned. His heart raced as he held his breath, waiting to hear the sound of her voice.

Groggily, in a deep husky voice a woman said, "Hello?"

"Janet?"

She cleared her throat. "Yes. Who is this? And what are you doing calling my home at this hour?"

Hatcher's ego doubled as if it were being filled with helium. A euphoric feeling of triumph swept over him when he heard her confusion. "Uh, Janet, you're in my home."

Janet's eyes shot wide open and she looked around the room. Nothing looked familiar. Then what happened that afternoon came racing to the surface. She looked at herself. She was nude and partially under a sheet. Her breasts were free and fully exposed. She pulled the sheet up over them and looked around the room to see if anyone was there and had seen her nakedness. All of a sudden she felt lots of moisture between her legs. She pulled the sheet back and looked. Her blood was everywhere.

"Are you still there, Janet?"

She closed her eyes and held the phone, wondering if she had made a huge mistake getting involved with Hatcher even if it was to avenge the death of her parents. She remembered the beer she had drank before the kissing began. And then everything that happened that morning unfolded in her mind.

"Janet."

She exhaled hard and said, "I'm here, Mr. Hatcher."

"I think we're way beyond formalities, but are you okay?"

"What did you put in my drink?"

Frowning he said, "Nothing. Nothing at all. Why?"

"You must have slipped me something. Why would I sleep to nearly nine at night when I got here before noon? And I'm still sleepy. I could use a few more hours to recover from whatever you gave me."

"What I gave you was all natural. It was all me. No drugs. Just pleasure."

"Then why am I feeling this way, like if I closed my eyes again, I may not ever open them again?"

"Great sex will do that to you."

"Someone has an ego, I see. I still say something was in the drink. Now . . . let's move on. You called for a reason, I'm sure. I hope it wasn't just to inflate your self-image."

"I just wanted you to know I'm close to finding Matthews. He should be coming to this restaurant in a couple hours. I haven't decided yet, but I was thinking of going down to the Coconut Groove Ballroom to have a word with him, but it might be a little noisy in there. I don't want to wait for him here. I'm told that this place will be full of people when the dance is over. I think I'll have a bite to eat and then walk down to the club and look for his car. If I find it, I'll just wait for him there."

"Call me as soon as you've finished speaking with him."

"Sure. Should I call you at home or at my place?"

She rolled her eyes and said, "Let your ego decide."

The line went dead. Hatcher laughed and called back.

"What, Mr. Hatcher?"

"That was rude. There's more to report. Do you want to hear it or not?"

She exhaled hard. "Even though it pains me to hear the glee of triumph in your voice, I will tolerate it for the duration of your report. Please don't tarry with it or play silly little games with me. I'm very serious about our agreement. Are you? Have you gotten cold feet now that you've gained access to my exclusive wine cellar?"

"That's an interesting way of putting it."

"It is, isn't it, but what you've just done is called a red herring. Please answer my question."

"Well, I gotta tell you, I have had second thoughts—"

Janet took a deep breath and screamed, "I know you're not re-neging on this deal after what I've done . . . not after what I've sacrificed."

Loving her response, Hatcher calmly said, "Again, if you'll al-low me to finish, I was going to say that I've had second, third, and even forth thoughts, but I'm in."

"All the way?"

Hatcher laughed and said, "Just like I was several hours ago when we were together."

"You have some ego, I'll tell you that much."

"So what are you saying, you don't want to give it another go?"

She exhaled hard again. "Can we stick to your report, please?"

"Sure. I have good news and not so good news. The good news is that Johnnie's car is here in South Carolina."

"And the not so good news would be what?"

"I've got the feeling she's not here. I think she came and left, which means she could be anywhere."

"Wait a minute. Tell me why you think she's not there."

"Well, our friend, Private Matthews, as his drill sergeant calls him, has found himself another woman—a Lieutenant Perry. He's at a dance up the block with her right now according to the cashier. That's all I know about her so far."

"Why would she leave her car in South Carolina?"

"It's an old car. Perhaps it broke down again and she asked him to keep it for her until she returns."

"Why do you think she went to him?"

"To reconcile, I suspect. He's given her lots of chances, but she was too much like her mother. I think the kid's had it with her. He probably introduced her to his lieutenant friend just to rub it in her face."

"So you think she's in San Francisco then?"

"That would be the logical next step."

"So what are you planning with Mr. Matthews?"

"I'm planning to do exactly what I told you this morning."

"Do you think he'll tell you where she went?"

"He probably won't tell me anything at first, but don't forget we have lots of leverage we can use against him. According to his sergeant, he's got grandiose plans of becoming an officer just like his lady friend. All of that can be used to persuade him to see things our way. Once I let him know what the score is, he'll talk."

"What time shall I expect your call?"

"As soon as I get to the airport."

"So you're definitely flying out to San Francisco tonight?"

"No. I'm coming back to New Orleans and I expect you to pick me up."

"Why would I do that? Take a cab home."

"You'll do it because we're partners. All the way. Didn't you say that a moment ago?"

"Mr. Hatcher." She paused and took a prolonged breath. "We are partners and I will fulfill my end of the contract, but I am not your personal Geisha. And I would appreciate it if you could remember that little detail. When we've completed our task, it's all over per our agreement."

"I fully understand, Miss Shamus, but this thing is far from over. Assuming she's in San Francisco, we still need to make plans to finish the job. Until *all* our business is concluded, I expect you to live up to *all* the details of the contract."

"Fine, but there was nothing in our agreement that says I have to be your personal chauffeur. So when you get in, take a cab to the Belle Glades. I'll be in the penthouse."

"Completely nude, I trust."

The line went dead. Hatcher laughed, and hung up the phone.

Chapter 25

"A pilot's license isn't enough."

J anet Shamus was still in Hatcher's bed looking up at the ceiling, thinking about the day she'd be able to take care of Johnnie Wise once and for all. Then, without meaning to, the romp she'd had with Hatcher came to mind. While she would never admit it, not even to herself, she had enjoyed everything he did to her. She had never felt so alive as when he was kissing her and touching parts of her body that she had been taught never to let the boys touch. Now she wanted him to touch her again just like he had before. But even though she wanted to do it with Hatcher again, she couldn't let him know that. She had to continue being contrary and aloof about intercourse and make him think it was a chore that she had to complete, otherwise she might lose control.

That's when it occurred to her that she could perhaps remedy her desire to engage in intercourse with Hatcher by bringing her rival's love interests into bed with them. She remembered the pictures of the men Johnnie had been with. They were all good-looking men. She decided that when she and Hatcher fulfilled their contractual obligation at the Belle Glades Hotel or anywhere else, she would close her eyes and let her imagination takeover. Instead of bedding Hatcher, she would bed Johnnie's lovers. She would get a measure of revenge by imagining Johnnie walking in and seeing it.

Satisfied she had come up with a plan to make meeting Hatcher irrelevant, she rolled out of his bed and took a shower. When she returned to the bedroom to dress, she saw her blood on the sheets again. She put her clothes on and then took both sheets off the bed, hoping her blood didn't soak through to the mattress. It hadn't. She then put fresh sheets on the mattress and remade the bed. She drove over to the Belle Glades Hotel and went to the check in counter.

"May I help you, ma'am?" the clerk said.

"Yes, I need your presidential suite."

"How long will you be staying?"

"I'm not sure. It could be a month or six months or a year. Who do I talk to about buying it?"

The clerk's mouth fell open. "Uh, I don't know. Let me get the manager out here."

A few minutes later, a short man wearing a blue jacket with a yellow hotel crest on it came out and said, "I'm Mr. Dalton. Am I to understand that you want to buy our presidential suite?"

"Yes."

"May I ask why, Miss . . ."

"I'm Janet Shamus and I'm the president of Buchanan Mutual. I want to buy your presidential suite as a residence and to conduct business, that is, if it's up to my standards."

"I'm not sure we could sell you the suite, Miss Shamus, but we'd be happy to let you have it on a monthly basis if it's up to your standards."

"Perhaps I should be speaking to the owner of this establishment."

"I'm afraid he's not available. Perhaps I could show you the suite and see if it's to your liking. And then in the morning, I'll contact Mr. Meeks and tell him what you're interested in doing."

"Mr. Dalton I don't think you understood me. I might be interested in buying his hotel. If I like the suite you're going to show me, get him on the phone tonight."

"I most certainly will. Now, if you'll follow me, I'll take you to your suite."

They took the elevator to the top floor and walked down the corridor to the end where Janet saw a set of double doors. Dalton opened a door and they went into the large living room.

"This is the best the Belle Glades has to offer as you might imagine. It boasts over four thousand square feet and it has all the latest technology. There is a master bedroom and two other bedrooms, each with their own baths. It also has a large eat-in kitchen if you prefer to cook your own meals. Or you can order room service twenty-four hours a day. I would stack our hotel against any hotel in the city, probably in the country for the matter. Rumor has it that the Hiltons have tried to buy the chain several times, but Mr. Meeks wouldn't sell. What do you think, Miss Shamus?"

"I don't know, Mr. Dalton. Let me take a look around and I'll let you know."

"I'd be happy to show you around."

"No need. I think I can find my way around. Thank you."

"Okay, well, if you need anything, anything at all, I'm only a phone call away.

Janet waited for Dalton to leave. Although she didn't fully grasp it yet, the feeling of power was rising within her. She noticed the effect it had on the desk clerk and Mr. Dalton when she mentioned buying the hotel. She walked around the suite, taking in all the luxury, the marble floors, the leather furniture, the state of the art kitchen, the China, and the silverware, the mirrors, the paintings, and the fireplace. She looked in all the rooms to make sure they were up to the standards of the mansion her grandfather had built. She definitely wanted to buy the suite or at least rent it until her business with Johnnie Wise was settled. She went back into the living room and picked up the phone and called Walter Patterson's office. Patterson was the private detective she hired who had investigated Hatcher. That's how she knew he was a marksman too. Patterson had also found out other details about Hatcher that she hadn't shared with him.

Patterson used to be Hatcher's partner and he hated Hatcher because he compromised their business by sleeping with the clients. He had warned Hatcher ten times to stop, but Hatcher responded by sleeping with Patterson's wife and making sure he found out about it. Then when Patterson confronted him, Hatcher gave him the beating of his life. Patterson's jaw was broken during the all out office brawl and had to be wired. He was unconscious for three days. In the meantime, Hatcher continued having relations with his wife and had told her that Patterson was out of town on a case. When Patterson's wife found out what really happened, she felt guilty; guilty enough to stop seeing Hatcher and nursed her husband back to health, which took four months. Obviously the partnership was over after that. When the clients that Hatcher was bedding found out they weren't the only ones, they got together and spread the word to their friends who were divorcing their husbands and sent them to Patterson who had opened his own agency.

"Walter Patterson."

"Mr. Patterson, this is Janet Shamus. Sorry to call you at this hour."

"No problem. What can I do for you, Miss Shamus?"

"I'd like you to go to Scottsdale, Arizona and have a talk with a man named Everett James. He's married and has a couple of kids, but he's having an adulterous relationship with Anita Jacobson, a pastor's wife."

Patterson remained quiet.

"Are you there Mr. Patterson?"

"Yes, I'm here. I'm writing it all down."

"Good. Once you find this man, let him know that I will completely destroy him if he doesn't do what I want him to do."

"Which is what, Miss Shamus?"

"I want him to let you know when and where he's going to meet Mrs. Jacobson. I want to know at least twenty-four hours in advance."

"May I ask why, Miss Shamus?"

"I'll fill you in later. Now how soon can you get to the airport?"

"Within the hour."

"Good. And by the way, I'm going to need my own plane. Please find three companies that make and sell them. Let them know who I am, and that they are in competition with each other."

"How soon do you want it?"

"Yesterday."

"That soon, huh?"

"That soon. And I'll need a couple pilots to be on standby. Let them know they'll be paid handsomely to be available at a moments notice to take me wherever I want to go. In fact, find several of them. I'll have them flown from wherever they are to New Orleans and interview them at my new suite at the Belle Glades or wherever I am. I'm going to be doing some traveling. Let them know I'll cover all their expenses."

"The Belle Glades? Why are you staying there?"

"I'm a grown woman now. I think it's time I got my own place."

"So you've got yourself a boyfriend, huh?"

"What makes you say that, Mr. Patterson?"

"You just avoided the question with a question. People who do that are hiding something. You all of sudden need privacy . . . another telltale sign of a man in your life."

"How long do you think it'll take to find the pilots?"

Patterson fought off a laugh when she didn't bother to deny she had a man in her life and he had found out. "First we need to know what size plane your getting and then we can find pilots to fly it. A pilot's license isn't enough."

"Okay, well, I need a plane as soon as possible—a luxurious plane . . . one that can fly anywhere in the world I want to go."

"I'm on it, Miss Shamus. I'll let you know when I've had a conversation with Mr. James."

Chapter 26

"They found her body, Lucas."

After devouring his cheeseburger and fries, Hatcher left the Blue Diamond restaurant and walked up the block, following the music as it led him to the Coconut Grove Ballroom. There were a number of black men outside smoking refers and drinking liquor from the bottle. Being the only white face on the street, Hatcher expected them to try to rough him up, but they didn't. And if they had, he was sure he could have handled them. If not, he had a firearm that could and a license to carry it just in case somebody ended up dead. He went inside to take a look around, hoping to get lucky and spot Lucas and get out of there before someone did something stupid. He wasn't about to stick around so many black faces with pent up rage against the white man. That just wasn't smart.

He went over to the box office and bought a ticket. He just wanted to make sure Lucas was in there, that way he wouldn't waste his time looking for his car when there were so many parked outside. Besides, he wasn't sure if he was still driving the same automobile. When he climbed the stairs and entered the ballroom, he was stunned to see so many white faces in there mixing among the Negroes, drinking and dancing with them like they were all the same. Then he understood why the Negroes downstairs didn't bother him. They were accustomed to seeing white people coming to the Coconut Grove. He decided to relax a little and blend in now that he could move around without attracting unwanted attention.

He made his way over to the bar and ordered a beer and then mixed in with the crowd. After about twenty minutes, he saw Lucas with a woman he presumed was Lieutenant Perry. He finished his beer and hung around for thirty minutes watching Lucas and his date, trying to determine how involved they were. The lieutenant was a looker and Hatcher could see how Lucas or any other man might fall in love with her in a heartbeat. And she was a college girl too; otherwise she wouldn't be wearing lieutenant's bars. Hatcher had seen enough. It was time to go. He decided to look for Lucas's car and wait, but first he had to relieve himself. It could be a long wait if the woman at the Blue Diamond was right. When he came out of the men's room, he bumped into an attractive Negress who had come out of the ladies room with several of her friends. After they both apologized, they locked eyes. The attraction was mutual. He was about to introduce himself when her girlfriends pulled her away and back into the ballroom with her eyes peering over her shoulder at him the entire time. That was an invitation, Hatcher knew. If he wasn't on the job and if he wasn't surrounded by Negroes who might all of sudden become unfriendly after the dance, he would have followed her into the hall for a chat. But if jealously reared its head and the Negro men decided to turn him into a piñata, he didn't have enough bullets to stop them all. So he walked down the stairs and out the glass doors.

He walked down the street and turned the corner where the parking lot was. It only took him a few minutes to spot Lucas's car. He opened the door, got in the backseat, and started thinking about how Janet Shamus knew he was a marksman. He wondered if she had hired someone to look into his background. It made sense to him because she had checked out everyone else in her circle of "friends". The first name that came to mind was Walter Patterson. He knew Patterson would love to reveal his secrets. While he believed and was sure she had hired someone to check him out, he was sure it wasn't Patterson. The stories Patterson could have told Janet would have turned her completely off and she had given herself to him. In fact she allowed him to be the first man to enter her. That's why he believed it had to be someone else. Otherwise, she would have never hired him. The next thing he knew he was fast asleep in the backseat.

The sound of car doors opening and closing and engines revving woke him up all of a sudden. He also heard heels clicking, men and women talking and laughing as they went to their vehicles. Unsure of how long he had been sleeping on the job, he looked at his watch, but he couldn't see the hands. He had no idea how long he'd been out, but he knew he needed to be alert. Lucas and Lieutenant Perry might be coming to his car any minute now. While he waited, he thought about the huge mistake that might have cost him his life if he was dealing with dangerous people; people who had motive to kill him. Lucas wasn't a killer and he didn't know Hatcher was there looking for him. He wasn't going to stop having sex with Janet Shamus, but he would make sure he got sufficient sleep after.

The passenger car door opened and a woman got in. Hatcher remained quiet. The woman didn't know he was there. Lucas got in and closed the door. He was about to say something to his date when Hatcher said, "Did you two enjoy yourselves?"

Lucas and Lieutenant Perry nearly leaped out of their skin.

"Who the hell are you?" Lucas screamed "And what are you doing in my car?"

"Relax, Lucas. I'm just here to talk to you. That's all. Can you give me a few minutes of your time? By the way, I watched you two in there and I gotta tell ya, both of you are sharp dressers and talented dancers."

"Talk?" Lucas said. "Talk about what?"

"I'm not sure you want the lieutenant to hear my questions. It's about Red River, Louisiana. You're familiar with the place, aren't you?"

If it were possible, Lucas' eyes would have bulged out of his head. His heart was pounding. His breathing became erratic and Cassandra was watching it all. She knew that whoever the man in the backseat was, he was a threat to Lucas.

"Who are you, sir?" she asked.

"Whoever you need me to be," Hatcher said. "Best thing you can do is get outta the car so I can have a private conversation with your boyfriend."

"My father is a lawyer and I know that if you're a cop, you have to identify yourself as a cop and show us your badge. Without that, I don't have to do anything and neither does Lucas. As a matter of fact, you're trespassing and we have every right to defend ourselves."

"You've got some mouth on you, you know that?"

"So basically you're saying you don't have a badge which means you're not with law enforcement. I suggest you leave before we beat you into a coma."

"I have a gun," Hatcher said.

"So what? Look around you, sir. You're surrounded by Negro men and they have guns too. I bet they would love to stomp you to death and leave your body in a white neighborhood. All I have to do is roll this window down and they'll pull you outta this car in no time flat. When they do, God help you."

She started rolling down the window.

"Hold on," Hatcher said, realizing this wasn't going according to plan. But he had to play it out anyway. The bluff still might work because Marla Bentley was a white woman and she was murdered by a black man. That was serious leverage—at least that's what he thought. "I just wanna talk to Lucas about a couple things. No need to get other people involved in this."

"Who are you?" Lucas asked looking at Hatcher through the rearview mirror.

"My name is Tony Hatcher. I'm a private detective."

"What do you want?" Cassandra asked.

Hatcher looked at Lucas and said, "You don't want her to hear this, do you? We both know what happened in Red River, don't we?"

Lucas was about to answer when Cassandra said, "Whatever happened in Red River, Louisiana has nothing to do with Lucas."

Hatcher said, "What kind of man are you? You let a woman talk for you?"

Lucas was about to answer, but Cassandra spoke first. "He's a smart man. The kind of man that knows when to keep his mouth shut. What else you got, Mr. Hatcher?"

Hatcher exhaled and said, "They found her body, Lucas. You know what that means, don't you?"

Lucas was about to turn around, but Cassandra touched his arm and said, "Whose body, sir?"

"Marla Bentley's."

"Oh, you mean Napoleon's wife? Is that what this is about? We know all about it."

Cassandra was running a bluff of her own. She hadn't heard anything about Marla being dead, but she was putting on a convincing show.

"If that's true, why don't you want Lucas to talk? Could it be because you're afraid of what he might say?"

"I am. All black men are afraid of what you crackers'll do when your precious white women open their legs to black men. And since this one is dead and Lucas was doing exactly what she wanted him to do, who knows what you crackers'll do. The police obviously couldn't find Mrs. Bentley's killer and you came all the way up here looking for an innocent man because you wanted her and she was giving Lucas what you wanted. Ain't that right?"

"Innocent? Did you hear that, Lucas? She really believes in you. You black studs sure know how to screw a woman, don't ya? After awhile they'll say anything or do anything you say, won't they?"

"Sounds like you're describing Marla Bentley. And for the record, I'm still a virgin. Now, is there anything else we can do for you?"

"Like I said, you've got some mouth on you, lieutenant."

"Yeah, but it's not like Marla Bentley's I'm sure. From what I hear, she likes to suck on things with hers."

Hatcher said, "So Lucas, you're saying you were never in Red River?"

"No," Lucas said confidently.

"And you didn't kill Marla Bentley?"

"No. I didn't."

"That's interesting because the guards at Angola say they intercepted several letters from Chicago. One of them talked of you meeting Marla Bentley at the Red River Motel. See where I'm going with this, Lucas?"

"I see where you're going, Mr. Hatcher," Cassandra said. "You obviously want something and you won't be satisfied until you get it. Now what can we do for you?"

"I'm looking for Johnnie Wise. Where is she?"

"I haven't seen her," Lucas blurted out.

Hatcher laughed. "You should have kept your mouth shut like the lieutenant told you. That's the first lie you've been caught in."

"I'm not lying."

"That's the second lie you've been caught in. How is it that Johnnie's car is at Fort Jackson and in front of your barracks? And don't tell me you drove it here. That would be the third lie. Like they say, three strikes and you're out."

Silence filled the car.

"So, *lieutenant*, you've finally run out of pithy come backs, huh?"

"I—"

"Shut up!" Hatcher yelled. "You're finished talking lieutenant." He looked at Lucas. "The car finished you. No more games. Now, where's Johnnie?"

"I don't know, all right?" Lucas said.

"How did you get her car?" Hatcher said.

"She came to the base looking for me."

"Go on. Spill it all."

"She came to the front gate and told the guards to tell me she would be at the train station until her train left."

"When was this?" Hatcher asked.

"I'm don't remember, man. Maybe a month or so ago."

"Did you meet her at the train?"

"No."

"So you didn't even bother going? I don't believe you. You loved her, didn't you?"

"I didn't say I didn't go to the station. I'm saying I didn't get there in time. And Cassandra was with me."

"Why do you think she came to see you? And how did you end up with her car?"

"I'll never know why she came to see me, but I think she came to apologize for what she did."

"Which was what?"

"She was seeing a couple white men besides the white man who raped her. I heard Earl Shamus's wife testify to it in court. That was it for me. She knew I heard it and I guess she wanted to apologize and leave New Orleans forever. Her car was at the station and the keys were still in it. I don't know if she left it for me or not. But I took it. I've been trying to sell it but so far I've been unable to."

"Why didn't you say that from the beginning instead of letting your *lawyer* speak for you?"

"Cassandra was right. Who knows what white folks are going to think when a white woman turns up dead? They don't seem to care who did the killing or why?"

"I believe you, Lucas. And don't worry, I won't tell the police anything. I need two favors for my silence though."

"What?" Lucas said looking at Hatcher through the rearview mirror.

"Take me back to the Blue Diamond. I left my bag with the cashier. And then I'll need a lift to the airport. I need to get back to New Orleans as soon as possible."

"Sure, no problem. Why are you looking for Johnnie anyway?"

"Her mother had another insurance policy with an insurance company from New York. I just wanted to make sure she got her money."

Lucas and Cassandra looked at each other, acknowledging that they didn't believe a word of what he was saying. Hatcher knew they didn't believe him, but he didn't care because he didn't believe them either.

Chapter 27

Pursuit

"What the hell happened in Red River, Louisiana, Lucas?" Cassandra asked when Hatcher got out of the car and entered the airport lobby.

"It was an accident," Lucas said. "I didn't mean it, I swear."

"Well, tell me what happened. I think you owe me that since I saved your ass."

"The short version is that we were in bed together and she told me that Napoleon had set me up so I would have to go to jail and then into the Army so he could have Johnnie."

"That's a reason to kill him, not her, Lucas. Why did you kill her?"

"It was an accident, I said. I liked Marla. I really did, but when she told me that she was in on it, I was so mad at her for not telling me what was going on, I grabbed her by the throat and the next thing I know, her neck snapped. What could I do? She was white and nobody would have believed it wasn't intentional. They wouldn't have cared. I would have been lynched on sight. You believe me, don't you?"

Cassandra exhaled and said, "I believe you, Lucas, but damn, you need to make sure you get outta the country as soon as you can."

"I know. But you know . . . something's been bothering me from the start. What does he want with Johnnie?"

"No, Lucas, what does who he's working for want with Johnnie. That's the question."

"You're right. When a black man kills a white man or woman, white folk lose their minds. This white man didn't."

"And he seemed bent on not telling anyone you killed Marla."

"He doesn't know, Cassandra. He was guessing. He guessed right, but he was guessing nevertheless."

"What makes you so sure?"

"I know because he was looking for Johnnie and he was threatening me to find her. If he knew for sure that I killed Marla, there's no way he'd let me get away with it. He would have told the police, and had me arrested, and then they would have beaten the truth outta me. But he didn't do that because they wanted something from me."

"What?"

"We just struck a deal."

"A deal?"

"Yeah. He keeps his mouth shut about his suspicions, and I keep my mouth shut about them killing Johnnie."

"Killing Johnnie?"

"Yes. Why else would he let a black man he believes killed a white woman go? He wouldn't unless that black man can put him in jail for killing Johnnie. Even if the cops don't believe me, the accusation would threaten his freedom. That means that whoever he's working for has big money or they're very important."

"Who do you think it could be?"

"It's either the Beauregards, or Meredith Shamus. Her husband bought Johnnie from her mother. Meredith paid Johnnie fifty thousand dollars to keep Earl's name out of the investigation. Meredith didn't know that Earl had nothing to do with Johnnie's mother's death."

"So Johnnie let her think he did and took the woman's money?"

Nodding, he said, "Yep."

"Um, um, um," Cassandra said, shaking her head.

"Okay, let's have it. Talk about how greedy Johnnie is. I can take it. I'm getting used to it."

"Not this time. I would've taken the money too."

"For real?"

"Yes sir. He raped her. His wife made up for it. As far as I'm concerned, Earl owed Johnnie that and then some. The problem is none of them knew that buying her would cause so many problems. Had Earl been able to look two years into the future and been able to see that poontang would ruin his life, he would have left Johnnie alone."

Nodding, Lucas said, "That goes double for me. Had I known I would end up killing a woman I really liked, I would have used all my strength to stop her from sucking me that day in their bedroom while Napoleon was waiting for me in his car. Now look at my situation. I've definitely gotta get to Germany and hope that Tony Hatcher never tells what he thinks he knows."

"We gotta warn Johnnie."

"How? I have no idea where she is," he said. Then it came to him. "I'll find her brother. He lives in San Francisco. I'll get my friend Nicolas to help."

"We better do it tonight. That's where he's going next, I'm sure."

Chapter 28

"Is this a board meeting or a romp, lady?"

Tony Hatcher's plane landed on the tarmac at two in the morning. After grabbing his bag, he walked out the glass doors and onto the street. For some reason he expected to see Janet Shamus parked at the curb waiting for him. But she wasn't there. He smiled and thought, "She must have been serious when she said she wasn't my chauffeur." Then he flagged a cab and headed for the Belle Glades Hotel. On the way, he thought about Lucas Matthews, Lieutenant Perry, and what he had learned from his trip to Fort Jackson. He knew that Lucas definitely killed Marla, but he didn't care. Why would he? He was in cahoots with Janet to kill Johnnie. He thought Lucas was lying when he said he didn't know where Johnnie was going. Soon he would know too—at least that's what he believed. As soon as they dropped him off at the airport, he walked inside, watched them drive off, and then went right back out and had a cabbie take him to the train station.

When he got there, he was lucky enough to talk to the same employee that sold Johnnie the ticket. She remembered her because she was so beautiful and she was waiting on her boyfriend who arrived later with another woman. Johnnie had purchased a ticket to Rhode Island with two stops along the way. The first stop was in Manhattan. The other stop was in Norwalk, Connecticut. She would be simple enough to find. The cabbies had to keep records of all their fares. The clerk said Lucas didn't ask where Johnnie was going. He and the girl he was with just took off running for the train as it pulled out of the station. He admired Lucas for telling only what he thought he had to tell to stay out of the electric chair. As it turns out, he didn't want Lucas to know that he knew more about Johnnie's whereabouts than he did. In a strange kind of way, he was glad that Lucas had found another girl. Johnnie would just hurt him again.

And Lieutenant Perry was sharp. She would be good for him if he had sense enough to hold on to her.

Hatcher figured Johnnie stopped in Manhattan to meet with a stockbroker or two because he fully believed she had the twenty thousand that Earl Shamus had withdrawn. He assumed that she was trying to rebuild her fortune with it. There was a very good chance that she would be successful because she had done it before. Everything is easier the second time around, he learned over the years. What had him puzzled was why she stopped in Norwalk, Connecticut. It would have been one thing if Norwalk was her final destination, but it wasn't. She bought a ticket so stopping there must have been essential. He was also puzzled as to why she was going to Rhode Island. He had watched her movements for months and he knew she had only been out of New Orleans once before her home burned down.

But he wasn't going to tell Janet Shamus all he had learned. The investigation was moving entirely too fast for Hatcher. He wanted to keep having sex with her on her dime. He'd catch up to Johnnie Wise, but it would be in his own time. First he was going to spend a little time in San Francisco. He might even head over to Chinatown and pick up a hot girl or two. Then he'd fly down to Los Angeles and go on a movie studio tour or find more hot girls. California was known for having a bevy of beautiful, long-legged willing women— at least that's what he'd been told. He thought that he might even be lucky enough to meet Lana Turner, his favorite actress. He had seen her in "The Postman Always Rings Twice" and couldn't get her out of his mind. He knew Hollywood starlets could be had because half the actors in Hollywood were closet homosexuals that wore panties—literally—at least that's what the boys at the pool hall said. The other half were cream puffs. A good shot to the belly would take all the fight out of whoever Lana was with and then she'd go back to his hotel for a week of passion.

An hour later, Hatcher walked into the Belle Glades hotel and walked up to the registration desk with pep in his step. His libidinous thoughts about Lana Turner had gotten him in the mood and when he got up to Janet Shamus' penthouse, he would satisfy his hunger with both of them even though only one woman would be in bed with him. The clerk had been told to give Hatcher a key when he arrived and then call ahead to let her know he was on his way up. Anxious to get the activities underway, he opened the door and entered. He saw Janet Shamus sitting at a desk full of official looking papers. He looked at his watch reflexively, wondering why she was working at that hour. Whatever she was doing, she was deep into it, Hatcher knew, because she didn't even bother to look up when he came into the room. All of a sudden the salacious mood he was in began to wane. He cleared his throat to get her attention.

"I'll be with you in a second," Janet said without looking at him.

"Let's go! I didn't come here to watch you work. I came here to get laid."

Still working, she said, "Mr. Hatcher I'm not a robot and I have more than one obligation. I have to work you in as best I can. If you wait a few minutes we can get started."

"Is this a board meeting or a romp, lady?"

"Both."

"I've been thinking about this for the last three hours. Believe me, this isn't how it played out in my mind."

She finally looked at him. She leaned back in her chair and folded her arms. "There's some beer in the fridge. Have one and it'll relax you. In fact have a few. You seem unbearably tense."

"How much longer are you gonna be?"

"About forty minutes. I've gotta go over payroll. Grab a couple beers and wait for me in the bedroom. I'll be in before you know it."

Hatcher looked around the penthouse. It was a nice joint, but he couldn't appreciate the step up from the cracker box he called a home. He walked into the kitchen and opened the refrigerator. "You want one?" he called out.

"Yes. Hopefully it'll have the same effect it had this morning and we can get this over with."

Hatcher stared at her. He had hoped to have relations with Lana Turner and ended up with a much younger and better looking version of Betty Davis. He was losing the urgency to enter her and he had definitely lost the desire for his favorite movie star. Nevertheless, he was still going to have his way with Janet because it was the only way to control the stiff flesh in his pants. "I guess I'll just find my own way there."

"I would have drawn up a map if I thought you were going to be a big baby about this. Jesus! You're gonna get what you came for and then you need to get out of here. I have a reputation to uphold."

"The reputation was shot to hell the moment you told the desk clerk to give me a key to the suite."

"He thinks you're my older brother, not my lover."

"So this is incestuous?"

"I've heard that sex isn't sex unless it's forbidden. Think about it for awhile."

Hatcher went into the master bedroom, turned on the radio, undressed, and got in bed. Then he opened one of his beers and drank it straight down. Then he opened the other and drained it too. Eight hours later, he woke up in bed alone. There was a note leaning against the lamp. He picked it up and read the following:

Mr. Hatcher,

You obviously needed your rest. In the future, please sleep in your own home. My suite is not a flop house. I've gone out to California to shop for an airplane. I'll be in Burbank looking at the Constellation and then I'll head over to Long Beach to look at a DC-6. I pretty much have my heart set on the DC-6. A Saudi Prince ordered it with all the trimmings, but he thought he ordered the DC-7. He told the people at Douglas to sell it for whatever they could get and put the money on the DC-7. Now all I have to do is find a couple pilots and I can go wherever I want. I assume that Fort Jackson was a dead end. Perhaps you can meet me out here since you have business to attend to in San Francisco. I'll be staying in a bungalow at the Beverly Hills Hotel. It's on Sunset Boulevard so it shouldn't be too hard to find. When you arrive, the first thing we'll do is make up for earlier this morning. I promise. Order room service if you like, but please get out to San Francisco immediately. That's Johnnie's last option unless you know something I don't.

Janet

Hatcher smiled. He realized she enjoyed that first romp more than he thought. He knew that if he had forced the issue a little when he came in, she would have gone along. He wanted to turn the San Francisco trip into a vacation, but with Janet Shamus already in California, it was too risky. And besides, he didn't have to look for hot women now that Janet was going to be his high-class whore for as long as they were in the Los Angeles area. He called the office to see if he had any messages and was surprised to learn that business had picked up considerably. He called all his creditors and they had all been paid off, including his house. He was suddenly debt free. A smile emerged and remained. That's when he knew Janet Shamus was prepared to go all the way with their plan and so was he. The only items left on his list were a new car, his nest egg, and unrestricted access to his benefactor's tight body.

Chapter 29

Masterson had taken great care in planning their get-a-way. He wanted to show Johnnie all the things he had seen as the son of wealth and affluence and when he traveled the world conducting missions for the CIA. He also wanted to change her notions about white people. He knew what Johnnie and most people didn't know about themselves. He knew their perceptions were geographically based, meaning their sphere of influence was usually myopic in scope, which often led to false conclusions. He had friends and enemies all over the globe, but it wasn't because of race; it was because of political acceptance and political differences. He had learned over the years that the race problem in the United States was due to political and financial expediency. He was hoping to be an instrument of change and bring racial politics to an end.

When they arrived in Paris, they took a taxi over to the luxurious and historic Hotel de Crillon. He chose that venue because it was near the major museums and the Faubourg Saint Honore shopping area. Talking had become easy for them and they talked until three in the morning which was when they fell asleep on the couch in each other's arms.

When Masterson opened his eyes, he saw Johnnie staring at him. He cleared his throat and said, "What's wrong?"

"Nothing's wrong, Paul. I'm just so happy. I've never met anyone like you. You're so generous and I know I keep saying this, but you don't ask for anything and you don't expect anything. Do you know how rare that is?" She didn't bother to wait for his response. "I've been thinking and I realize you were right when you said people have been using me for so long that I've come to expect it. When I was in Jackson, Hank and Lucille even tried to use me until I put a stop to it. They wanted me to work extra hours so they could make more money, but at first they weren't planning to compensate the new girl in town with the movie star looks when they knew more people were coming into the restaurant to see what all the fuss was about."

Masterson looked into her eyes and said, "So you have movie star looks, huh?"

"Uh-huh. My mother told me that all the Baptiste women were gorgeous and that women would always be jealous of us. From my experience, she was right on that too. I've learned on my own that when you have beauty and money at the same time, the level of hatred increase several notches. But, I'm getting used to it."

"Why don't I order us some breakfast and continue this conversation on the terrace like we did in Nice before we had to go on the lamb."

She laid her head on his chest and said, "Can't we just lay here for just a few minutes?"

"Sure, I suppose we could just lay here, relax, and talk some more if you like."

"I like," she said, and kissed his cheek.

He stiffened.

Smiling, she said, "What was that?"

"What was what?"

"You know what? That hard thing trying to poke a hole in my stomach."

Masterson sat up and then walked over to the phone and ordered breakfast. Then he said, "I'm gonna clean up. I'll meet you on the terrace in twenty minutes. The kitchen said our food should be here in thirty minutes. I'm starved, are you?"

"Yes, but I want to talk about that erection you got. Is that the first time that happened since we've been together or what?"

"I'll see you in twenty minutes."

"That's fine with me. But when we meet on the terrace, my first question will be about your erection. So you go on in the bathroom and clean up, Mr. Cowboy Preacher. And when you come out, we'll have that conversation."

"Do you realize that's the first time you've called me that since I picked you up at the train station?"

Smiling, she said, "Yes. I remember the first time I said it in Jackson. You made me hot then too. So saying it now seemed appropriate. Sooner or later, you're going to have to fulfill your duties as my husband. The bible teaches that the husband's body belongs to the wife and vice versa. Ain't that right, Mr. Cowboy Preacher?"

Nodding, Masterson said, "It does."

"So sooner or later, you mine."

"That goes both ways," Paul said, returning her smile.

Twenty-five minutes later, the newlyweds were on the terrace having breakfast when Johnnie said, "I just love your cologne. What's it called?"

"It's called, Monsieur Marquay. It came out about four years ago."

"I'll buy some for you on your birthday."

"That would be a nice gift. I look forward to it."

"Can I ask you something?"

"Sure."

"Will you answer me?"

"If I can, yes."

"What's your greatest fear?"

"Take a guess."

"Death?"

"That must be your fear, Johnnie."

"No it isn't."

"Sure it is. Most folk have a great fear of the unknown."

"And you don't?"

"Of the unknown, sure, but death for me couldn't be categorized as the unknown. I know who I belong to and where my soul is going when I leave this world. Most folks have a great fear of death because they are unsure if they're going to heaven or hell. When death knocks and you're uncertain of your eternal destination, you've got reason to be fearful. What gets me and other preachers is that folks know they're going to hell and then make a joke out of it, saying stuff like, 'Well when I get to hell, I'll have a bunch of friends there with me,' like there's gonna be a party down there or something. But what's strange to me Johnnie is that I don't think I've ever heard a Christian say, 'When I get to heaven, I'll have a bunch of friends there with me.' Kinda makes you think, doesn't it?"

"Like I said, Paul, you're a different breed. Just so we understand each other, I know you just switched the subject again. You think that talking about heaven and hell is going force to me to think about that rather than the question I asked you, which again is what's your greatest fear? Those Central Intelligence people are good, because you avoid questions better than a wife messing around on her husband. I know one thing about you."

"Oh yeah? What's that?"

"If you start messing around on me, I'll catch you because you either don't want to lie to me or you don't know how to lie."

Masterson sipped his coffee, looked directly into her eyes and said, "So what are you revealing about yourself? Are you inadvertently telling me you do know how to lie? Is that what I'm to infer, Johnnie?"

"Of course I do, Paul. I'm a woman. We come out of the womb lying because we have to. Society teaches us to behave the way we behave. So we blend in. We conform to the mores of the day."

"So it's society's fault women lie, huh?"

"Yes. You can't tell a man the truth."

"Really? And why not?"

"Men can't handle a truthful woman and they don't want to. Well, wait, there are two kinds of men that can handle truthful women but they are diametrically opposed to each other. Can you guess what kind of men I'm talking about?"

"I can."

"Are you a betting man, Mr. Cowboy Preacher?"

"I love it when you call me that."

"Uh-huh. I'll make sure to whisper it in your ear when we finally do it. I'ma say give it to me Mr. Cowboy Preacher! Give it to me! Give-it-to-me!"

Masterson swallowed hard.

"Did that make you hard again, Mr. Cowboy Preacher?"

"No comment."

"I know it did."

"Am I a betting man was the question, right?"

She shook her head. "What is your greatest fear, Paul? You've got to keep up."

"I've been known to gamble on occasion."

"What's on the line?"

"If I win, you stop trying to force the issue. We'll get to it in due season."

"And if I win?"

"We do it right now."

"Can we do it on the table?" Johnnie said staring into his eyes to see how the foreplay was affecting him.

"Not on the table out in the open."

"Then out here tonight in the dark when no one can see?"

"How about in the bedroom with the lights out?"

"How about in the bedroom with the lights on?"

"I can do that. The answer to your question is the preacher and the pimp."

"That's right. Now, when are we gonna do it?"

"Hey, you just agreed not to force the issue."

"I'm not forcing the issue. It's a simple question, besides didn't I just admit that women lie from the womb? You're so gullible to be a roughneck preacher. Let's get back to the original question. What is your greatest fear?"

"Promise not to hold it against me?"

"I promise."

Masterson exhaled hard and deliberate like there was a revolver pressing against his skull, right behind his ear. Then he said, "My greatest fear is running into Anita Wilde again."

"Do you mind if we talk about her?"

"Yes."

"So we can't talk about her?"

"I didn't say that. You asked me if I minded. I do mind, but I will talk about her. I'll tell you everything, but do we have to talk about it now? Let's talk about it over lunch. I've planned a marvelous day of shopping and then a picnic under the Eiffel Tower. How does that sound?

"Sounds great. And we'll talk about Miss Wilde then?"

"Yes."

"Why do you want to know about her?"

"Because she's the competition. You're a good man, Paul Masterson and I want to hold on to you for as long as I can. Since you're worried about Miss Wilde that tells me I should worry about her too."

"But she's thousands of miles away."

"True. But unless we make Paris or Nice or some other exotic locale our home, she could interrupt our marriage. I don't want that and I know you don't want that. But temptation is difficult to handle."

"Yes it is. But be honest here, okay?"

"What do you mean?"

"You know that if you would've stayed in South Carolina with Lucas and left me waiting at the station, I might've left you for Anita, right?"

"Would you have left me waiting at the station?"

"Not on purpose."

"But you would do it with her?"

"Honestly, I don't know. What about you? Would you do it with Lucas?"

"Yes. And you would do it with Anita Wilde. Perhaps you don't know that, but I do. You loved that woman and perhaps you still do. You're afraid to admit it, which means you'd be in trouble if you ever saw her again."

"That's what I like about you, Johnnie."

"What's that?"

"You admit to lying, but you have a way of getting to the heart of things—the truth of a thing. Well, are you ready to get some shopping done?"

"Yes!"

"Let's go. But we'll stop by the Louvre first okay?"

"Okay."

Chapter 30

"I mean you call yourself a preacher but you're sinning against God."

After spending several hours in the Louvre, which had opened in 1793, having seen lots of masterpieces, including the Venus de Milo, the Mona Lisa, Victory of Samothrace, works from Greece, Egypt, Rome, Islamic Art, sculptures, and an endless number of paintings, they headed over to Rue de Faubourg Saint-Honore to do some shopping. From there they went to Place de la Concorde, Champs-Elysees, Rue de la Paix, and finally Avenue Montaigne. Johnnie spent a small fortune on all the latest brand name dresses, skirts, blouses, hats, purses, bras, panties, watches, perfumes, colognes, an assortment of jewelry, a couple of mink coats with stoles, and an endless number of shoes for every outfit. Paul, on the other hand, picked up a couple of suits, a tuxedo, and one pair of shoes. They had returned to the Hotel de Crillon several times that day to drop off the things they purchased. He gave the bellhop a few American dollars each time to take their bags up to the suite.

It was five o'clock when they made it back to the hotel for the night. They were heading over to the elevator when the desk clerk called out, "Mr. Masterson, Mr. Masterson."

He saw the desk clerk beckoning him to come over. He looked at Johnnie and said, "Get the bellhop to help you take the bags to our room."

"I don't mind waiting."

"That's okay. I'll see what he wants and I'll be right up. We'll have dinner on the terrace. I promised you lunch under the Eiffel Tower and I didn't deliver. So we'll have dinner and look at its bright lights, okay?"

"Okay. Do you mind ordering dinner for me while I take a quick bath?"

"Sure. No problem."

She stretched her neck up and kissed him on the lips and felt her private place twitch. She wanted him and she didn't want to wait any longer, but she turned around and headed over to the door to get a bellhop. Masterson wanted her to be a lady, she knew, and even though she'd love to get naked with him and have sex in every corner of the suite, she would be a lady until it was time to not be a lady.

Masterson watched Johnnie as she walked over to the bellhop's station. He had an idea what the desk clerk wanted. He thought that he had gotten a message from Marcus Yarborough. If the desk clerk had a message, Johnnie would find it strange that someone knew where they were, especially since they weren't supposed to tell anyone they had left the country. More important, if he did have a message, she would want to know what the message said. He couldn't tell her anything so he sent her to their suite to get her out of the way and to keep her from asking questions he didn't want to answer. He walked over to the desk and said, "I'm Masterson."

The desk clerk handed him an envelope and said, "Your tickets arrived an hour ago, sir."

He took the envelope out of his hand. "Thank you. I was wondering if they would show up in time."

"You're welcome, sir."

Masterson opened the envelope immediately and saw that he and Johnnie had tickets to see The Phantom of the Opera at Garnier Opera House. Yarborough had written him another note. It read: The men's room at intermission. It was a simple note, but it had Masterson questioning what to expect. Who was he supposed to meet? Did they have the information he wanted? Or was he going to receive more instructions? He headed over to the elevator and went up to his suite. Upon entering, he went straight to Johnnie's adjoining suite and knocked. Hearing no response, he cracked open the door and said, "Are you decent?" Hearing no response a second time, he entered her bedroom and walked over to the bathroom door. He knocked.

He heard Johnnie say, "Come in." And then he heard her laugh.

"Listen," he said. "I've got tickets for the Phantom of the Opera. Put on something nice when you're done in there. I'm wearing the tux I just bought."

"Is this a fancy place?"

"Yes. I'll tell you all about it over dinner."

"You'd do anything not to talk about her, wouldn't you?"

"What are you talking about?"

"You know what I'm talking about. I'm talking about Anita Wilde. You promised to tell me about her under the Eiffel Tower while we ate lunch. Remember?"

"It wasn't me who tried to buy up the whole town, was it?"

"So it was my fault we didn't have the picnic?"

"Well, let's see. I think I bought about four or five items and it took all of an hour or so. How many items did you buy and how many hours did it take you to buy them?"

"Well why didn't you stop me?"

"Because I didn't want to talk about Anita and spending thousands of dollars on you was the best way to do it even if I would be breaking my word to you to do it."

Laughing she said, "I'm glad you admit it."

"I'll order dinner and see you on the terrace in a little bit."

An hour later, Johnnie stepped onto the terrace wearing a backless white crushed crepe formal gown with elbow length white gloves. Her hair was up and the diamonds in her ears sparkled. It made her feel good when she saw Masterson's mouth fall open. She said, "The next time you wanna take me to a nice place, I need to know in advance. This is all I could come up with on such short notice. A girl needs to plan for these things."

"Looks like you did okay to me," Masterson said, smiling.

"Okay?" Johnnie said, smiling. "Is that all you can say?"

"That's all I dare say without getting into trouble. Otherwise, we'll never make it to the Garnier."

"That's fine with me. We can go another time if you want."

"We've got box seats and they weren't cheap, Johnnie."

"I was just letting you know you had options, Mr. Cowboy Preacher. You've chosen to see some old opera instead of helping take this gown off. That's why I chose white by the way. I mean, I'm still a virgin as far as you're concerned."

"Yes you are. Now sit down and let me tell you all about Anita Wilde like I promised. And look, you can see the Eiffel Tower. It's all lit up just for you."

"Just for me?"

"Cost me a fortune."

"I like those kinds of lies, Mr. Cowboy Preacher. Keep 'em comin'."

"Dinner's here. We've got about forty-five minutes to get to the theatre."

"So that means you're going to rush the story, huh?"

"No. I've already eaten so that I could tell you what happened without interruption. So . . . ya ready?"

"Yeah. Let me say my grace first." She closed her eyes and bowed her head for a few seconds. Then she said something inaudibly and then she looked at Masterson and said, "Okay, I'm ready. Let's hear the Anita Wilde story."

"You know part of it already so I'll just tell you what you don't know, okay?"

"Not okay. Start from the beginning. I remember what you said in Jackson and if you lie or leave anything out, I'll know and I'll never forgive you, Paul Masterson."

"I had just preached what I thought was a powerful sermon and I thought the altar would be flooded with sinners wanting to be saved. Now, what you've got to understand is that my congregation had outgrown two buildings in a matter of months and we were about to outgrow that one too. I remember seeing people running to the altar after one of my sermons. Anyway, this time only Anita came to the altar. She was wearing a white dress."

"I bet it wasn't like mine."

"No it wasn't. She told me she was a sinner and she needed to be saved. She said she didn't wanna go to hell. I had her repeat the sinner's prayer and she did. When I think back on it, I should have seen it coming, but like I told you, arrogance had me."

"I remember you saying that," Johnnie said, "Go on."

"First off, you've got to understand, the woman was gorgeous, okay? I mean she was a knockout, period, end of story. Anyway, she called and said that she needed help and she wanted me to counsel her."

Johnnie stopped eating and said, "You knew then, Paul. Right then and there you knew she wanted you to have sex with her, didn't you?"

He exhaled and said, "Looking back on it, yeah, I did. I mean, now it's obvious, but back then, it was pretty foggy."

"Hmph. The fog was your lust for a pretty woman; that's all that was. But go ahead."

"Anyway a voice inside my head told me not to meet with her, but I rejected the voice and told myself she needed me."

"Did you ever ask yourself why the voice was telling you not to meet with her?"

"No."

"You didn't ask the voice why because you didn't want to hear the answer, did you, Paul?"

"I'll tell you what. You tell me the story and I'll just correct you when you miss the mark. How 'bout that?"

"Aw come on, Paul. Don't be like that. I won't interrupt you anymore, okay? I just don't want you lying to yourself. You gotta deal with this or it'll get you later."

"I met with her a few days later and I asked her to tell me what she needed help with. She said she couldn't tell me because she didn't feel comfortable talking about it. It wasn't the first time I'd counseled a person and they had trouble opening up to me."

"After awhile, she was wide open, wasn't she? And you went all the way up in her, didn't you? Because you couldn't deal with being in the same room with such a beautiful woman, could you? Sooner or later, she was crying on your shoulder, telling you how badly her life had been and how men were taking advantage of her. You felt close to her and you hugged. Both of you felt a spark of excitement. You looked into each other's eyes and you knew then not to do anymore counseling sessions, but you did, didn't you? Then you stopped praying, didn't you? You found yourself looking forward to seeing her and having conversations with her. Before long, you weren't even sitting behind your desk. You were sitting on a couch or something and she was wearing suggestive clothing. You could see her cleavage and you knew then to get her outta your office, but you ignored the voice again. You found yourself trying to peek down her blouse, hoping to see the edges of her nipples. You told yourself you'd only steal one little peek, but she dropped something on the floor and when she bent over to pick it up, you saw everything, didn't you? Once you saw her naked breasts, you wanted to see the rest and you wouldn't stop until you did, would you? To make a long story short, you ended up having sex with her right there in the church, in your office, on the couch or on the floor, right?"

"Now you know what happened."

"How close was I?"

"You missed on the breasts thing. She kept squirming in the chair she was sitting in. I asked her what was wrong and she said her back itched."

"Her back, Paul? Are you serious? And then what? She took off her blouse and unsnapped her bra and told you to scratch her back?"

"Pretty much, yeah."

"How often were you seeing her? How many times a week?"

"Four sometimes five times a week."

"And this went on for a year?"

"Close to a year, yeah."

"Four or five times a week, Paul?"

"About that."

"So you went up in her somewhere between seventy-three times and ninety-one times."

"Oh, no. It was a lot more than that. We did it multiple times when we met."

"How many times?"

"Three or four."

"Three or four? That comes to either two hundred and nineteen times or three hundred and sixty-five times. So either you did a year's worth of screwing in ninety-one days or seven months of screwing."

"Hey, I told you I couldn't leave it alone. Now, what else can I tell you?"

"Nothing. I'm jealous. You went up in her that many times and I can't even get a sample. The sad part is I married you and can't get any, she didn't and took all mine. That's messed up."

"I think you're looking at it the wrong way. I married you and I want to know you because I don't want the marriage to be one of convenience. I didn't know her all that well, I did what I had to do with her, and we didn't get married. You have my name, she had my lust. At some point, I hope to offer you my love and I hope you'll take it."

"When, Paul?"

"When you're at least eighteen, otherwise it's like I'm having sex with a child. There's something wrong with that. I know other men did it and I know we're married, but to go up in a girl that age?"

"What's gonna change in eight months, Paul? What? Is my hymen going to grow back or something? What?"

"If I had a daughter your age, I wouldn't want a man my age having sex with her."

"Even if they're married?"

"Well that would be okay."

"What's the difference?"

"The difference is my daughter would be in love and hopefully the man who married her would feel that same way. We're not there yet. And until we are, we're gonna wait." He looked at his watch. "Now, are you finished eating. The car should be waiting for us."

A few minutes later, they were on the elevator. Johnnie said, "What's the show supposed to be about? That way I'll have some idea of what to expect."

"Well, let's see. It's an unconventional love story inspired by an accident that took place in 1896 when a grand chandelier fell and killed somebody. A man named Gaston Leroux wrote a novel in 1909 about the actual opera house we're going to."

The elevator doors opened. They stepped out into the lobby and headed for the door where their car was waiting.

"So is this a true story or is it based on a true story?" Johnnie asked.

"I think the only truth is that someone was killed by a falling chandelier and there is an underground lake and other things you'll see in the show."

The doorman pulled the door open for them and they stepped out onto the street.

"Mr. Masterson?" the driver questioned.

"Yes."

The driver opened the door for them while saying, "I'm Ralph. I'll be driving you over to the Opera House."

"Thank you," Masterson said and tipped him.

In the car now, Johnnie said, "Okay, so how is it a love story?"

"Well, the main character is a musical genius, but he's hideous to look upon. He falls for a young ingénue named Christine, but she's engaged to a guy named Raoul."

"So Christine's messing around on Raoul?

"Kinda, but not really."

"So she's using the genius and she's being true to Raoul?"

"Let's just watch and see what happens, okay?"

"Okay."

The limousine stayed on Place de la Concorde and circled the fountain in front of the Hotel de Crillon and then turned right on Rue Royal. Minutes later they were on Rue Scribe and stopped at Opera Garnier.

Johnnie's eye lit up when she saw the building. When they entered The Grand Foyer, her mouth fell wide open when she saw its magnificence. The Garnier was full of the rich and famous—at least that's what Johnnie thought. The women wore fine apparel that she wouldn't have been able to afford even if her money hadn't burned up in the fire. She understood why Napoleon Bentley wanted to bring her to Paris. She wondered what he was doing now and if he was looking for her. If he was, she was glad he hadn't found her. She was free and she was happy for the first time in a while. She was happier with Masterson than she would have been with Lucas because Lucas knew what she had done behind his back. She knew he might never be able to forgive her for that.

Her head continued swiveling as they climbed The Grand Staircase, which split at the landing. They climbed another flight and entered their box. She gasped when she saw the view they had of the stage. The rich red décor, the columns covered in gold, and the chandelier had her shaking her head. She didn't know people built places like that for entertainment. She looked at Masterson and said, "Rich people got it made. That's for sure."

Masterson laughed and said, "There's a lot of truth to that, Johnnie. But it isn't all that it's cracked up to be."

"Really?"

"Really."

"So you would rather be poor than rich?"

"I didn't say that."

"Answer the question, Mr. Cowboy Preacher."

Masterson leaned in and whispered in her ear, "You keep calling me that and you won't make it to eighteen."

Johnnie leaned over and was about to whisper in his ear when the house lights went down. Instead she breathed in his ear and then put her hand in his crotch. He stiffened in her hand. She stroked him there and whispered, "Now you listen to me, Mr. Cowboy Preacher, I'm only removing my hand because I'm too much of a lady to keep doing this in public. But we do have a suite waiting for us later."

Masterson whispered, "Thanks for having mercy on me."

At the intermission, Masterson left their box to meet his contact in the men's room. As to be expected, the men's room was packed, but unlike the women's room, the lines weren't nearly as long and they moved along rather quickly. Eventually, Masterson got inside, he went to the urinal, did what he had to do, but there was no sign of his contact. He washed his hands longer than necessary, waiting to be contacted, but nobody said anything. Finally he left, wondering what happened.

As he was heading back to his box the usher at the entrance said, "Your cufflink was found in the third box on the left."

"Thanks. I'll get it."

He walked down to the box and went inside.

Marcus Yarborough said, "Tony Hatcher is definitely on your trail and it won't be long before he figures out that you two are together. He's already been to Fort Jackson and talked to a kid named Lucas Matthews."

"Did Matthews tell him anything?"

"I think he did, but not intentionally."

"What makes you say that?"

"Matthews and the woman he's seeing, First Lieutenant Cassandra Perry, took Hatcher to the airport."

"Why would Matthews do that unless Hatcher had something on him?"

"We have reason to believe that Matthews killed the wife of a mobster named Napoleon Bentley. She was found in her Cadillac in Red River, Louisiana. We found out that Matthews had taken a bus to Red River when he got out of Angola Prison."

"Do you think Bentley might kill the kid over this?"

"No. Bentley's done. Iced by the Italians over the woman you married."

"What?"

"You heard me the first time."

"Earl Shamus is dead. Why is Hatcher still on the job?"

"Janet Shamus hired him. We have reason to believe she's got a vendetta of her own now that her old man is dead. And she has the finances to pull it off, if that's what she wants to do."

"What about me? Are they looking to kill me too?"

"Right now they don't know you two are together. When they run out of leads and still can't find your wife, they'll look for you and when they can't find either of you, they'll put it together and then both of you will have a bull's-eye on your backs."

"So what makes you think Matthews told Hatcher something without realizing it?"

After Matthews and the lieutenant dropped Hatcher at the airport, he went inside like he was about to take a flight back to New Orleans. But he only waited until the kid and his new girl pulled off. Then he hailed a cab and went to the train station. Do I have to tell you what he found there?"

"So he knows Johnnie took a train to Manhattan, Norfolk, Connecticut, and then to Rhode Island."

"And it won't be long before he goes to a cab company and finds out about the fares."

The house lights dimmed and the curtain was rising.

"Anything else?"

"Yeah. Let's step in the hall for a few minutes." When they stepped out, Yarborough continued, "What's it gonna take to bring you back into the fold?"

"What are you offering?"

"For now, protection for you and your wife. But we'll need you to move certain things in and out of certain countries."

"And if I don't move these things for you? Then what?"

"There's only so much we can do for you, Paul. The Vietnam thing is starting to heat up. The French are about to lose over there. In another month or two, they'll have to pull out, if they can. What'll happen when they finally pull out, Paul?"

"We'll step in. We can't afford to let the North conquer the South."

"If we don't have our people on the ground over there, we may have our hands full too. Any war is a fluid situation. As you know, once we go in, lots of people will die. We'll have to stay in there until we win because we can't afford to lose. The French are getting their heads handed to them. We don't feel they can hold on much longer. Once the bullets start flying, there's no telling when and where it'll end. We'll bomb them day and night if we have to. Nobody wants that, Paul. The Russians are backing the North. So we have to back the South. A few good men could make the difference. What do you say? Will you help us out? If not for me, do it for your country. We need you more than you think."

"I've got a wife to think about now. And she's in trouble. I will not abandon her."

"We take care of our own. Since she's with you that makes her one of us. Whatever problems she has, we have. If we get involved, I guarantee her safety."

"How? By killing Hatcher and Janet Shamus?"

"If that's what it takes for your wife to be safe."

"Then I'm back on the hook for how long?"

"Just until this Vietnam thing is over. After that, you're a free man again."

"Well you know what, Marcus? The French invaded that country over one hundred years ago. Maybe it's time they left. And frankly, given what happened to the French, I don't think Vietnam is worth the trouble. So if it's all the same to you, I'll pass. I'll protect my wife on my own."

"If you change your mind, we'd love to have you back with us, Paul."

"If you won't help me, Marcus, don't hurt me either. If Janet Shamus and Tony Hatcher come after us, stay out of the way."

And with that, Masterson returned to his box.

Johnnie whispered, "Where have you been? I thought you left me here."

"It was a long line," Masterson whispered. "I'm sorry."

She reached out and laced her fingers with his and whispered, "I'm glad you forced me into the Flamingo Den that night not so long ago. And thanks so much for taking me to Nice and bringing me to Paris. I've never had more fun in all my days. What you've done for me in just a few days almost makes up for everything that's happened to me."

Masterson whispered, "You're welcome. Now let's enjoy the show."

It was about three o'clock in the morning when Johnnie entered her husband's bedroom. She had been up waiting for him to fall asleep and then she would be in charge. She had made up her mind. There wasn't going to be anymore waiting. She was going to get him and he would be powerless to stop her. The idea had come to her when Masterson had gone to the men's room. On the way back to the Hotel de Crillon, she talked about the Phantom of the Opera and how wonderful it was; especially since they had seen it in the theatre that inspired Gaston Leroux's Gothic novel. She had played the good little girl, knowing that Masterson was going to think that she would want to talk about the conversation they had in their luxury box. She made sure the conversation was about the show and didn't veer from it. When it was time to go to bed, she went to her suite and he went to his. In his room now, she quietly walked over to the bed, careful not to bump into anything.

Looking down at him, she watched him sleep for a few seconds. He was lying on his back on the left side of the bed. Then she went to the other side of the bed. Her heart sped up as the excitement of what she was about to do filled her mind. Before pulling back the covers, she took off her nightgown. Completely nude, she got in bed with her husband. She moved over until she could feel his body heat. Then she reached over and massaged his crotch until she felt him rise in her hand. When he woke up, startled that she was in bed with him and touching him, she grabbed his testicles and squeezed.

Masterson groaned. "What's going on? What are you doing?"

"It's time we had a real conversation, Mr. Cowboy Preacher."

"Okay, but do we have to have it now?"

"Yes."

"Okay. Are you going to let me go?"

"Eventually."

"What do you wanna talk about?"

"Your hypocrisy."

"My hypocrisy? What do you mean?"

"I mean you call yourself a preacher but you're sinning against God."

"How?"

"Are we married?"

"What?"

"Answer the question. Are we married?"

"Yes."

She shook his testicles and said, "Answer me. According to the bible, who do these belong to?"

"Well, uh . . ."

She applied a little pressure to get his attention. When he groaned, she said, "Answer me."

"You."

"That must mean I can do whatever I want to it. Is that right?"

"I guess."

She applied pressure to ensure that he complied. Then she pulled at his underwear. "Lift your behind." When he did, she tightened her grip a little with one hand and then she kissed him there. A moment or two later, she heard him moan and she knew she had him. A few minutes later she was on top of her husband, in complete control, giving him what he had been fighting. She could tell that by the time she was finished with him, he would never resist her again.

Chapter 31

"I have a proposition for you."

J anet Shamus was sitting in the parking lot of the Malibu Hotel in Scottsdale, Arizona with Walter Patterson waiting for Everett James, Mrs. Jacobson's current lover, to show up for their hurried impromptu romp. They figured he would arrive first because he had already gotten the room earlier. Normally, they wouldn't dare meet on a Sunday night, but when Pastor Jacobson's father called and told him his mother was ill and might die, he took the first flight out to Toledo, Ohio, his hometown, giving the simmering lovers an opportunity to douse the blaze. Mrs. Jacobson had left a message for her lover to call at his answering service. Everett James immediately informed Patterson and Patterson called Janet at four that morning, after Hatcher had fallen asleep. She was planning to go to California the next day, but postponed to get Anita Jacobson's attention.

Janet found her new life so exciting, and the power she wielded was addicting. With the exception of Tony Hatcher, everyone did what she told them. She liked that about Hatcher, but she wanted to control him too. Given enough time, she was sure she would. She had something he wanted and enjoyed. He wanted it so much that he was willing to kill for it. Hatcher had said that he was willing to commit first degree murder because he was in debt. She knew there was truth in that, but she also believed that he wouldn't be satisfied with his end of the bargain. He'd want more and he might even try to blackmail her to get it. That's why when he completed his end of the deal, she was going to kill him too. Otherwise she would have to pay him and have sex with him for the rest of her life. That's why she had him investigated. That's why she slept with him. That's why she paid his bills. That's why she invited him to the Beverly Hills

Hotel. She needed him to think he was in control when in fact she was and would always be.

Janet looked at Patterson and said, "How difficult was it to get Mr. James to cooperate?"

"Not too difficult. One blow to the solar plexus and sound wisdom was all it took. He, like most men, loves his wife, but felt the need to roam. He doesn't want her to find out what's going on. He just wants the thrill Mrs. Jacobson gives him. If he divorced his wife, it would be all over. I've seen it happened time and again. In a marriage, selfishness and frustration interrupts the relationship and separates men and women. Then temptation comes in and lures them to illicit, titillating relationships outside their marriages. But they rarely work. I've never seen it work myself. But other PIs have told me they've seen it happen. Personally, I don't believe it, but maybe I don't want to. There's something sleazy about a person that would do something that lowdown."

Janet thought of what her father had done to her mother. Her conscience slapped her hard on the cheek and told her to stop what she was planning and to move on with her life. It reminded her that she was in an enviable position, being the head of Buchanan Mutual and its subsidiaries. It reminded her that she and her sisters would be worth over a billion dollars within the year, but she fought with her conscience and prevailed when she envisioned her mother and father lying in their coffins. And poof, her conscience had been sufficiently suppressed and she could again focus on the task at hand. She told herself that it was justice and that she was only doing what the law couldn't or wouldn't do. Johnnie's image came to mind. She pictured shooting her in the face from long range. She had been practicing for weeks with a sniper's weapon in the shooting range her grandfather built. She had gotten good. At first she thought it was dangerous to kill Johnnie with a rifle because of the attention it would attract. Then she convinced herself that no one would care that she was dead. In fact, lots of people would be glad she was in her grave.

"There he is, Miss Shamus. And right on time too."

"Do you think she'll show?" Janet asked, watching Everett James climb the stairs and enter his rented love nest.

"Of course she will. She can't help herself at this point. As a matter of fact, here she comes now."

They watched as Mrs. Jacobson checked herself over, put on some lipstick and perfume. Then she fluffed her hair, got out of the car, and hurried up the stairs. Everett opened the door and they fell into each other arms and kissed passionately, like they were madly in love, but hadn't seen each other in over a year.

With her hand on the doorknob, Janet said, "How long should we wait?"

"Just a few minutes. People that have affairs have no time to waste. They have to get back home to their husbands and wives and continue the farce of a marriage they have for the children's sake. Then they sit around spending lots of time trying to figure out the next set of lies they planned to tell to get their piece of heaven."

Janet couldn't stand hearing Patterson talk about her father like that, even though he wasn't talking about her father at all. She knew that whatever he was saying was equally applicable to the man responsible for her birth. Again her conscience demanded attention, but she said, "It's been five minutes. Let's get up there."

"See what I mean about being in a hurry. They didn't even bother turning the lights off. People having an affair don't have to set the mood. They just act like animals in heat."

Patterson reached in the backseat and grabbed the leather pouch with all the information Janet would need to convince Mrs. Jacobson to cooperate. Janet grabbed the camera. Standing outside the room, they heard Mrs. Jacobson's passionate sighs. While Janet tried to stop giggling, Patterson carefully slid the key James had given him earlier into the lock and slowly turned the knob to the right. He looked at Janet, who was holding the camera, and nodded. Then they burst into the room.

Mrs. Jacobson's legs were high in the air while her married lover plowed into her ferociously like it would be the last sex he'd ever have. The bedsprings and Mrs. Jacobson's open mouth were screaming as if they were in competition for a coveted trophy. Janet snapped off a picture. A bright flash of light appeared and disappeared. She popped out the bulb, replaced it, and snapped another picture before Mrs. Jacobson realized they had been caught.

Mrs. Jacobson's eyes shot open and she desperately tried to get James out of her, but he was determined to finish and he did while Patterson and Janet looked on, laughing hysterically. James's movements slowed, but he kept plowing until he had fertilized her soil. Then he pulled out of her, grabbed his clothes and put them on, panting all the while.

"*You* bastard!" Mrs. Jacobson yelled. "You knew about this and set me up?"

"I'm sorry, Anita," James said, as he continued dressing. "You gotta believe that. I had no choice in the matter. It was either do this or he was going to tell my wife. I would have lost everything. I'm sorry. It was fun while it lasted."

Patterson looked at James and said, "Scram. Miss Shamus will handle the rest."

James ran out of the room and down the stairs. A few seconds later, they heard a car door slam, an engine start, and tires screeching.

On his way out, Patterson said, "I'll be right outside this door if you need me." He looked at Mrs. Jacobson and said, "Don't do anything stupid. Listen to what she says and you'll be just fine." Then he handed Janet the pouch and left them alone.

Janet stared at Mrs. Jacobson, who was cowering under the sheet. As the sound of her sighs filled her mind, Janet wondered if that's how she sounded to Tony Hatcher when he broke into her closed sheath and reshaped it.

"Who are you?" Mrs. Jacobson said, "And what do you want?"

Janet almost pitied her. She had been caught and photographed in the throes of passion. It had to be humiliating. Janet said, "Why don't you take a shower, and then get dressed. We'll talk when you come out, okay?"

Stunned by her compassion, Mrs. Jacobson kept her eyes on her captor while sliding off the bed. Careful to keep the sheet up to her neck, she stood up and wrapped the sheet around her backside, walked into the bathroom.

When Janet saw the door closing, she said, "Please leave the door open."

Mrs. Jacobson stopped in her tracks, swiveled her head to the left and looked over her shoulder at Janet and with a sexy grin said, "What did you have in mind honey?" Then she turned around and dropped the sheet, giving her captor full viewing access to her fleshly assets.

They stared at each other for a second or two.

"What do I have to do to keep my husband from finding out about this?"

"Have you no, shame, Anita? Have you forgotten your Tupelo, Mississippi roots?" Shaking her head, Janet continued, "What would your sharecropper father and mother say if they saw you now?" Mrs. Jacobson mouth fell wide open. She was about to say something, but Janet raised her hand, stopping her and said, "Don't say a word. Please . . . just take a shower and think about your situation. When you finish, come back out *fully* dressed with a serious change in attitude, and let's have a conversation. I have a proposition for you."

Chapter 32

"You okay, Miss Shamus? What's going on?"

Half an hour had passed by the time Mrs. Jacobson came out of the bathroom. Her hair was wrapped in a white hotel towel. She was still completely nude, but she showed no signs of modesty when she walked over to the table where Janet was waiting and sat down in a chair across from her as if she were fully dressed, hiding her sensual curves from human eyes. Mrs. Jacobson had adopted the same attitude as the character in the fairytale, *The Emperor's New Clothes*. She had thought the thing through in the shower and she was prepared for whoever Miss Shamus was. She locked eyes with Janet who was totally distracted by Mrs. Jacobson's nakedness, which was part of Jacobson's plan. She wanted her opponent off balance when the joust began, giving her a decisive advantage during the game of words they were about to embark upon.

"Shall we begin," Mrs. Jacobson said, taking command of the situation. "Miss Shamus, is it?"

Clearly rattled by her supposed victim's nonchalance, Janet's hand shook as the adrenaline flowed when she reached inside the leather pouch to get the instruments of persuasion she would need to sell the proposal she was about to pitch.

Mrs. Jacobson saw Janet's hand shaking and knew the impending threat wasn't coming from an experienced extortionist. "How old are you, Miss Shamus?"

Janet took a breath and held it. She too realized she was in over her head. But the game was afoot and she would play it out, hoping the threat of exposure would be enough to coerce Mrs. Jacobson into relinquishing the information she wanted. Even though she was nervous, she still expected to win the game because she had all the leverage. She pulled out a photo and answered, "The same age you were when you met this man." She placed Paul Masterson's photo on the table and watched her opponent's eyes widen.

Mrs. Jacobson picked up the picture and looked it. A warm smile swept across her face. She returned the photo to the table, looked at Janet, and said, "How do you know Paul?"

Feeling more confident now, Janet reached into the pouch and grabbed another photograph and placed it on the table. "I would think you would be more concerned with how I know this man."

Mrs. Jacobson lowered her eyes to the table briefly, saw a photo of her husband leaving his church, and then locked eyes with Miss Shamus. "I already know how you know Judah. So let's not do this little dance. Let's cut to the chase. What do you want, honey? How can I help you and your friend get what you need?"

Stunned by the ease with which Mrs. Jacobson had responded and the fact that she was naked and her breasts moved every time she spoke, distracted Janet again. She found it difficult not to look at her breasts and now Mrs. Jacobson's nipples had hardened right in front of her, as if she was being sexually stimulated by their conversation. Janet wished she hadn't told Walter Patterson to leave them alone. She needed him now, but her pride wouldn't allow her to ask for help.

"You mind if I smoke, honey," Mrs. Jacobson asked.

Needing time to catch her breath and think, Janet said, "No. Go ahead."

Mrs. Jacobson casually walked over to the nightstand and grabbed her purse. "Is this your first time doing this, kid?"

Feeling insulted, Janet defiantly said, "I'm not a kid."

Mrs. Jacobson came back to the table and sat down. "Would you like a cigarette?"

"No."

Mrs. Jacobson reached into her purse and pulled out a .38 revolver. She pointed it in Janet's face, cocked it, and said, "This is your first time, isn't it, *kid*?"

Janet's eyes nearly bulged out of her head and she started hyperventilating, wheezing uncontrollably. It never occurred to her that Mrs. Jacobson could bring a gun to an adulterous romp.

"I oughta blow your head off for what you're trying to do," Mrs. Jacobson said. She kept the gun in her face until she closed her eyes and accepted her death. Now that she had Janet's attention, she uncocked the revolver and put it on the table. She reached into her purse again and grabbed her cigarettes and a book of matches. Still watching her would-be blackmailer hyperventilate, she tapped out a cigarette, put it in her mouth, and lit it. She took a long drag, inhaled, and said, "I oughta let you die in here." She blew out the smoke she had taken in and continued, "Then I could let your friend in here and make him finish what Everett started and then blow his brains out. Everett would have a devil of a time explaining to the police how two people ended up dead in a room he rented and it would serve him right for jamming me up like this." She listened to Janet wheeze a little longer before reaching in her purse and grabbing a paper bag. She rounded the end and blew into it. Then she handed it to Janet and said, "Breathe into this and you'll be just fine, kid." She took another deep drag of her cigarette and watched as Janet's breathing slowed, returning to normal. She flicked her ashes into the ashtray and said, "Now . . . what's this all about, honey?" She picked up the pouch and emptied its contents on the table.

"I can't tell you that," Janet said, feeling like a fool.

"Sure you can. I've got the gun."

"Is everything okay in there, Miss Shamus?" Patterson said, after knocking three times.

Mrs. Jacobson emptied the bullets onto the table. Then she went to the door, opened it, and gestured for him to come in.

Stunned when he saw Mrs. Jacobson was naked, he stared at her breasts and her nether region much longer than he should have. He forced his mouth to close before entering the room. "You okay, Miss Shamus? What's going on?"

"She had a gun, Mr. Patterson. We didn't account for that."

"No we didn't," Patterson said.

Mrs. Jacobson went back to the table and sat down. Then she took another drag of her cigarette.

"We've got you dead to rights," Patterson said. "Miss Shamus thinks you can help with something. I don't know what. But you're caught and you're a pastor's wife."

Mrs. Jacobson puffed her cigarette again. "So eighteen-year-old Miss Shamus here is running the show and you don't know what's going on either?"

Patterson nodded a couple times.

Mrs. Jacobson released the smoke through her mouth and nose while saying, "Mr. Patterson, do you mind waiting outside. Let me figure out if I can help you or not. If I can, I will. If not, please be on your way, okay?"

Patterson looked at Janet. She nodded. He looked at all of Mrs. Jacobson and said, "I'm gonna need to hold on to your firearm, ma'am."

Mrs. Jacobson smiled when she saw him staring again. She opened her legs wide and said, "Fine, but I keep the bullets. I wouldn't want you to accidentally shoot yourself and bring the cops here. If that happens, we're all in trouble."

Patterson fought off his laughter, took another long look at her nether region while her legs were open before picking up the gun, and left them alone again.

Mrs. Jacobson puffed her cigarette, blew out smoke rings and then stubbed out the butt in the ashtray. "What can I do for you, kid? And what does Paul Masterson have to do with all of this?"

"I want you to do what you did to Masterson again."

Mrs. Jacobson pulled her head back and frowned. "Why?"

"Because the woman he might be with hurt me and my family."

Mrs. Jacobson looked at the photos and said, "This woman?" She was holding a picture of Johnnie.

Janet nodded.

"And you don't know if he's with her or not?"

"No. But I'll find out soon."

"Jesus Christ. It's amateur night. Busted by a couple of novices. I must be slipping. The answer's no and, honey, you're plan would have never worked."

"Why not?"

"Because you've got nothing on me, that's why. Nothing I can't survive anyway."

"But I could show the pictures to your husband and your sons. That's what I've got on you."

"Leverage is only leverage when the person you're blackmailing gives a damn if someone finds out their secrets. I don't, Miss Shamus. That's what you don't understand."

"But I can still embarrass your husband and your sons will never see you as they once did."

"You sure could, but you wouldn't be hurting me. You'd be hurting my husband and my sons. I'll survive this. Trust me. When I finish explaining why I did what I did, he'll feel like it was all his fault and forgive me. And my sons will forgive me because they'll believe that I had to do what those pictures show because of my past. That's the story I'll tell. They'll feel sorry for their mother because they couldn't bear to see the real truth even though it's staring them in the face. I've survived a whole lot worse than this."

"I'll have copies stapled to every telephone pole in Scottsdale. How do you think that'll go over with the congregation?"

"What's the congregation going to say when they find out? They'll demand that he divorce me of course, in which case you'll be responsible for breaking up a Christian family. Is that what you want?"

Janet looked at the floor.

"Consider this. How will my sons, Abraham, Isaac, and Jacob ever live it down in school? They'll be the butt of every cruel joke because their mother's a whore."

Shocked that Mrs. Jacobson described herself that way, Janet stared into her eyes, and tried to see the soul that lay behind them. All she saw was what was left of a woman who under different circumstances might have made better choices. That's when she knew that Mrs. Jacobson was no longer among the living. She knew there was nothing she could do to her. There was nothing she could hold over her head to control her, but still, she listened attentively to everything she had to say, hoping to gain some insight into who Anita Wilde had been and how she became the tortured soul who became Anita Jacobson.

"So you see, Miss Shamus, I have no fear of what you might do to me, or with those pictures you've taken. I am what I am and I'll always be what I am. I cannot become the doting wife and angelic mother. Sure, I can pretend for several hours a day and fool those who need me to be what they need me to be. But once, sometimes twice a week, I have to let loose and be who I am and what I am. It's the only time I feel alive and among the living, even if it's only for a few stolen minutes or a couple of stolen hours. I do what I have to do here and I do what I have to do . . . for my boys and my loving husband . . . and everybody's happy. It's an elaborate sham, sure, but I bet that most of the homes in this country are a sham as well—perhaps more of a sham.

"Pretending to be a dutiful pastor's wife is a small price to pay for what I get here . . . in this place of sin and unrestrained deca-dence. And I will go on paying that price until I'm found out, which, considering the pictures you took, won't be long hence. In the long run, you'll be doing me a gigantic favor. You'll be setting me free from the farce I live day by day. What you didn't know, what you couldn't know when you cooked up this plot to trap me is that I've been longing for the liberation that truth offers. Lying is more work than you can possibly imagine. Living two lives, having to keep track of everything I say is the albatross that hands around my neck.

"So you see, Miss Shamus, you can't hurt me. You can only hurt those who foolishly love me. You can only hurt those who have complete faith in me and live and breathe because of me. You can only hurt those whose lives will be shattered when you unleash the god-awful truth. You're about to set off the Hiroshima bomb right here in Scottsdale, Arizona. Imagine if you will, the residual destruc-tion, and the carnage those photographs will cause. Those pictures will rock the very foundation of my husband's congregation and Christendom in general when it's learned that the first lady has never been faithful to her godly husband. And the boys she gave him . . . Abraham, Isaac, and Jacob, who were named after the fathers of the faith are not even his children, but are bastards and their whore of a mother has no idea who sired them.

"This scandal will cause hundreds, perhaps thousands to leave the church and pursue their own fleshly instincts. I will be their excuse to do what I do without shame. I will be the poster child for their own sensual desires because no woman, especially a pastor's wife, should be caught dead doing such things. You'll be destroying their innocence. Me . . . I lost mine a long time ago." She lit another cigarette, took a deep drag, inhaled, and blew out the smoke. "Earlier, before I took my shower, you asked me if I had any shame. My answer is no. And to prove that, watch this." She took another drag of her cigarette and then walked over to the bed. She sat down and picked up the phone and dialed a number. Looking into Janet's eyes, she said, "Everett, I know you can't talk, but I want you to know everything's all right between us . . . Oh, you're alone. Your family's gone? No, I'm not mad. I know they had you over a barrel sweetie . . . I understand. Yes, I forgive you. When are the wife and kids returning? Really? Come on back to the Malibu and let's finish what we started before we were so rudely interrupted . . . Yeah, they're gone . . . I'll tell you about it when you get here . . . An hour? Okay, see you then. I love you too." She hung up the phone, crossed her bare legs, and took another drag of her cigarette. "You see, Miss Shamus, this was all a colossal waste of everybody's time. Do run along. I told Everett you two were gone."

Thoroughly humbled by what she'd heard and the resolve of the woman she had planned to intimidate and ultimately control, Janet collected the blackmail photos of Mrs. Jacobson's sons, her husband, Everett James, Paul Masterson, and Johnnie, and returned them to the pouch. Then she walked to the door and put her hand on the knob. She turned around and said, "I'm sorry for all of this."

"Don't worry about it, kid. Like I said, I've had a whole lot worse happen to me. This was nothing."

"Given your performance, and the way you've lived your life, and the unfeeling attitude surrounding you, I'm sure it has, Mrs. Jacobson. Whatever happened to you to turn you into what you are now must have been nothing short of evil incarnate."

"It's not too late for you, Miss Shamus. You've got your whole life ahead of you. If you don't stop now, you're looking at your future. Take a good long look before you leave this room and know for sure that what you see is waiting for you and will have you too."

"Perhaps it will, but what must be done will be done even if it costs me my life."

"It undoubtedly will."

Janet turned the knob and was about to open the door when Mrs. Jacobson offered her final parting shot. "Just so you know, even if I had everything to lose, and you caught me in the same position, I still would've never helped you do whatever you're trying to do to Paul. He's still the only man I ever truly loved and the one thing I regret. He had the biggest cock I ever tasted."

Janet looked her up and down, disgusted with her for being what she allowed herself to become, while at the same time pitying Anita Jacobson and her family. There was no profit in revealing her awful truth and therefore she wouldn't be responsible for breaking up her family. She would leave that dubious task to Mrs. Jacobson. She knew that even though she wasn't going to tell Judah Jacobson, Anita's affairs would eventually be found out. When it finally came to the surface, she hoped that Mrs. Jacobson would be forthright enough to tell her husband the "paternal" truth as well. "I'll have Patterson bring in your gun just in case your date doesn't show up."

Mrs. Jacobson set a short laugh free. "Was that last barb a double entendre?"

Nodding, "Yes. They won't know it until the hereafter, but you'll be doing your husband and your sons a favor."

"You have quite the sense of humor for a girl of eighteen years. Nevertheless, I'll give your *suggestion* all due consideration."

When Mrs. Jacobson heard the door close behind Patterson, a sigh of relief found its way out of her mouth. Her bluff had worked marvelously. The last thing she wanted was to give up all her comforts and start all over. She knew that if she'd had a more experienced and a more ruthless blackmailer, she would have never pulled it off. A ruthless blackmailer would have told her husband and posted the pictures on telephone poles out of spite. She practically ran to the door and locked it. Breathing heavily from the stress of being caught in the act and having to maneuver her way out of it, she inhaled deeply to calm her frayed nerves. Then she turned off the light and peeked outside to see what Miss Shamus and Patterson were doing. They were standing near a car talking. Then they got in and pulled off. She turned the light back on and sat down at the table. She pulled her personal phone book out of her purse and flipped through it. When she found Masterson's number, she closed her eyes and whispered, "Please God, let this still be his answering service."

"Evangelist Paul Masterson's office, may I help you?"

"Yes. I'd like to leave an urgent message. Could you have him call Anita Wilde at home no matter what time it is, day or night. The number is . . ."

"Got it, ma'am," the operator said.

"Has he been picking up his messages regularly?"

"He was until about a month ago."

"Is he still using the service?"

"All I can tell you is that his bill is paid until the end of the year."

She hung up and wondered where Masterson was and if he was okay. Before she knew it, she was vividly reliving their trysts which excited her. An hour later, Everett James was back at the Malibu Hotel. Mrs. Jacobson's legs were in the air again and her screams could be heard in the parking lot. They acted as if nothing had happened. When it was over, she took another shower. She came out of the bathroom fully dressed. Then she pulled the lamp cord from the socket, picked up the lamp, and broke it over her lover's head. She walked over to the door, grabbed the knob, and then turned around. Blood was running down the side of his head.

"What was that for?"

"That was for setting me up in the first place and putting my family in jeopardy. My husband is a good and decent man and so are my boys. Now . . . will you be here on Wednesday?"

James nodded.

"The next time someone approaches you, tell me about it and I'll handle it. Get over to the emergency room. You might need stitches. See you in a few days. I love you, sweetie."

"I love you too."

"And Everett, if this ever happens again, I'll kill you. Do you understand?"

He stared at her for a long minute, trying to figure out if she was serious or if she was scared and frustrated they had gotten caught and there were pictures.

She repeated, "Do you understand?"

He nodded.

With that, she left him there trying to stop the bleeding.

Chapter 33

"Yes. Now. Right now."

J anet Shamus took the next flight out to Los Angeles. She still had a plane to buy. But on the flight, she thought about what had happened at the Malibu Hotel, and knew she was lucky to be alive and if something like that happened again, next time good fortune may not be with her. So far nothing had gone according to plan. She remembered that Hatcher had told her that there were always variables that could not be predicted. Now she knew he had not exaggerated. Then she imagined just how badly things could have turned out as she wondered what would have happened if Mrs. Jacobson had pulled the trigger instead of being a mentor of sorts and taught her a valuable lesson.

From that moment forward, she was going to assume it all. Everyone had a gun. Everyone had nothing to lose. Everyone is willing to die for something. She wasn't going to underestimate anyone again. She then assumed that Hatcher knew about Patterson, and her plans to kill him. She was going to do everything in her power to persuade him to think otherwise. After the Malibu Hotel incident, she knew she was going to need his expertise in her pursuit of vengeance. That meant she had to cater to him, make him feel like he was the conquering king and she was his prized possession, his consort to do with as he pleased whenever he pleased for as long as he pleased. She had to make him think he was in charge, running the show, coming up with all the ideas, drawing all the logical conclusions. She had seen her mother do it with her father. She had seen her grandmother handle her father's father in the same fashion. When she thought about it, she realized that women were in charge of everything. They just didn't know it. Now that she did, she was going to make every effort to win Hatcher's heart. Possession of the heart was the secret to controlling anyone, she understood from observing her mother's relationship to her father. And in so doing, coerce Tony Hatcher into being both her slave and her unwitting stooge.

The moment she decided to do whatever it took to control Hatcher, her conscience kicked in again, telling her it was time to lick her wounds and leave Johnnie Wise alone and walk away. Again, she imagined the double funeral she had attended, and seeing her parents lying in their coffins, and her sisters leaning their heads on both her shoulders, crying their eyes out. And thus she strengthened herself and pressed on, determined to do what she thought needed to be done. She would have to plan better, she told herself, but no matter what, what happened at the Malibu Hotel could not happen again.

At that moment, a nude image of Anita Jacobson came to mind. In a strange way, Janet admired her. She was obviously intelligent, strong willed, articulate, and incredibly fearless when she faced the dismantlement of her wonderful life in affluent Scottsdale, Arizona. She didn't even flinch when she was threatened with blackmail. In fact, she skillfully turned the tables on her would-be extortionist. That's when Janet realized that she would have to have nerves of steel too. She couldn't allow anything or anyone to put her in a no win situation. She decided she would be equally fearless. Equally fierce. Equally resourceful when confronted with secrets that could embarrass her if they ever surfaced—not that she had anything worth blackmailing her for. Tony Hatcher was the only person who could put her behind bars for conspiracy to commit murder, but he'd be under her spell soon enough. Later, when he had served his purpose, she would dispense with him too.

She thought about fear, what it meant, and how it affected people. An incident in the kitchen came to mind. Her mother had told her to be careful with her "good" dishes. At the time, she was only nine years old and she had broken one of her mother's favorite dishes. The fear of being spanked ripped through her and made her shake. Her heart pounded. Her conscience told her to tell her mother the truth and accept whatever punishment that went along with being careless. Her mother had spanked her before and the pain on her backside reminded her that it would soon revisit her. She grabbed the broom and dustpan and swept up the broken dish and put it the trash.

Fear ripped through her again when she realized that when her father took out the trash, he would see the broken dish and tell her mother and she would be caught. To cover her tracks, she removed half the trash, and put the broken dish and the remaining fragments in the center of the can and then covered it with trash. Whenever she saw her mother, fear would suddenly surround her and make her nervous with the anticipation of being questioned about the missing dish. But it never happened. After awhile, seeing her mother didn't make her nervous anymore. Later, she overheard her mother on the phone accusing someone of not returning her dish from Thanksgiving dinner. Janet knew she had gotten away with it. The fear of being caught never returned.

After she retrieved her luggage, she hailed a cabbie to drive her over to the Beverly Hills Hotel. She smiled when it occurred to her that she would be the proud owner of a brand new DC-6 in less than twenty-four hours. She couldn't wait to see it. No more standing in lines. No more living by an airline schedule. It was going to be marvelous. She realized that if a Saudi Prince had ordered it especially for himself and his wives, it was going to be sensational. It would have all the modern conveniences and she was going to get at least thirty to forty percent off. She wondered how long it would take to find qualified pilots who could navigate the world if that's what she decided to do. That's when it hit her. What if Johnnie Wise left the country? What if she wasn't even in America anymore? If she were a black woman and someone thought she had killed a white man, she would do her best to flee the country because she wouldn't be safe in any state. But where would she go? Janet wondered. The obvious answer was Canada. They spoke English and French up there and she didn't have to have a passport to get in, she realized. Although she had never been there, she assumed that living in Canada would probably be like living in America. Then she considered the alternatives. She could go to England. They spoke English there, but she would have to have a passport. It occurred to her that if Johnnie spoke French, she might be adventurous enough to go to France. But again, she would need a passport.

She walked into the lobby of the Beverly Hills hotel. Tony Hatcher was there waiting for her. She walked up to the front desk and hoped he wasn't stupid enough to follow her up there. She didn't want people thinking she was a whore. When the desk clerk told her the room number and gave her the key, she repeated the room number just in case Hatcher hadn't heard. She couldn't wait to tell him about the conclusions she'd drawn. She made her way through the lobby and over to her bungalow. It was smaller than what she was accustomed too, but it would do. She was only planning to be there for a day or so. Nevertheless, she unpacked her suitcase and put her toiletries in the bathroom. A moment or two later, she heard a knock at the door.

Janet checked herself over in the mirror. Hatcher wanted sex and she would give it to him. She unbuttoned the top three buttons and went to the door and opened it.

Hatcher walked in like he owned the place. He handled her roughly, and she let him. Like he did the day before, he plunged in with both lips. His hands explore her ample rump and her thick bust. The pleasure that touching her gave him, ordered him to continue without regard for how she felt about it. Pleasure demanded more pleasure and he obeyed like an infantryman. When he felt her returning his lust without restraint, he kissed her harder and tugged at the buttons on her blouse until one broke.

"Let me do it," she said, wantonly, but thinking, *before you rip it you idiot*. She watched how he looked at her as she slowly unbuttoned her blouse. She saw the hunger in his eyes. He looked like a rabid dog foaming at the mouth. She pulled off her blouse and let it fall to the floor, keeping her eyes on his lust, holding him at bay. She could tell he thought she was taking too long. He wanted her to hurry up so she went even slower, teasing him, building to the moment. She wanted him to want her so badly that he couldn't stand it any longer. When he finally entered her flesh, she would have him. Little by little, he would surrender his soul to her. With both hands around her back, she unzipped her skirt and let it fall to the floor. With nothing but a slip, panties, and bra to hide her simmering flesh, she stood before him, drinking in his urgent need to quench his thirst. She didn't know why, but she had never felt more beautiful than she did at that moment. At the same time, she never felt more powerful, or more in control. She almost laughed in his face when he ripped off her silk slip and panties.

Seconds later she would feel him ripping into her flesh. Again she fought the urge to laugh out loud because he wanted her so much that he didn't even bother to take off his clothes. He just unzipped his pants, pulled them down, and forged ahead while they were still in the living room on the carpet. She expected to feel the piercing pain of her flesh being forced open, but it wasn't nearly as painful as the day before and it didn't take long to feel the pleasure the pain of entering promised. Moments later, she felt all his muscles tense, his movements slowed, but he continued his expedition, searching, it seemed, for something that could only be found deep inside her.

Whatever he was looking for, she knew she was looking for it too when she heard herself sigh synchronously to his cadence. Using both her hands, she grabbed his hair and pulled until she could see his face. She kissed him hard, opening her warm mouth to taste him and feel his hot breath. Then she held on tight and rode the wave like a surfer on the Pacific. She was losing herself during the romp and she didn't care. She wanted him to take her where he had taken her before. She was almost there. When she realized her sighs added to his pleasure, she put her mouth to his ear and let him hear her ecstasy. It was musical in tone and it drove him wild.

Moments later, only the sound of their breathing returning to normal filled the bungalow. Panting she said, "You missed me, huh?"

Looking at the ceiling fan that was spinning on the lowest setting, Hatcher breathing heavily said, "I think it was the other way around."

She said, "I wasn't the one who ran at you and I certainly didn't tear any of your clothing off."

Hatcher said, "Well, all I can say is it didn't take you long to get into it. So you must've wanted it too."

"Let's agree that we both wanted it, okay, Mr. Hatcher?"

"I'll go along with that."

"Good. Now, tell me why you're not in San Francisco."

"You know why."

She laughed and said, "Is it because you couldn't go another day without seeing me?"

"I could go another day without seeing you, but I couldn't go another day without thinking about doing what we just did."

"Oh, guess what I figured out on the way here?"

"What?"

"Would you think I'm crazy if I told you where I think Johnnie went?"

He looked at her, frowned and said, "Do you know something I don't?"

I know lots of things you don't think I know, Mr. Hatcher and when I'm ready, you'll have a lot to answer for. Now's a good time to go into my act of letting you think you're in control. I'll play the dumb woman role. I'll build your ego until it reaches the stratosphere if that's what I have to do.

Janet offered a smile and said, "I wouldn't say I know something you don't. I mean you're a private detective with lots of experience. I'm new to all of this. You know what, I feel like such a fool for even thinking it. Why don't you tell me what happened in South Carolina."

"No. Tell me what you're thinking."

"Forget it. You'll make fun of me. It seems so silly now that you're here. At first I thought my conclusions made perfect sense. I thought you would immediately agree with me, but now it doesn't make much sense."

Intrigued, Hatcher said, "Well tell me what it is."

"You promise not to laugh and think of me as a silly little schoolgirl trying to be a grownup with unrealistic theories that don't stand a chance at bearing fruit?"

"I promise."

"Okay, but don't laugh."

"I won't."

"Okay, here goes," she said, looking into his eyes. "What if she left the country?"

"Johnnie? I doubt it."

"See, I told you it was silly."

"Tell me why you think she may have left the country."

"The most obvious reason."

"Which is what?"

"She a Negress, Mr. Hatcher and she killed several white people. If you were a Negro, and you had twenty thousand dollars, what would you do? Where would you go?"

"Hmm. That's a thought."

She hit him playfully and said, "You're not serious, Mr. Hatcher. You're playing with me, aren't you?"

"No. Seriously, you might be onto something." He reached down and pulled up his underwear and pants. He realized that she had thought the thing through better than he had and he was the one being paid to figure out where Johnnie Wise might be hiding. It occurred to him that she might figure out that he was taking longer to track Johnnie down than was absolutely necessary. He decided he better come clean because if she found out that he was holding out so he could keep having sex with her, she might just turn on him. Although she didn't fully understand it yet, she had plenty of juice to turn his life into a living hell. He knew that when she realized just how much power she wielded, she would make him pay for not delivering the justice she sought sooner when it was within his means to do so. Zipping his pants he said, "I found Lucas Matthews in South Carolina."

"Great. What did he say?"

"He didn't say anything at first. But after I let him know I knew he killed Marla Bentley, he softened up a bit."

"Are we going to have to take care of him too?"

"No. Matthews isn't going to say anything."

"What makes you so sure?"

"You said it yourself. He's a Negro and he killed a white woman. He can't say anything without incriminating himself. And if he talks to the police once the deed is done, he knows he's going back to Angola and he's never getting out. On top of all of that, Lucas has found himself a girl at Fort Jackson. A real looker too. He's moved on. I'm sure he cares about Johnnie, but let's face the facts. She screwed at least three white men that we know of. Being a Negro, it's gotta mess with his head."

"What do you mean?"

"Matthews has to wonder why his girl, for whatever reasons, kept laying down with white men. It would bother me if a woman I loved kept seeing Negro men."

"Hmph. That's the difference between women and men. It would bother us if the man we loved, loved another woman the same way he loved us or more. Playing with a woman's emotions is a very dangerous game. I don't understand why men think physical love for him doesn't equate to emotional love to the woman wearing the ring he gave her. That ring symbolized his undying love and devotion to her."

"You mean her worship."

"Yes. Being a queen is our right as women, even if our territory ended at the edge of the property. Don't you understand that?"

Hatcher looked into her eyes and saw the sincerity in them. "To be honest with you, I never thought about it that way."

"And that's why you're divorced. You don't understand a woman's need to rule. It's been bequeathed from mother to daughter, all the way back to Eve. We must rule, Mr. Hatcher. It's what drives us."

"Excuse me. . . how old are you again?"

She kissed him.

"What was that for?" he said.

"That was for not laughing at me earlier and for recognizing that I have value. It was for recognizing that while I will always defer to your judgment, I have a mind too. And maybe we can plan this thing together. I know I don't know nearly as much as you, but I'm willing to learn. I know I'm young, but I have money and people do what I say. You tell me what you need and I'll see to it that you get it. But help me get my vengeance on the woman who killed my family and I'll give you anything you want. You'll never have to worry about paying your bills as long as I'm alive."

"Whatever I want?"

"Anything. You name your price."

"Well you've already done just about everything you said you'd do. The only things left are my car and the nest egg."

"What would you need to feel financially secure for the rest of your life?"

"I don't know, I haven't thought that far into the future."

"A million?"

"You'd be willing to give me a million dollars?"

"No. I wouldn't give you a million, but I would pay you a million. There's a difference."

"Let me get this straight, you're going to pay me a million on top of everything else you've already done?"

"Yes."

"What's the catch?"

"No catch. And it isn't generosity either. It's business. I want that bitch to die, okay? That's it. No absolution. No Forgiveness. No mercy. To be that ruthless, a man has to bury his conscience."

"And you've buried yours?"

"I'm working on it. That's why I know you've got one too. At the moment of truth, you might change your mind. You're going to find Johnnie Wise, Mr. Hatcher. Of that I have no doubt. Now . . . what else did you learn from Mr. Matthews?"

"He told me she took the train to Providence, Rhode Island."

"Rhode Island? Why would she go to Rhode Island and how does that help us? Isn't it possible that she bought the ticket to Rhode Island and got off somewhere else to throw you off her trail?"

"It's possible, but I doubt it."

"Why?"

"She doesn't know for certain that someone is looking for her."

"But Mr. Hatcher, what if she found the tapes in her room at the Clementine?"

"She already took care of that. She told everybody she was going to East Saint Louis, remember?"

"Hmm, I see. What's our next move, Mr. Hatcher?'

"I've gotta find out why she stopped in Manhattan and Norfolk, Connecticut. You've given me an idea."

"What?"

"She could be going to Canada. It makes sense. She was going north. She could go all the way to Canada. I mean why not?"

His eyes widened a bit.

"What?"

"This is a long shot, but what if she is going to Canada, but thinks she'll need a passport? What if Norfolk, Connecticut has a passport office?"

"Couldn't she get a passport in Manhattan or Rhode Island? You said she was stopping in those places too."

"Yes she could, but the lines would be so much longer. Nobody wants to wait in lines like those except people trying to get into the country."

"Don't you think you should check Manhattan too?"

"I think Manhattan's a waste of time. I think she went there to invest her money. What we need is a US map. That way we can see better what she did. It'll probably save me a ton of time."

"They had a lot of maps in the lobby."

"Yeah, but are they what we need?"

She went to the phone. "I'll call the front desk and find out if the hotel has one."

"Hopefully they will."

"This is Janet Shamus, I'm wondering if you have a map of the United States . . . sure, I'll hold."

"If not, I'll have to get one from a filling station. But I'd love to have one now while it's fresh in my mind."

"Oh, great that would be wonderful. Could you bring it here? In about five minutes? Do you mind sliding it under the door? I may be in the shower. Great. Thanks."

"He's got one, I take it."

"He's got one in his car. He's going to bring it over."

"Do you think we could get something to eat? I'm starved."

"There's a menu on the desk in the corner."

Hatcher grabbed the menu. When he saw the prices he was glad he didn't have to pay. "Are you going to have something? I can afford it. I've got a Diners Club card."

"I'll have something, too, but I'll take care of it. How would it look if I had single occupancy and I paid for it with a card that has your name on it?"

"I understand."

"I'm thinking of ordering the Grilled Jumbo Shrimp, Smoked Salmon Canapé, and Crab cakes."

"Sounds good to me."

"Would you like some wine, Mr. Hatcher?"

"Sure, why not."

She ordered their food and then went into the bedroom. When she came out, she was wearing a white robe. "Do you mind lighting the fireplace? It's a little chilly."

"No problem."

Janet saw the map on the floor in front of the bungalow door. "The map's here. I'll look it over while you're starting the fire."

"Listen, I'm having second thoughts on the Canada theory," Hatcher said as he started the fire. "I mean why not go straight there from South Carolina? I understand she wanted to invest in Manhattan, but she had investments before and she had never been to Manhattan as far as I know. Why go now? I'm thinking she wanted to meet the people she was about to trust to handle her money. She's leaving the country and she doesn't know when she'll be back. Makes sense to me. What do you think?"

"You're right, Mr. Hatcher. Besides, she's probably thinking about what Sharon Trudeau did when she trusted her or something."

"Do you have to keep calling me Mr. Hatcher? Would you please call me Tony?"

"I suppose you'd like to call me Janet."

"I would. Yes. Is there anything wrong with that?"

"I guess not, considering our plans. Just don't fall in love with me, okay? You're not the marrying kind," she said playing him. She offered him her sensuous eyes and continued, "And I don't want my heart broken. I'm sure you've broken lots of hearts, haven't you, Tony?"

"I've broken a few," he said, making his way over to the kitchen table where Janet was with the map.

"See Tony, when we start at New Orleans, it looks like she's got a plan. If she were going to Canada, why not go straight from Fort Jackson. What's in Providence?"

Hatcher thought for a second and said, "Maybe it's not a what, but a who?"

"Who? It wouldn't be Paul Masterson, would it? I mean that's way out there, don't you think?"

"I do think its way out there, but that doesn't mean you're wrong. There's a steady progression of her going northeast."

"Do you know where Masterson is?"

"No. I haven't been looking for him. There was no reason to before now."

"Why not send someone to Houston to find him?"

"I could do that, Janet, but then if he's with her, we might have to take care of the preacher too. Then I'd have to take care of one of my own guys because he would know too much. No. Let's just stay on her. This execution must be surgical or not at all. That's why we plan. That way we avoid a high body count. One murder is complicated enough. Now . . . if Masterson's with her, we'll know soon enough. But look at the map. The shortest way to Canada, is north through West Virginia. Then go northwest through Toledo, Ohio, and on to Detroit, and you're in Windsor."

"Why go to South Carolina to begin with, Tony? That's what I don't understand. Was it just to see Matthews or did she have another agenda?"

"To see if she could win him back, I guess."

"If she was there to win him back, she must have been conflicted."

"Why do you say that?"

"If a woman drove that far for a second chance, there's no way she wouldn't wait for him. Trust me, if her goal was to win him over, she would have been far more persistent. There's no way a woman who loved a man would leave without seeing him. She would have waited at the gate all night if she had to."

"When she learned he wasn't at Fort Jackson, why didn't she go to the Negro side of town looking for him? If you're right, there must be some other explanation."

"Maybe she went there to say her final goodbyes."

"She said those in the courtroom the day he heard your mother's testimony. Nevertheless, I agree with you. If she wanted him back, she would have stayed until morning, I would think. But she didn't do that. Why?"

"Maybe she was on a schedule."

"To see stockbrokers she's never met? To go to Norfolk, Connecticut, a place she's never been? I don't think so."

"What then?"

"If Paul Masterson helped her with your father's body, he may very well be with her now. And since she went to Rhode Island, he may have been there waiting for her. If she left the country, he probably went with her. Otherwise it makes no sense to meet him. Assuming she did meet him, they left these shores going east; otherwise, why not meet here, in California?"

"But he hardly knows her, Tony."

"True, but she's a very beautiful girl and she likes white men. That makes sense to me."

"But he's an evangelist, Tony. I can see him helping her because she was in trouble. But I don't see him leaving the country with her."

"Again, she's a beautiful girl. And even though he's a preacher, he's a man first. His flesh gets hard just like mine. And like any other man, once it gets that way, he wants to stick in a woman's flesh. If you doubt me for one moment, consider the Anita Wilde situation. How does that happen if he's above that sort of thing? It doesn't. It happened because he's not above it. If he'd get involved with a beautiful sex kitten like Anita Wilde, there's a very good chance he would get involved with Johnnie. He saved her from three bikers in Jackson. That undoubtedly drew her to him and they were staying at the same hotel. It is therefore possible that he ravaged her in his hotel room and they are now in cahoots. Once he sampled her merchandise, he no doubt found it difficult to stop. It would have been like a drunk falling off the proverbial wagon. A reformed drunk could go years without drinking, but after one drink, he'd be drinking for days, perhaps years. I submit that the pleasures of the flesh have the same effect on a man whether he's a member of the clergy or not. In fact I would say that because he's of the cloth, the temptation to give in to wanton desire is more formidable for him than the rest of us mortals because he's supposed to be an example." He paused for a second and thought. Then he shook his head in disbelief. "It can't be."

"What, Tony? What are you thinking?"

Hatcher exhaled heavily and said, "What if he was so guilt-ridden for having had sex with her, that he felt the need to marry her?"

"But he's white and she's Negro. That's against the law."

"Not everywhere. Some states allow it."

"And you think Rhode Island does?"

"There's only one way to find out. And get this, Janet, if he married her, not only does he have conjugal rights, but they cannot be compelled to testify against each other. Don't you see? It's the smart move. He's also the son of a rich man, which means he has the resources to hide abroad."

"Hmm, it is the smart move. Do you think . . . maybe we should get married too?"

Hatcher looked her in the eyes. "Are you serious?"

"Yes. Why not? You told me that there are always unpredictable variables, right? Why not cover ourselves. It wouldn't be a real marriage or anything. That way we won't be compelled to testify against each other either." She silenced herself for a few moments when she saw Hatcher contemplating the possibilities of having access to all her money. When she thought he was on the verge of rejecting the idea, she continued. "You've said many times that Johnnie Wise didn't kill my father. Given what we now know, it's possible that they covered up what really happened that night. For all we know, Masterson walked in on them having sex and my dad was so afraid, he had a heart attack.

"Because everything would've happened so fast, Masterson then might have felt compelled to help her because he would have been implicated if the police showed up. If the police show up, an investigation ensues and they might find out about Anita Wilde. If they do, they might just think what we're now thinking, Tony. Masterson may have thought of this too. It was probably his idea. Then to make sure they could never be prosecuted, they got married and left the country so they would never have to explain what happened that night. And Masterson gets to have guilt free sex with her for the duration of the marriage. All I'm saying is that if we're right, they were smart to marry. We need to be equally smart. We don't have to get married today or anything because we don't know where they are. But when we find them, maybe we should marry as soon as we take care of them. What do you think?"

Still looking at the map, Hatcher said, "I think you want to get married because you feel guilty about what we're doing in a hotel room. I'm sure your mother and your father would prefer you were married if you're going to be indulging in the pleasures of the flesh. I understand. But marriage? To me? I think you should really think about that. Don't you want a husband and a family?"

"Yes, I want those things. But considering what we're planning, we really ought to cover ourselves just in case something goes wrong. I have lots of money, but I don't know that it will keep us out of prison, do you?"

"No, I don't. That's why we have to be careful. We have to plan."

"And we have to keep our plans to ourselves, right Tony?"

"Right." Her robe had parted, offering him a close-up of the scenic mountains on her chest. He reached out and pulled her to him. "Come here."

With her hands on his chest, she pulled her head back. Smiling she said, "What? You want me again?"

"I do," he said softly.

"I see why you said the preacher would find it difficult to stop."

He kissed her hard on the lips. Then he moved her robe over her shoulders. It fell to the floor. Looking into her eyes, he fondled her breasts. She closed her eyes for a moment and enjoyed the feeling he gave her. He kept his hand on her breasts while he kissed her again. When the moment was right, he picked her up and sat her on the table.

"No, Tony. Not yet."

Kissing her neck, he said, "Yes. Now. Right now."

She lifted his head from her neck, looked into his eyes. She could tell he was drunk with passion. She said, "Tony our food is going to arrive any minute now. Let's wait, okay?"

"I can't wait," Hatcher said and dropped his pants again. "I can't stand it."

"Wait, wait, wait," she said, knowing he wasn't going to. But resisting his advances made her want him all the more. When she felt him inside her again, she held on tight and said, "Oh, Tony. You make me feel so good."

When it was finished, he laid there, half naked, with his head comfortably on her breasts. She held onto his head and they drifted off to sleep. A few minutes later, they heard someone knock and yell, "Room service." They looked at each other and laughed.

Chapter 34

"Hey, it's a hotel. Figure it out."

The next morning, Hatcher took a plane to Connecticut, where he rented a car and drove to Norfolk, which was about 35 miles northwest of Hartford. It was a smallish town located in a mountainous area. From what he could tell Norfolk was only about nine miles long. There was a lawyer's office or two, an insurance company, a filling station with a service garage, a bank and a hair salon. He was driving down Freemason Street when he saw a sign that read: The Norfolk Police Museum established 1919. He was stunned that such a small town would have a police museum and that it had been around for 35 years. By his estimation, the population couldn't have been more than fifteen hundred people, and that meant Johnnie Wise would stick out, particularly since he hadn't seen one black person in the town—not that he'd seen many people to begin with.

He went into an empty diner and ordered a cheeseburger, fries, and a Coke. He was hungry, but he mainly was there to get information. He figured that Johnnie might have come to the same restaurant in which case the proprietor would probably remember her. He sat on one of the stools in front of the counter. Charlene was the name of the woman who owned the place. She was very friendly and probably very lonely too, Hatcher figured by the way she stared at him. If he was willing, he thought she would invite him to her place for dinner and anything else he may have wanted but was afraid to ask.

After some small talk, Hatcher told her he was an investigator for the Buchanan Mutual Insurance Company and that he was looking for Johnnie Wise because the company didn't realize until recently that her mother had two policies and Buchanan Mutual owed her ten thousand dollars. He knew it was better to stick as close to the truth as possible. That way he couldn't get tripped up easily if Charlene turned out to be another Lieutenant Perry. Working for Janet Shamus meant he was working for Buchanan Mutual as far as he was concerned. He showed her a picture of Johnnie. Charlene remembered serving her a bowl of chili, a grilled cheese sandwich, and a glass of ice cold lemonade. He could tell that Charlene liked Johnnie, which wasn't a surprise. Everybody liked her except her family, excluding her brother of course. According to Charlene, Johnnie was there to get a passport, which could be done in one day with proper identification. After hearing about her tragedy, Charlene called the City Clerk's office and told her younger sister, Barbara, that Johnnie was on her way over.

When he finished his meal, he thanked Charlene in the back of the restaurant for about fifteen minutes. She was very grateful. Hatcher thought it was the least he could do.

Then he went over to City Hall and learned that Barbara issued Johnnie a passport even though she didn't have any identification whatsoever, which didn't surprise him at all. He understood that beauty opened doors for women who possessed its magical power. It also got them a seat at the table because people automatically assumed that a good-looking woman was innocent. And when a beautiful woman smiled, people gave her just about anything she wanted. Add a hard luck story to all of that, and people would give them the world, which is probably why Johnnie also told Barbara about the man who had rescued her at the Flamingo Den in Jackson. Johnnie went on to tell her that she was going to Providence, Rhode Island, to marry him and they were going to travel abroad, but she was smart enough to tell her that she didn't know exactly where they were going—she also left out the fact that he was white. She told Barbara that her fiancée had made the arrangements. Of course Barbara thought it was a fairytale that she wished had happened to her and issued the passport without further inquiry.

Hatcher then drove back to Hartford and flew to Hillsgrove Airport in Warwick, Rhode Island and took a twelve minute cab ride over to Providence's Union Station, where he saw a line of Checker cabs parked outside the train terminal. He smiled, knowing he was just that much closer to finding his prey because undoubtedly, one of the cabbies had picked Johnnie up. He must have questioned thirty cabbies before he found the one who remembered her. Hatcher gave the cabbie a fifty dollar bill and he told Hatcher he had picked up a white man and brought him to the station, where he waited for thirty minutes. When he came out, he had a black woman with him—a real looker. He then took them to City Hall. Then he took them to Camille's where they had a bite to eat. Then he brought them back to Union Station.

Hatcher then went inside the station and talked to the clerks, and showed them pictures of Johnnie and Paul Masterson. Normally, a clerk wouldn't remember one couple from another if they both had the same skin color, given the traffic. However, Hatcher knew Johnnie and Masterson would be easy to remember because of color prejudice. He knew that anyone who had anything to do with them would in all likelihood remember because mixed couples attracted a lot of attention. All he had to do was supply their names and the approximate day they left. The clerk checked the manifest and told him they had gone to Manhattan. He slipped the clerk a fifty and took a cab over to Camille's. It was a long shot, but he was hoping to find a waiter that may have overheard their conversation. He was hoping to narrow down where they were headed. Masterson was ex-military with a top secret file. Hatcher suspected that Masterson was linked to the Intelligence community. If he was right, there was a pretty good chance Masterson wouldn't leak anything to anybody, but he had to be sure.

Camille's was a dead end, but City Hall was an information bonanza. A clerk showed him the application for their marriage license. Masterson's address was in Providence. Hatcher figured he must have recently purchased the house. Apparently the newlyweds were planning to make Providence their home. It made sense too. Rhode Island was one of the states that allowed blacks and whites to legally marry. He found the home and took a look around. He looked through the windows. There was no furniture and no appliances, which made sense. Every husband knows that the wife decorates the house and chooses the appliances. He talked to a few of the neighbors, but none of them ever saw Masterson. Depending on how long they would be gone, someone would invariably have to cut the lawn and trim the bushes. So either the Mastersons were only going to be gone for a couple weeks, or he had hired a lawn service for the duration. Assuming Masterson hired a lawn service, they would need to be paid. If that was the case, Hatcher knew that it might be possible to track them down that way.

It was about six o'clock by the time he got back to the airport. He called the Beverly Hills Hotel, but Janet wasn't there. Then he called his office in New Orleans to see if he'd gotten any messages. He hadn't, but business was booming in his absence. He looked at his watch again. His plane was leaving for Manhattan at 7:10. Just before his plane boarded, he called the Beverly Hills Hotel again and left a message to call him at the Hilton in Manhattan. On the flight he realized that he was coming to the end of the road. Even if he knew the country and city the Mastersons had fled to, he would have to deal with the language barrier. He didn't speak any foreign languages. Masterson on the other hand could speak several. Even Johnnie could speak French.

He was tired and hungry. He checked into a suite at the Hilton and ordered lobster, fries, a salad, and a of couple beers. He was getting used to the good life. Having someone else paying the bills while he traveled around the country had him seriously thinking about Janet Shamus's offer of marriage. *What if something did go wrong? She'd have my back because I could bury her and I'd have her back because she could bury me.* It was a great arrangement and an excellent plan for getting away with murder. He imagined himself living in the Buchanan mansion, having servants and riding around in a chauffeur driven limousine. He could even create a position for himself at Buchanan Mutual. People filed false claims all the time and they needed to be investigated before the company cut the checks.

He wondered how it would work with a precocious young woman like Janet. He realized he had to control her, which meant he had to get her mind. Once he had that, her body had no choice but to obey him. The best way to attack her mind was to be the hard guy he was. He knew most woman didn't go for the crème puffs; the guys they could control. They wanted the guys that wouldn't take their crap; guys that would slap 'em around and then bang their brains out. He knew they also loved the hard truth because most women were liars themselves. Even though Janet was a rare beauty, he wasn't going to let her know that. He'd let the other suckers fall all over themselves trying to get her while he would slap her around and bang her every other day. Before long, she'd be his. Satisfied he'd come up with an idea to get his hands on the Buchanan fortune, he turned on the radio and listened to his favorite shows and the Associated Press updates. Before he knew it, sleep was upon him. He was in a deep satisfying sleep when he heard someone knock on the door. He didn't know anybody in New York, so he figured they must have the wrong room and fell back to sleep. Someone was knocking again. This time it was a little louder.

"Yeah," Hatcher said angrily.

The knocking was louder.

"Yeah!" Hatcher screamed.

No response. Bam! Bam! Bam!

Hatcher snatched the covers off and fast-walked across the room. Then he snatched open the door ready to unleash a hail of obscenities to whoever dared interrupt his sleep only to find Janet Shamus standing there with a bottle of Chardonnay, cheese, crackers, and strawberries.

Smiling she said, "Well, aren't you going to invite me in? I believe we have some celebrating to do, don't we?"

Hatcher knew it was time to go into his act. She had obviously flown across the country to get what only he had given her. She was simmering. He could tell by the look in her eyes. She had probably been thinking about what they were going to do all the way to New York. "What the hell, Janet? I called you a couple of times."

She tried to walk in, but he stopped her.

"Aren't you going to let me in?" she said, smiling.

"You should've called first. I've got a broad in here."

Janet's smile evaporated. "What?"

"Hey, didn't you tell me not to fall in love with you?"

"Yes, but . . ."

. "Listen kid, the best way not to fall for dame is to have lots of dames. We're partners, okay? Nothing more. Now, scram before you wake her up."

"Where am I supposed to sleep?"

"Hey, it's a hotel. Figure it out. Save us both some trouble, call first the next time."

He shut the door and watched her through the peephole. She was just standing there looking confused and frustrated. Twice she was about to knock on the door and changed her mind. Then she turned around and left. Hatcher laughed out loud. Then he got back into bed and fell fast asleep.

Chapter 35

"But not impossible, right Tony?"

Hatcher opened his eyes and looked at the clock. It was a few minutes after nine. Sh-Boom (Life Could Be A Dream) was playing on the radio. He smiled because the uptempo song by The Crew-Cuts made him think of how his life would turn out if he played Janet Shamus just right. He closed his eyes and remembered the look on the face of a woman who wanted to become his future wife when he denied her what she wanted. She was so stunned, so disappointed. If he didn't know that she had come from humble beginnings, he would have thought his rejection was the first time someone had told her no. He figured it had been a month or so since she came into power. As far as he was concerned it had gone to her head. She was getting too big for her britches. Someone needed to take her down a few pegs. And he was just the man to do it. He got up and showered. Then he brushed his teeth in the marble basin and then applied some shaving crème to his face and removed it with a straight-edged razor. When he finished, he applied some aftershave and dressed. His phone rang. He sensed that it was Janet.

"Hatcher," he said gruffly.

"Is your *whore* gone?" Janet said.

"Why?"

"I thought we might have breakfast in my suite and discuss our plans to get married among other things."

Hatcher smiled, pleased that he hadn't overdone it. But he still had to play hard. He couldn't make it too easy for her. "Married? I thought I told you I didn't want to get married when we were in Los Angeles."

"No, Tony. You said you thought I only wanted to get married because of what we were doing, remember?"

"Same difference."

"Are you coming up here or not?"

"No. You come down here."

"I will not be bedded on the same sheets your whore slept on."

"I got news for you. We didn't do any sleeping."

"Tony. Are you coming up here or not? I've ordered you breakfast. Why won't you come up here and enjoy it with me?"

"Do you have any clothes on?"

"Why? Do you need me to be naked?"

"Yeah. I do."

"It can be arranged, but you better be here in five minutes."

"What's the room number?"

"You're the detective, Tony. Five minutes," she said flippantly and hung up.

Even though he wanted nothing more than to find and enter her, Hatcher knew he had to do the opposite of what she wanted. Instead of being lead by his wanton desire, he went over to the window and looked down onto 42nd Street. His phone rang, signaling him that more than five minutes had passed and Janet had run out of patience. He figured she was sitting there, waiting for him to show up like he was her plaything.

When five minutes passed and he didn't knock on the door, she was confused. He had gotten rid of her and talked harshly to her the previous night. Now he was acting as if he could take her or leave her when just a few days ago he had made a deal that he could have her whenever he wanted until the deed was done. From what she could tell, he enjoyed her, which was why she didn't understand his reluctance to have her again. She had to know what was going on. What had changed so suddenly? Was the woman still in his room? Was he still having relations with her now in the hotel room she was paying for? Or was she overreacting because he didn't know what room she was in? She called his room to find out if he was on his way or still in his room. When he didn't answer, she assumed he was on his way. She gave him another five more minutes to find her and when he didn't show, she'd called his room again.

Hatcher heard his phone ringing a second time. He knew it was her and he wanted to answer. He would never admit it, but he liked Janet Shamus. He knew her desire for power was growing and if he didn't stop her, it would consume her and consequently him. He watched the diplomats enter and leave the United Nations building and wondered if they'd ever accomplish anything. They had been meeting since 1945 and there had still been wars. The phone stopped ringing. He watched Checker cabs pick up and drop people off at Grand Central Terminal, wondering if it would be worth the time to visit their dispatcher's office. He still needed to know if the Mastersons left the country by air or sea. He hoped the Mastersons were in a romantic mood. If so, they would have boarded a ship instead of flying over. He still hadn't figured out what he was going to do about the language barrier. He heard a knock at the door and looked at his watch. Twenty minutes had passed. A gleeful smile crept across his lips.

As he made his way over to the door, he heard pounding, followed by, "Tony Hatcher! Open this door this instant!" He opened the door and heard Janet say, "Just who in the hell do you think you are? If you want to have sex with your whores, you do it on your own money. Is she still here? I demand that you get rid of her immediately."

Hatcher didn't bother answering. He just reached out and grabbed her by the lapels of her blouse. Then he snatched her into his room and closed the door. He kissed her hard on the lips. She fought to get away, but he forced her to kiss him and then he forced her into his bed. He heard her say, "Don't make me do it on this bed. Don't make me." Not long after she said those words, he made her and she loved it.

When she heard The Chordettes singing, Mr. Sandman, she laid her head on his chest, sighed and said, "I just love this song, don't you?"

"It's okay, I suppose," Hatcher said. "I'm partial to Tony Bennett's Rags to Riches myself."

"Really? Why?"

"I'm surprised you'd ask, given the way your grandfather treated your family."

She stretched her long neck up and kissed his cheek. She returned her head to his chest and said, "He eventually came around. Now you and I are enjoying his money, aren't we?"

"Yeah, but look how long it took? Jesus! You'd think the man would show more concern for his daughter even if he did hate her husband."

She kissed his bare chest. "It's good to know you care, Tony."

"Who said I care? I'm just pointing out the obvious. That's all."

"Sure you do, Tony. You're just afraid of falling in love with me. I understand."

"So did you buy your plane?"

"If you want to change the subject, that's fine," Janet said, after hoisting herself up on her elbows and looking down in his eyes. "What's your story, Tony?"

"My story?"

She laid her head back on his chest. "Yes. What do you believe in?"

"I believe in self-determination. Meaning, I determine how my life turns out. No one else. I'm in charge of everything and I like it that way. Most people blame others their entire life for what happens to them. Not me. I make everything happen good or bad. What about you, Janet? What do you believe in?"

"Revenge."

"Revenge? Is that all?"

"Right now, that's enough. It keeps me focused and moving forward. I think about it day and night. If I could, I'd dream about it too."

"Geez. You're obsessed. I'd think a dame like you would believe in love."

"Not me, Tony. Never. My mother believed in love and what did it get her? It got her a broken heart when she learned that daddy wasn't true to her. The sad part about it all is that daddy couldn't even be true to her after her death. She had only been dead for a few days and he ran off to meet his whore."

"Maybe he loved her."

"Is that supposed to be an excuse, Tony?"

"No. I'm just saying. Love does that to people."

"And that's why you and I will never fall in love, right, Tony? Promise me you won't let us fall in love."

"I promise. It'll never happen. It does screwy things to peoples brains. That dopey preacher, Paul Masterson, fell in love with Anita Wilde and look what happened to him. She's a beautiful girl. Young. Hot body. I could see it happening. Maybe that's how your father felt about Johnnie Wise. What do you think?"

"Okay, Tony. Let's say my father loved his whore. What did it get him? It got him a heart attack. It got him the physical manifestation of what he did to my mother's heart."

"Do you hate your father, Janet?"

"No. I love him dearly no matter what he did, but the truth is, he couldn't be faithful to my mother or his family and it killed him."

"If that's what you believe, why are we going after Johnnie?"

"The same reason people blame the devil, if there is one. People believe that if the devil wasn't around to tempt them, they'd behave."

"So if Johnnie was never alive, your father would've been true to your mother and the whole chain of events would've never occurred?"

"That's exactly what I'm saying. It all started with Johnnie and Marguerite Wise. They are the root of all my family's problems. I'm going to make sure she doesn't have a chance to do it again."

"Even though she's married now? You still want to go through with this?"

She raised herself on her elbows again and looked down into his eyes. "So . . . when were you going to tell me about this new development?"

"I was just waiting for the right time."

"The right time? Immediately is the right time."

"Hey, I called you twice, remember? I guess I could've left you a message detailing my findings and leave the cops a trail that leads directly to our doorstep."

"Are you with me on this or not, Tony?"

"I said I was, didn't I?"

"Are you sure? There's no room for second thoughts or remorse. If you can't pull your weight on this, I need to know now. I've fulfilled my end of the bargain, Tony. I've paid off all your bills, including your home. I've given you my purity. What more can I do? Find a husband for your ex-wife so you can stop paying alimony? Tell me what more you want and I'll get it for you. But don't you dare back out on me now."

"I'm in."

"All the way?"

"All the way. Now, were you serious about paying my ex-wife's boyfriend to marry her?"

"I'm sure something can be arranged. I'll tell you what, I can make sure he either goes along, or he loses everything, including her. Then I'll send her a charming man who'll marry her, and get you off the hook."

"You'd do all that for me?"

"Not for you, Tony. For revenge. That's what this is about. Don't lose sight of that."

"How would you do it?"

"My grandfather had an enormous amount of contacts. He was into everything."

"Oh, yeah? What about Ocean liners and airlines."

"Those too. We insure everything and everybody. I've got several rolodexes full of numbers. I can get us almost anything. Take your ex-wife's boyfriend, Antonio Mendez. He's a mechanic and he owns a landscaping business. First I can have his employer's bank to call in his loan. He probably doesn't have the money. Then I have one of my people throw him a life preserver. With my man in charge, I have Mendez fired. Then I can easily call in Mendez's business loan and break him. With no money, I'm sure your ex-wife will have to get rid of him eventually. But before all of that, I'd have to find someone to woo her before all of this happens. A woman has to have options. She'll be true to Mendez for a while, but with no income, she'll take the man I hire."

"Yes. Yes. I like that. Buy a great house in the Garden District and let them live there."

"Done. I hear that Ethel Beauregard left her home to her cook, Katherine, but the neighbors don't want her living around them because she's a Negro. They're going to force her out and I'll buy it.

What you've got to understand, Tony, is that all of that is going to take time. If I do it all at once, it'll look suspicious."

"I understand. Then, after they've been married for a sufficient time, he'll lose his job and he won't even own the house. Then she'll come to me, begging for the mercy she never showed me. I like it. Put that in motion."

"I've done a lot for you Mr. Hatcher and I'll do this too. I swear it, but you better deliver Johnnie Wise's head on a platter."

"I will, but you've gotta understand that this could take years."

"I don't care if it takes ten years."

"It might take that long if we don't get lucky. Now . . . I tracked her to Norfolk where she picked up a passport. She told a of couple sisters her sad story. One of the sisters worked in City Hall where they approve passports. I tracked Johnnie to Providence where she married the preacher. He bought a house there and that might be the way to find out where they are without leaving much of a trail."

"What do you mean?"

"The way I figure it, the house is in a good neighborhood. He's gotta have a landscaper to keep the property looking good even though he's not there."

"So?"

"So? Are you kiddin' me? The landscaper's gotta get paid for services rendered. We find out where the checks are coming from. Masterson's got a house in Houston too. If he hasn't sold it yet, he will. That's another way. Again, all of this takes time. The other thing is to find out what ship they left on. That'll tell us where they went."

"What if he didn't go by ship? What if they flew?"

"Either way, we need to get the manifests and find their names. The sooner we do that, the better, but again, it must be handled delicately and quietly. The more people know about this the greater the chances of getting caught. I'm pretty sure I can find the cabbie that picked them up from the train station. They have to record where they take their fares. Once we have that, we know the date they left and the mode of transportation. I'm betting they went by ship. It's more romantic than flying."

"Assuming you're right, find out what ship they left on and I'll see about getting the manifest. How soon can you find the cabbie?"

"Now that's tricky. There are a lot of cab companies here."

"What can I do to help?"

"You start working on finding out about the ships and airlines. In the meantime, I'll check on the cab companies. It'll take awhile, but we could find them. How soon do you have to get back to New Orleans?"

"I've taken extended leave. Phillip Seymour is running things while I'm gone. And I've spoken with my sisters too. Mildred is moving in until further notice. We all love her and she can be trusted to handle my sisters properly until they're ready for college. It'll be two years for Marjorie and four years for Stacy. Hopefully we'll find them long before then."

"When did all of this happen?"

"I took care of everything yesterday morning after you left. Then I bought the plane and flew all night to see you. I think you owe me an apology for last night."

"Why? Because of the broad I had here?"

"No. Because you didn't get rid of her when I showed up."

"So you don't want me bangin' other broads?"

"Not unless its business. If you've gotta have sex with a woman to get valuable information for our cause, fine. If not, I'm available if you need that sort of thing. I mean that was part of the bargain you made, wasn't it? Or have you grown tired of me already?"

"No promises on that."

"Okay, Tony. But at least call me first. Can you do that?"

"I'll give it some thought. In the meantime, we're looking at major problems with the Mastersons being overseas. I don't speak any foreign languages. Do you?"

"I speak French and a little Italian, but that's it."

"I guess I'm the only bonehead in New Orleans who doesn't speak French. My mother told me one day I'd regret it and now I do."

"I can teach you."

"Good. It might come in handy, but if they're on the move as I suspect Masterson is, we still might have a major problem getting information while we're tracking them. That's probably why Masterson took Johnnie out of the country. He knew it would be hard to find them."

"But not impossible, right Tony?"

"Not impossible."

Chapter 36

"You ever hear of a guy named, Michelangelo?"

T he cab stopped in front of the historic Excelsior Hotel in
Rome, built in 1906. The doorman opened the cab door and
Johnnie got out. Her mouth fell open when she beheld the
elegance of the lobby through the revolving glass doors. She thought
she had seen it all at the Negresco in Nice and then the Hotel de
Crillon in Paris, but so far the Excelsior in Rome topped them both
and she hadn't even been inside yet. With wide-eyed wonder, she
forgot Paul, who was wearing his trademark Stetson, which
screamed "I'm an American" to the Roman onlookers, was with her.
She followed the doorman up the red carpeted steps, inside the
Excelsior, and onto the sparkling marble floor of the lobby. She felt
her husband take her hand. He was leading her somewhere, but she
couldn't take her eyes off of the soaring ceiling, and the chandeliers
that hung from them.

"This is a palace," Johnnie heard herself say.

"Paul Masterson," the man behind the check-in desk said. His
Italian accent was thick. "It's been a while since we've seen you.
Still saving souls I hope."

"How you doin', Vito?" Paul said. "It has been a while and yes,
I'm still in the saving souls business."

"Good to hear. So . . . who is the lovely creature with you?" Vito
asked.

"This is Johnnie, my wife," Masterson said, smiling.

"Really? Vito said, smiling. "When did this happen?"

They showed him their gold wedding bands.

In Italian, Vito said, "For shame. A rich man like you and you
didn't buy your beautiful wife a diamond." Shaking his head he
muttered, "Tsk, tsk, tsk."

"If I find the right one, I'll get her one here," Masterson said in Italian. "It's a surprise so don't say anything."

Wondering what was going on, Johnnie, in French, said, "What did he say?"

In French, Masterson said, "He says you're the most beautiful woman he's ever seen and if I wasn't careful, he'd take you from me." Then he looked at Vito and in English said, "Is our room ready?"

"The Villa La Cupola is always ready for you, my friend." Vito looked at Johnnie and said, "Mrs. Masterson, you're in for a real treat. Is this your first time in Rome?"

"Yes it is," Johnnie said smiling, "You're the first person to call me by my new name. It sounds great, like it fits me."

"Vito, will you make us reservations for dinner in about an hour? I wanna show my new wife how beautiful your city is at night."

"Sure, sure, Paul," Vito said and signaled a bellhop. "No problem."

A few minutes later they were standing outside the Villa La Cupola. They went inside the magnificent 11,700 square-foot suite. If Johnnie's mouth could have hit the floor, it would have. Paul gave the bellhop a generous tip and closed the door.

"Well, it's not much, but its home for the next four or five days or more if we want it," Masterson said.

Looking up at the domed ceiling, fascinated by the paintings on it, she said, "Not much? Oh, Paul, I didn't know the world had places like this in it. And to be here for four or five days or maybe even longer, I don't know what to say except God has given man great gifts and if men can do this with those gifts, heaven is going to be even more spectacular than I ever imagined."

"Let me show you the place," Masterson said. He opened a door and they walked into a room with walls lined with wood, complete with built-in bookshelves with books already on them. A large desk was its centerpiece and a red cushioned chair sat behind it. "This is the library. My mom and dad used to bring my brothers and sisters in here and we'd all read classic novels. Then after we read for a couple hours, we'd share what we'd read with one another."

"You must've had a great childhood, Paul. From what I see, it was nothing like mine back in Sable Parish."

"I did have a wonderful childhood and I had the best mother that ever lived. She reared us to be good and decent people. She taught us to treat others the way we wanted to be treated."

"She must've grown up poor then. Rich people don't treat poor people the way they wanna be treated."

"My mother's parents were rich, but they were obviously decent people even though they didn't want my mother to marry my father because they thought he wasn't good enough. She left it all and eloped with him. According to my father, she never complained when ends didn't meet."

"Wait a minute. You're saying your father was poor and then struck it rich?"

"Well, not poor, but far, very far from rich and what we have now."

"So you're telling me that rich folk aren't the tyrants most poor folk think they are? They are good and well-brought-up people among the rich?"

"Yes. My mother was that way and I gotta believe her mother was that way too. Don't despise the rich because they're rich, Johnnie. It's the rich that built this hotel you called a palace. It's the rich that provide jobs and make this world a better place. Sure, you're going to have greed among the rich, but there's greed among the poor too. So what we're talking about is class envy. I'm just saying that if you have a problem with the rich, become rich yourself and be just the opposite of what you think rich people are; do all the things with your money that you think rich people should be doing with theirs."

"I don't despise the rich, Paul, but I do envy them. I won't lie about that. Having plenty of money makes it easier to sleep soundly at night. Can't you understand that?"

"I can," he said. "Let me show you the theatre."

"The what?"

"You heard me." They walked down the hall and when they came to the room he was looking for, he opened the door and they went in. "I remember being in here when I was a kid during Christmas time. We'd come in here and watch movies. The staff would bring us buttered popcorn and cold drinks."

Johnnie sighed and shook her head. "Paul, I'm wondering if you have any idea just how good you had it."

"To be honest with you, no I don't think I do. Christmas in Rome, Paris, Monaco, Madrid, Switzerland or even Sydney, Australia was the norm. I remember overhearing my parents talking about going to Berlin, but my father didn't think it was safe."

"Too bad we can't have any kids together. I'd loved to give my daughters and sons a fraction of what you had as a child and none of what I had as child. I'd love to be the kind of mother to them that your mother was to you. But I guess everything happens for a reason. I just wish I knew what God was thinking sometimes, ya know? I just wanna make sense of it all so I can be all right with everything that's happened to me so far."

"I understand," he said, and laced his fingers with hers. "Come with me." They went further into the suite. He opened another tall door and said, "This is the master bedroom. We're gonna christen the bed when we come back."

Bright reds offset by beige filled her eyes. The bed was huge and the canopy almost touched the high ceiling. There was a fireplace and a cherry wood armoire. A chandelier hung in the center of the room. She looked at her husband and asked, "Is it me or does every suite you choose have a terrace?" Moving quickly, she walked over to the veranda to take a look at the city. It was getting dark, but she could still see most of Rome. When Masterson came outside with her, she pointed and said, "What's that dome over there?"

"Oh, that little thing," Masterson said. "That's the dome of St. Peters."

"Can we see it?"

"Sure, if you like," Master said. "I'll make sure our driver takes us by there tonight. Tomorrow or the next day, we'll take a closer look during the day, okay? When we come back, we can watch a movie. We have over a hundred movies to choose from."

As they looked out on Rome, a cool breeze swirled around them. Masterson stood behind Johnnie and warmed her with his love. In the quiet, as the sun set, he thought about Janet Shamus and what she was doing at that moment. He wanted to know what she would do when she found out they had left the country. Would she give up then? Or would she pursue them and try to dispense her own brand of justice? He kissed Johnnie on the neck and held her tight. He was falling for her. She was still so very innocent in spite of it all. He looked around the city, surveying it, trying to pinpoint where a sniper might hide to kill them if Janet Shamus took things that far. He knew that being in another country in some ways made it easier to kill them if the killer was patient enough. He thought about accepting Marcus Yarborough's offer.

He didn't want to get involved with the agency again, but to protect Johnnie, it might be necessary. If he got involved with the agency again, he might have to kill again and he would have to lie to his wife about where he was going and what he was doing. Another problem that might creep back into his life would be the desire for a variety of women. He'd seen a couple Italian beauties in the Excelsior already. Being a minister of the Gospel always drew beautiful women to him. After the Anita Wilde problem, he had sworn he wouldn't let it happen again. But it did happen again in foreign countries on lonely nights. However, the past few years, he rededicated himself to his faith. He had been celibate and he was in control, but he knew who he was on the inside and he wanted to steer clear of the darker more decadent part of himself.

"Hey, where are you, Mr. Cowboy Preacher?"

"Huh, oh, I'm just enjoying the breeze and being so close to my wife."

"Come on. Let's get a little bit closer. Let's christen that bed right now," she said, and grabbed Masterson by the hand and dragged him back into the bedroom. She had been ravaging him for the past two days and there was no fight left in him. She knew that he would eventually forget about the seventeen years she had been alive and he had.

After the "christening", they had a delicious dinner and talked lovingly about what they were going to do the next day, the places they were going to visit, the shopping. After dinner, Masterson paid a cabbie to drive them to the Pantheon, the Colosseum, the Roman Monument, St. Peter's Basilica, and the Trevi Fountain. When they returned, they went into the theatre and watched Gregory Peck and Audrey Hepburn fall in love in the picture that launched Hepburn's career, Roman Holiday. It had been shot in Rome a year earlier in 1953. After the film, they made love until they were exhausted.

With her head resting on his bare muscled chest, she said, "Paul, did I thank you for showing me the time of my life?"

"Many times," he said. "Thank you for letting me show you the time of your life."

"You're welcome," she said. "What are we doing tomorrow?"

"We're sleeping in."

"You're tired, huh?"

"Yes. Aren't you?"

"Yes, but I'm afraid that if I go to sleep, I'll wake up and it'll be all over."

"I promise you it's not a dream even though you'll wake up in the morning. Now . . . let's get some sleep. We've got a busy day tomorrow."

"Where are we going first?"

"You ever hear of a guy named Michelangelo?"

"Yeah. Isn't he a painter?"

"Yes, but people have forgotten that he was a great sculptor long before he painted his masterpiece. I thought it appropriate that we start our own Roman holiday by going to the Sistine Chapel first. Now stop asking questions and let me sleep."

Before Masterson drifted into slumber land, he made up his mind to accept Marcus's offer on a provisional basis. He hadn't been as happy as he was with Johnnie since he was a little boy visiting the very hotel they were in. He wanted to go on feeling happy with her, but he knew that they could never be in the blissful state for long if Janet Shamus was still on the hunt. He knew that if she would look for them even though they were no longer in the United States that could only mean one thing. She was going to kill his wife and he wasn't going to let that happen. He told himself he'd have to risk getting involved with women and having to kill again if he was cornered by an enemy agent, but he thought he could handle both without crossing the line and entering the dark world again.

He convinced himself that giving Marcus what he wanted would keep his wife alive. He told himself his wife had been through enough the last two years and she deserved to be spoiled to make up for some of what happened to her. He thought about all the things she had told him, and despite it all, she was still a person who cared what happened to others. For all those reasons, he was going to give her everything and when she had it all, he would find something else to give her. When he made that decision, he knew that one day there would be a reckoning and he told himself that he would pay the toll, having no idea what it would cost him. Then he drifted off to sleep.

Chapter 37

"Wouldn't it be dangerous to meet your family now?"

Masterson was confused. His contact was supposed to be at the Sistine Chapel and he never showed. They had been in there for hours, looking at the works of Michelangelo. He wondered what happened. Was his contact dead? Had he been captured? If he was in custody, did he know who he was supposed to meet? Did he know what Masterson looked like? Did he know he was at the Excelsior Hotel? Having been an agent, he knew that things changed quickly. Agents had to improvise all the time. It was possible that his contact knew they were touring the city and he would try to make contact later. So as he showed Johnnie Rome, he kept drinking water to have an excuse to get away from her. If they were being watched by his contact, he needed to have an opportunity to collect the envelope he was carrying.

When they returned to the hotel, he waited for Johnnie to change and then went into the library, closed the door, and grabbed Charles Dickens' *A Tale of Two Cities* from the bookshelf. That way when Johnnie came looking for him, he'd have a viable reason to be in there. He called Yarborough to find out what happened. The woman on the phone said he was unavailable, which meant that he was actively involved in an operation, and could be anywhere in the world at that moment. He took out the envelope and stared at it for a long minute, contemplating whether or not he should open it. He had been a courier before and knew it was possible that the letter he was holding had a microdot in it. He assumed the worst case scenario. His contact had been caught and the only reason the authorities weren't there to arrest him was because his contact hadn't broken yet.

He decided to burn the document, but first, he would read it to see what kind of mess Yarborough had gotten him in. He tore open the envelope and took out its contents. There were three blank pages of papers. He put the papers back into the envelope and then back into his pocket. If Johnnie saw the envelope, she would have questions and he didn't want to lie to her. He would dispose of the envelope later. In the meantime, he sat there, trying to figure out what was going on. Was he a decoy? On occasion, the agency misled its operatives in an effort to mislead other interested parties. The important thing was that the operative believed the operation was real. Another possibility was that there was never a mission to begin with. Playing games was something Yarborough excelled at. But if that were true, what was the point, Masterson wondered. Was Yarborough sending him on a fake mission to give him a taste for adventure again without endangering his life?

"Paul, where are you?" Johnnie called out.

"I'm in the library."

She came to the door and said, "What are you doing in here? I thought we were going to watch a movie."

"You ever read Dickens?"

"Yes. Huckleberry Fin and a Christmas Carol. Why?"

"What about this one?" He held up A Tale of Two Cities. "Ever read it?"

"We can skip the movie and you can read it to me in bed."

"I was wondering if we could start a tradition of reading and then telling each other what we read. Would you like doing that with me?"

"I would," Johnnie said, smiling. "Too bad your family doesn't know about me. What would they say if they knew you ran off and married a black girl?"

"I would hope they would say, 'When can we meet her?'"

"So your mother would be okay with her baby boy married to a Negress?"

"I would hope so."

"But you don't know, do you? That's the real reason you wanted to run off with me, isn't it? That way, if it doesn't work out, you'll never have to tell them. They'll never know and we can't have any babies together so there'll be no black children in the Masterson family, huh? We're not in any real danger, are we Paul?"

"I ran off with you because we are in danger . . . you more than me for obvious reasons. As for my family, it may be a problem for them. I don't know. I wasn't raised to prejudge people. I would hope that my mother and father are exactly what I am. After all, I'm a combination of their gene pool and the environment they provided."

"I guess I have to accept what you say, but I'd love to meet them and see for myself."

"Pack your things. We'll leave first thing in the morning."

Johnnie stared at him, trying to determine whether he was serious or not. "I thought you said there were people coming after us."

"I did."

"Wouldn't it be dangerous to meet your family now?"

"Probably. But if you want to endanger your life, it's up to you. I don't recommend it. I could call them and let you speak to them, but the phones may be tapped. If I'm right and there are people looking for you, we'll be giving them a big clue as to where we are and where we've been. So . . . what do you want to do? Watch the movie, or put our lives in danger?"

She walked over to the desk and took him by the hand. Then she led him to the theatre and they watched Gone with the Wind.

Chapter 38

"So then Hatcher and the black broad can be eliminated?"

It was noon the next day when Tony Hatcher and Janet Shamus
finally left the Hilton and got into a cab. Janet laid her head on
Hatcher's shoulder and sighed. Hatcher held her hand and then
their fingers laced. She kissed his cheek and returned her head to his
shoulder. Hatcher told the driver to take them over to Pier 84. The
cabbie pulled into the thick 42nd Street traffic, occasionally watching his passengers in the rearview mirror. Truck and car horns blared
as movement slowed. The cabbie joined the cacophony of horns and
yelled obscenities at other New Yorkers. When another cabbie
pressed his middle finger against the window, the cabbie rolled
down his window and in typical New York fashion, yelled, "Give
that finger to ya mother, ya fat palooka!" Both cabbies had thick
New York accents and yelled obscenities back and forth at a stop
light. When the light changed to green, the cabbie looked in the
rearview mirror again, shrugged his shoulders, and said, "The nerve
of some people, eh? I've been living in this city all my life and the
people never change. What can you do?"

Janet elbowed Hatcher and when he looked at her, she whispered, "Show him the pictures." Hatcher frowned like he knew it
was a waste of time. Janet returned his frown with one of her own
and took the envelope out of his hand. She took out the pictures and
looking at the cabbie through the mirror, said, "I'm wondering if you
wouldn't mind taking a look at a couple of pictures and telling us if
you recognize the people in them. They may have been a previous
fare about a week or so ago. You may have picked them up at the
train station."

Looking at Janet in the rearview mirror, the cabbie said, "What's in it for me?"

"Ten bucks," Hatcher said.

"What if I don't recognize them?" the cabbie said.

"Listen, pal, what do you think this is?" Hatcher said. "You give us nothing, you get nothing. It's as simple as that. You won't get a better deal anywhere in the world."

The cabbie stopped at a light and said, "Sure, I'll take a look. Let's see 'em." He took the pictures Janet handed him, looked at them, and said, "Beautiful broad for a spade. Why ya lookin' for 'em?"

"Have you seen them or not?" Hatcher barked.

"No. Never seen 'em."

Hatcher looked at Janet and said, "See what I mean? This might take forever."

"I said *I've* never seen 'em. What if I know the cabbie that might've picked these two up at the terminal? What do I get then?"

Janet said, "If your friend recognizes the people in those pictures and remembers where he took them, I'll give each of you fifty dollars cash."

"Fifty bucks!" he looked at Hatcher in the rearview mirror and said, "Is she on the level, pal?"

"If we get the information we need, yes," Hatcher said. "What makes you think your friend might know the people in the pictures?"

"First off, he ain't a friend," the cabbie began, "I can't stand the jerk, but money is money. I've got bills to pay just like the next man. And there's no end to 'em. Am I right or am I right? Anyway, this guy, Larry's his name, was talking about them for three freakin' days that guy. I told 'em I says shut the hell up about those two or I'll give ya a beatin'. To be honest with you, he got on everybody's nerves talkin' about those two."

"Are you sure it was these two?" Hatcher asked.

"What are you, stupid, pal? I just freakin' told ya I don't recognize those two. Geez! The crap ya gotta put up with to earn fifty bucks."

"Where's your friend?" Janet asked.

The cabbie looked at Janet in the mirror and exhaled hard. "Are you deaf, lady or what? Did I not just say he's not my friend? Geez! What a freakin' couple. Anyway, he's probably still at the hotel waitin' on a fare. If not, all we gotta do is sit tight. He'll be back within the hour I'm sure."

"Take us back to the hotel," Hatcher said.

"Sure thing, pal," the cabbie said. "Let me get this straight, I get fifty bucks if he recognizes the spade and the white man she was with, right?"

"Right," Janet said.

"And I get the full fare too, right? We ain't deducting the fare, right?"

"Right." Hatcher said.

"No matter what he tells ya, I get to take you to the address, right? That way I get another fare."

"You'll be compensated, sir," Janet said.

"I'll be what?" the cabbie said looking at Hatcher.

"You'll be taken care of. So will the other cabbie if the information pans out," Hatcher said.

The cabbie stopped near the entrance of the Hilton, parked, and got out. He looked back into the car and said, "I'll check with the other drivers to find out if they know where he went and how long he's been gone. That way we'll know how long a wait it'll be. I gotta leave the meter runnin' though."

"If he doesn't show in half an hour, we need to get over to pier 84," Hatcher said.

"Keep your shirt on. Here he comes now," the cabbie said. "Get the cash ready and come with me." Hatcher and Janet followed him. "Hey Larry, I gotta dame and her father looking for that couple."

"What couple?"

"You know the one . . . the fat cat cowboy with all the dough that had the beautiful nigger broad on his arm. You couldn't stop talkin' about 'em. Now you can't remember 'em?"

"Yeah, I remember. You said you'd give me a beatin' if I brought it up again."

"Don't worry, Larry. Today's your lucky day. The lady's got a hundred bucks she's trying to get rid of."

Larry rubbed his chin while looking at Janet. "A hundred bucks, huh?"

"Yes, Larry," Janet said, "Fifty each. Do you recognize either of these two?"

Larry looked at the pictures and said, "Yeah. I recognize both of 'em."

Janet and Hatcher looked at each other and smiled. They knew they had hit the jackpot. Things were going to move so much quicker, they were thinking.

"I don't see how I can give yous the information you want. Not without being well taken care of."

"What are you looking for, Larry?" Janet said. "And what am I getting for my money?"

"Well, you see, lady, judging by the pearls around your neck and the diamond bracelet you're wearing, and the rest of your outfit, I take you for a rich broad, see? Besides, I saw you two come outta the Hilton and the Hilton ain't cheap, see? I can't even afford to go to the can in there. Ya probably got a lot of dough—a lot more than fifty bucks, see?" He looked at Hatcher. "And you, you look like a cop, but you ain't otherwise you would've flashed your badge by now and threatened me with a minor charge of some sort. But you didn't. That means you're either her bodyguard, or a private detective." He returned his eyes to Janet. "What I have is where I dropped them and everything they said in my cab. I told my wife about the couple and where they were going. My wife's Italian so she gets all loud-mouthed with me saying how can a colored woman snag a rich white cowboy and wonders how she ended up with me. Then she starts with the 'you never take me anywhere crap'. I ask you, do I need this? I'm bustin' my ass fourteen to sixteen hours a day and what thanks do I get? Now I can't get her to get me a freaking beer outta the fridge. And when I wanna hide the high hard one, she ain't interested, all because some colored broad married herself a rich white man. For all the grief I get over this I wish I would've kept my mouth shut. So guess what? I need one of them expensive trips too. And I wanna stay in one of them fancy hotels they're stayin' in over there. I'm thinking round trip tickets to Hawaii for me and the missus. What'll you say?"

"If I can verify your information, it's a done deal," Janet said.

"Hey, wait a freakin' minute," the cabbie said. "He gets a Hawaiian vacation and I get fifty bucks? What gives? You two would've never found him if it wasn't for me. I want something too."

Hatcher said, "You agreed to the fifty and that's all you get. You don't have the information we need. He does."

"What about my fare?"

"You'll get your fare, okay pal?" Hatcher said, frowning. "Now relax."

"Do I get the tickets to Hawaii or not?" Larry said.

"Only if your information can be verified," Hatcher said.

"I need to hear her say it, mister." Larry said. "She's the one with the dough, right?"

Janet said, "How do you plan to verify your information?"

"I'll tell you what I'm gonna do," Larry said. "I'm gonna give you a freebie and tell you that the purser will not only confirm what I tell you, but he should be able to give you far more details since he was on the ship with them, but he's gonna need a little payola too. They probably stood out being the only mixed couple on board, I'll bet."

"So they left the country on a ship, huh?" Hatcher said.

"That was your freebie," Larry said. "The name of the ship is going to cost you."

"If it pans out, I'll make sure you take your wife to Hawaii," Janet said.

"When you leave here, I won't ever see you two again," Larry said. "How much money ya holdin'?"

"A couple thousand," Janet said.

"I'll take it," Larry said.

"Take us to the purser and we'll talk to him," Janet said. "If he can give us the details, you'll get the money plus the Hawaiian vacation on me."

"Hey! What the hell's goin' on here?" the cabbie said. "You told me I would get the fare for taking you to your next stop."

Janet opened her purse, pulled out two hundred dollar bills, and said, "Does this cover your fare, the tip, and the fifty I promised?"

The cabbie smiled greedily and said, "And how."

"Let's see the two grand, lady?" Larry said. "As soon as I see it, I'll take you to the dock and you can talk to Melton yourself."

Janet counted off the two thousand and showed it to him. His eyes lit up and he said, "Hop in. I'll be with you in a second. I wanna talk to this palooka." He waited until Janet and Hatcher headed for his cab and said, "What's the idea, pal? You made your deal and I made mine. Next time ask for what you want, but don't blow a man's only chance at takin' his wife on a Hawaiian vacation with a couple grand in his pocket."

"They're in your cab, Larry," the cabbie said. "Looks like we pulled it off."

"You were great, Bill, but what the hell's goin' through Yarborough's mind? Why don't we just pop 'em and be done with it? What's all this cloak and dagger crap?"

"Let's get something straight. We don't kill our own people unless we have to. No matter what, those two are Americans first. We're here to save their lives not take them. Besides, the old man is hoping that when the moment of truth comes, they'll change their minds. The old man wants to give them that chance. Lots of people talk about killing but few can do it. He says right now Buchanan's granddaughter is angry, but sooner or later she'll calm down. And with them two bangin' each other, she's bound to get pregnant and when that happens he's hoping it'll give her a whole new perspective on life and her responsibility to her child."

"Well why are we leading her to Masterson? It makes no sense if we're trying to protect them all."

"We're protecting them all. Buchanan was a great patriot. His granddaughter has the potential to be one too. The old man owes Masterson. I don't know what or why, but he's made it clear nothing is to happen to him either."

"So then Hatcher and the black broad can be eliminated?"

"If we can save Masterson's wife, we save her. Hatcher . . . we'll see."

Chapter 39

The Ultimate Puppet Master

Marcus Yarborough was deeply indebted to Paul Masterson because he had mentored his troubled son, Marcus Jr. When young Marcus was floundering in school and had no sense of direction, Masterson was able to reach him when no one else could and had helped him focus. Masterson then helped young Marcus set goals, which was why he was now at Yale and thriving academically. Before Masterson stepped in, Yarborough had given up and written his son off as a failure despite the advantages he had been given. For those reasons, Yarborough would protect Masterson and his wife even though he had turned down the offer extended at the Opera House in Paris. The history between Yarborough and Masterson was typical in that Yarborough had recruited him some seven years earlier when Masterson had a death wish. While it would seem unlikely that the Central Intelligence Agency would recruit a preacher into its ranks, it wasn't. The Agency used people from all walks of life to achieve its ends. Many of whom were doctors, lawyers, maintenance people, teachers, and a number of well-known people in show business.

In the beginning, Yarborough was going to use Masterson for as long as he could like any other Agency asset, but the preacher from Houston had grown on him over the years mainly because of the relationship he had developed with his son. However, Yarborough had serious doubts that Masterson was ready to go into the field. In fact, Yarborough didn't think that Masterson would make it through his first mission in Burma. Masterson was to use his authentic clergy credentials to pose as a missionary to get pictures and collect information on the drug lords in the Golden Triangle. Drug trafficking was big business and could be traced back to 1757 when the

British East India Company took over the opium trade. By 1840, the British were importing 2000 tons of opium into China, which led to the first Opium War. The war was bloody and it lasted for three years. Thousands of Chinese died when they tried to stop the British from bringing the addicting substance into Canton. The Chinese signed the Treaty of Nanjing, which forced their ports open. By 1858, the British were importing 6500 tons of opium.

The Agency saw great moneymaking potential to fund its future clandestine operations, but they needed to know who all the players were. Masterson accomplished missions in Burma, France, China, India, Turkey, Spain, Brazil, Argentina, Morocco, Algeria, Libya, Egypt, and Saudi Arabia. He had made contacts in Iraq and Iran before he left the Agency. Masterson thought he was doing reconnaissance to prevent another world war, but when he found out he had been used to help form an alliance with Lucky Luciano and certain government officials that made it possible to bring illicit drugs into the United States, he was furious with his supposed friend. Intelligence officials were concerned about the New York ports being sabotaged. The deal with Luciano was to ensure the safety of the docks, but it eventually led to another deal in Marseille with the Corsican mafia that twenty years later would become known as the "French Connection". Yarborough tried to show him the big picture, but Masterson didn't want to see it. Masterson wanted Yarborough to bring it to an end, but much like the British East India Company discovered a hundred years earlier, exporting drugs had gotten too big and too profitable to stop.

Yarborough had set the New York operation in motion before he went to Paris. He was reasonably certain Masterson would refuse to rejoin the Agency he had come to despise, but he gave it a try anyway. His operatives had been watching Janet Shamus and Tony Hatcher, making note of their progress and reporting it to Yarborough. He and several of his men were in the room next to Hatcher's. Another team was in a suite next to Janet's. Both teams were listening to everything Hatcher and Janet talked about and knew of their plans. Yarborough decided to help them get the information they needed a few days earlier when Janet Shamus went to Hatcher's house. He had five operatives disguised as cabbies waiting for

Hatcher and Janet to come out of the Hilton. He had a few more operatives in key positions at the docks who were instructed to behave like racists to allay any suspicions that might arise as a result of their "luck". The purser was one of them. Yarborough would feed them information leading them to the Masterson's.

Yarborough and his operatives had listened to Tony Hatcher and Janet Shamus making love through headphones. When they finished, Hatcher suggested that they move up to her suite for a bite to eat and more lovemaking. Yarborough went to the room they had next to Janet's suite where the other team was and listened to them make plans to stay in for the day. They were planning to look for the cabbie that picked up the Mastersons the next morning, which gave his team all the time they needed. As far as Yarborough could tell, Hatcher and Janet had no idea they were being led to their own destruction, if they didn't changes their minds. In the meantime, Yarborough and his operatives would know exactly where they were at all times.

Chapter 40

"Do you have any feelings for me?"

Yarborough was standing on the deck of a yacht with a pair of binoculars to his eyes, watching and listening to Hatcher and Janet talking to one his operatives, disguised as the purser of the Independence. The operative spun an intriguing tale, some of which they had learned from the real purser under the banner of "National Security". Nevertheless, some of the story being told was so outlandish that it rang true and if Yarborough didn't know they had been working on the story for a few days to make sure it sounded authentic, he would have sworn the operative was telling the truth about the Mastersons and the eight day journey to Nice. The operative offered lots of specifics, like the diamond studded dresses Johnnie had worn to the nightly formal dinners and all the accouterments. He talked of her having over a hundred pairs of shoes. All of it was true too, but not when they boarded the Independence. Masterson bought her the dresses and shoes when they went to Paris. Yarborough was satisfied that Hatcher and Janet Shamus were convinced the information they received from his operatives was authentic. Now, his team would watch them and give reports to Yarborough while he focused on the war between the Vietnamese and the French.

Hatcher and Janet left the dock and hurried back to the East Manhattan Hilton, where they each made long distance calls. Hatcher made his calls to New Orleans from the lobby and had gotten an update from Hawkins on what was going on with the cases Janet sent his way. Other than the need to hire more personnel, everything was going smoothly in his absence. Hatcher told Hawkins that he'd be out of the country following a lead on a present case. In addition to some personal information, he also told Hawkins to hire as many investigators as he needed to sufficiently cover all the cases and that he would be back to New Orleans as soon as possible.

Janet first called her pilots who were on twenty-four hour standby and let them know she wanted to go to Nice within the hour. When the captain told her they couldn't leave for at least twelve hours because they hadn't had sufficient sleep for the journey, she was furious and threatened to fire him. The captain managed to calm her down by telling her they could leave within the hour, but they might end up in the Atlantic. They needed the sleep for her protection. She apologized.

Janet then called the mansion to talk to her sisters, Marjorie and Stacy. They both wanted her to come back home. When they asked her if she was still after Johnnie Wise, she lied to them, telling them she just needed some time to herself. Her sisters didn't believe her and begged her to come home, but she refused. After an hour of reasoning and crying, they gave up. Of all the things they said, the only thing that made her hesitate was when they told her they were afraid that she would end up like their mother and father. Then she talked to Mildred and let her know that she could be reached at the Negresco Hotel in Nice. She promised to call the moment she checked into her hotel room.

Hatcher called Janet from the hotel lobby and said, "Where are you?"

"I'm sorry, Tony. I forgot to tell you we can't leave until tomorrow. The captain said it would be dangerous to fly unless he and the copilot had enough sleep."

"But I've already checked out."

"I haven't. Come on up. I'll order dinner and we can talk."

"I'm on my way."

A few minutes later, Janet opened the door and flung herself into Hatcher's arms. "Thank God, it's almost over. We almost have her."

Hatcher went inside and said, "Yeah. It's almost over. Now we have to decide how she dies."

"A bullet in that pretty face of hers. That's how."

Hatcher shook his head and sighed. "We're trying to get away with this, remember? If she dies that way, there will be lots of questions. And if you shoot her in the face, don't we have to shoot him in the face? Otherwise he may never stop looking for us. But if it's an accident, no one is looking. We move on with our lives."

"Then we push her off a balcony or something."

"I'm thinking she gets run over by a hit-and-run driver. It happens all the time. The trick though is that the driver has to get away, or he'll have to answer a lot of uncomfortable questions."

"What are we going to do?"

"First we gotta find them."

"And then?"

"The purser said they were going to Nice, and that they were traveling the world. Who goes to France without visiting Paris, Marseilles, and Monaco? We gotta check those places out." Hatcher quieted himself and thought. Then he smiled and said, "I've got it."

"What?" Janet said, smiling, expecting something wonderful from him.

"I've told you about the language barrier, right?"

"Right?"

"For most people traveling aboard there would be a language problem, but not for this guy. Remember his military record. He's speaks a number of languages so where then would he go?"

"To the countries he feels most comfortable, right?"

"Guess what else?"

"What, Tony?" Janet said, beaming.

"If your pilots need a flight plan, so does Masterson. He's got a plan. He's had one from the moment your father died. Think about it. They planned to take his body back to New Orleans to throw the police off. They planned for Johnnie to tell everybody she was going to East St. Louis, but that's not where she went. Johnnie planned to come to Manhattan. She then went to Norfolk to get her passport. Then they met in Providence, got married, caught a train back to Manhattan, and then boarded the Independence all in one day. They had a plan then and they've got one now. And another thing, they were in the presidential suite on the Independence, which means he's spending big bucks on travel. When you put a girl in the presidential suite on the Independence, you can't put her in some cheap hotel. No. It's gotta be first class all the way from that point forward. She'll never be satisfied with anything less."

"What are you saying, Tony?"

"All we have to do is use your grandfather's contacts at the airlines and find out what reservations they have. Then we check the best hotels in the cities and that's where they'll be."

"You think so?"

"They're staying at the Negresco, right?"

"That's what the purser said, but what if they're trying to throw us off their trail again?"

"Okay, but they did go to Nice. We know that for a fact. We'll check into the Negresco and snoop around. And if we find that they went to Monaco or Paris, we'll go there too. We'll find out what hotel they stayed in and if it's first class all the way, we'll conclude that I was right. We'll know their modus operandi. From there it'll be a matter of getting ahead of them."

"Oh, Tony! You've made me so happy! I love you!"

They locked eyes for a moment.

Janet turned away and said, "Uh, I didn't mean that, Tony."

"But you said it."

"It was just my excitement about the progress we've made. That's all."

Hatcher turned her around and looked into her eyes. "You do love me, don't you, Janet?" Then he kissed her. "Say it again," he said looking into her eyes. "Say it." He kissed her again, but more passionately. "Say it."

She flung her arms around him and with desperation, said, "Oh, Tony, I do love you. God help me, I do."

After more kissing and fondling, he was in her again and she loved it. The combination of sex with Hatcher and her hatred for Johnnie Wise had become a toxic love potion and she couldn't get enough of either.

Lying in bed, breathing heavily, she kissed him and put her head on his chest and said, "I don't know what's wrong with me. I can't seem to get enough of this. Can you?"

"No," he panted. "It's the best ever."

"The best ever? Do you mean that?"

"Yes. I mean it. I've never been more stimulated in my life. I don't understand it."

She lifted her head and looked into his eyes before saying, "Am I better than my mother, Tony?"

The question caught him completely off guard. His eyes bulged and he said, "What are you talking about?"

Still looking into his eyes, searching them for truth, she said, "You know what I mean. You've been with my mother, haven't you?"

Hatcher pushed her off him and swung his feet to the floor and said, "That's ridiculous. Your mother was a saint. You shouldn't talk about her that way."

Janet sat up, rested her back on the headboard, pushed her hair back, and said, "There can't be any lies between us, Tony. None. Talk to me. How did it happen?"

"It didn't. Your mother was a saint. You've gotta believe that."

"Look at me, Tony." With his back to her, he swiveled his head to the left and looked into her eyes. "I know you were with my mother, Tony. So don't you freakin' lie to me about it, all right? Now . . . what the hell happened? Was she just another conquest or what? I want the truth, damn you!"

"The truth is that your mother was a saint, okay? But even saints aren't perfect."

"So you took advantage of her?"

"If that's what you need to believe."

"What are you saying?"

"You sure you want the truth?"

"Yes."

"How about giving me some truth first. How long have you known?"

"For a few weeks."

"How did you find out?"

"Your ex-partner."

"Walter Patterson?" He watched her fold her arms and nod. "What else did he tell you?"

"You know what he told me, Tony. He told me that he begged you to stop sleeping with your clients and you kept right on doing it.

Then you had sex with his wife and broke his jaw during an altercation in your office. Was he lying?"

Hatcher hung his head and said, "I'm sorry, Janet."

"So it's all true then?"

"All of what you've said so far is."

"So what the hell happened, Tony?"

"What made you bring this up now, Janet?"

"I'm in love with you, Tony. That's why. It was just business at first, now it's this. I tried not to love you, but I do. So help me move forward, Tony. Tell me how it happened."

Hatcher exhaled and said, "At first she was just another dame that came into my office looking for answers to questions she already knew the answers to. She knew your father was seeing someone, she just didn't know who. She hired me to find out. I did what she paid me to do. After I gave her pictures and my notes, I thought that was the end of it. Then she called me later on Christmas Eve and told me she wanted me back on the case. I met with her a few days later and she told me your father had gone to see Johnnie on Christmas Eve. There was an ugly confrontation and Johnnie slammed the door in your father's face. Your mother was humiliated because she had paid Johnnie fifty thousand dollars to end the relationship with your father. When she slammed the door in your father's face, she knew Johnnie had kept her end of the bargain. It was your father who couldn't leave Johnnie alone. For evidence of this, consider what your father did just two days after your mother died."

"Stop straying, Tony. Stay focused on the question. How did it happen?"

"I'm getting there. You think this is easy. Jesus. The next day, or rather the next night she called and asked me to meet her at my office. There was a lot of crying. I got the feeling I was the only person she could talk to. So I listened and I listened some more."

"What happened, Tony?"

Hatcher exhaled hard and said, "I thought she needed to be held and so I held her. I let her cry on my shoulder and then she kissed me."

"So you took advantage of her."

"No. I tried to stop your mother. She was a saint."

"But you couldn't stop yourself, could you?"

"It wasn't like that. I felt sorry for her. She was deeply hurt by it all. She wanted revenge and she asked me to help her get it. She said that if her husband could sleep with another woman, she could sleep with another man."

"So you helped her get her revenge, huh?"

He nodded.

"How many times did you help her get revenge, Tony?"

"Just the one time."

"So it was a mercy lay, huh?"

"In that particular case, yes. I swear. The other broads were different. They weren't saints. They were lookin' for an excuse to get banged. So I banged 'em. They got what they came for and I got a free piece without having to wine and dine 'em. Goin' out on dates costs and I was broke with the divorce and all. But your mother, she was different. She did it just the one time and then she went back to your father and made it work. That's the truth. Ya gotta believe me."

"I do believe you."

"A moment ago you said you loved me. Was that the truth, Janet?"

"It was and it is."

"Then why go through all of this?"

"I've been thinking about what you said when we were in Beverly Hills. You had said you thought I wanted to get married because of what we're doing. I've concluded that there was some truth to that. I wasn't raised this way, Tony. I was raised to wait until marriage and that's still with me. I've also been thinking that if this thing goes bad, we should be married long before we do what we have to do. That way it won't look like we married the moment we knew we were suspects. So tell me. Do you have any feelings for me? Do you love me?"

Hatcher reached out and took her hand. He kissed it and said, "I think there is something there. Is it love? I don't know, but I do have genuine feelings for you, Janet."

"That's good. We can build on that."

"You think we can? Even after everything I told you."

"Yes. You told the truth. To be honest, I didn't think you would. I thought you would deny it to the bitter end. I'm gonna take a shower. Why don't you order us some dinner and then I'd like to talk to you about my sisters."

Chapter 41

"Please don't turn me into a whore."

"One thing you gotta understand," Hatcher was saying. It had been an hour since they'd eaten. Now they were in the living room discussing their plans. "When we get to Nice, we're gonna have to stay there a reasonable amount of time."

"Why?"

"Because when you bought that plane, you bought two witnesses that might one day testify against us. I'm suggesting we go to Nice as tourists, but we fall madly in love and get married. We go to Monaco or Cannes or whatever to show a pattern. We'll have receipts for everything that supports our alibi. We basically have a wonderful time in front of all who see us when in reality we're hunting down Masterson and Johnnie. Now, I gotta tell you, Janet, there's an inherent problem with that."

"What?"

"They are leaving a trail too."

"I see. So our trail can't look as if we were following them around the world."

"Exactly, which is why we need to find out where they're going, get there before them and simply wait. It could take quite some time, but we've gotta be patient to get away with it. Do you understand, Janet?"

"I do."

"No. I mean we have to be extremely, extremely patient."

"I'll try. What if we chartered a yacht? Or what if I simply purchased one?"

"Hmm, I suppose we could do that. That way we don't have a trail of visiting the same hotels. But this thing is going to cost a fortune and a yacht means more witnesses. You've got to ask yourself if it's worth the money to carry this out, Janet."

"My mother and father are dead because of her and her mother and you ask me if it's worth it? Buchanan Mutual and its subsidiaries are going to top a billion dollars within the year. As president, all of it can be used at my discretion. What's a nice yacht going to cost me? A few hundred thousand?"

"You may be able to get a vessel for that amount, I don't know. But you'll need a crew too. Then there's maintenance, food, fuel. It could add up. And then you've gotta think, how long will you keep it if you buy it?"

"According to Phil Seymour, when I spend, I'm to try to relate everything to business, which is why you have an expense account. I'll check with my accountants and see if I could write it off as a business expense. That way I don't have to worry about it. It'll take care of itself on tax day. What else can we do to ensure we escape the hands of the law?"

He looked at his watch. "It's seven o'clock. That means its midnight in Paris. That's another thing. Time might be important. The east is always ahead of us. We'll probably have to factor that in somehow. For now, let's make a few calls to find out the numbers to some hotels. In the morning, we go to the bank and get lots of coins and make the calls from the lobby. Or better yet, we go to Grand Central Terminal and make the calls from their phones. Anybody could be calling from there. If the cops check, they'll find out that we only called Nice from this hotel, which will mean nothing because we're going there to vacation. It makes perfect sense. And your pilots will tell them, if asked, that you wanted to go and got angry with them when we couldn't leave immediately."

"I'm starting to understand why there has to be so much planning. There's so many ways to get caught."

"Right. We haven't even taken weather into account yet."

"Weather? How would that make a difference?"

"Well, if there's a thunderstorm, most people stay indoors. Even if they came out, our vision would be impaired by the rain. The streets would be slick and that might make it difficult to get away in a hurry if we had too. If the rain comes on the day we catch up to them and they're leaving the next day, we'll have to start all over, won't we? Murder isn't the primary goal, Janet. Getting away with it *is*. You've got to remember that because if we find them and you see her, you've got to be able to use incredible restraint until the right moment. Do you understand?"

"Yes."

"I sincerely hope so. Let's make the calls to Nice. Then we get some sleep and keep planning on the plane tomorrow. We've got to go over everything until it becomes second nature. But when we're in public and especially in front of your pilots, we have to be all smiles. We have to be the happy couple that everybody remembers to make it hard for them to envision us being plotters of murder."

Hatcher thought it would be better to arrive in Nice at about twelve or one o'clock in the afternoon. In order to achieve that with the time difference, they left at about ten o'clock at night. He thought the Negresco lobby would be full of people checking in and out. They could use that as cover to ask questions the desk clerks would easily forget. He figured the entire trip would take about fifteen hours, which included the eight hours it would take the DC-6 to fly into London to refuel. Then it would be another five hours or so to Nice. They had been to the bank to get the coins they needed to make numerous overseas calls from Grand Central Terminal. They left with the phone numbers of fifty luxury hotels in Europe. It took a little longer to refuel in London than anticipated and they didn't get to Nice until two-thirty. By the time they got to the Negresco, it was three and the lobby was full of people. The delay couldn't have worked out better and the clerks were bilingual.

"May I help you, sir?" The desk clerk said.

"Reservations for two under the name Hatcher."

The clerk grabbed the registration book and flipped to the reservations for the current day. "Ah, yes. Here it is. You're going to be with us for four days. Your suite is ready."

"A couple of friends of ours were here a week or so ago. The Mastersons. We were wondering if we could get the same room they had."

"I'll check. You say they were he a week or so ago?"

"Yes . . . a cowboy and a colored woman."

"Ah, yes. The Mastersons. I remember now. Wonderful couple. They were very much in love. They checked out early. But I'm afraid the room is being used by another guest."

Hatcher decided to gamble and said, "Yeah, they said they were going to Paris, didn't they Janet?"

"Rumor has it they were going on an expensive shopping trip in Paris," the desk clerk said.

"Can you recommend any five star luxury hotels near the shopping area in Paris?" Hatcher said to the desk clerk. "If we decided to go there and do a little shopping, I don't wanna have to go clear across Paris to do it."

"There are a number of hotels in the heart of Paris, but I would only recommend a few of them if you're looking for five star luxuries."

"Great. What are they?"

"Well, I'd start with the Le Meurice. Then there's the Hotel de Crillon and the Hotel Pont Royal."

"Do you mind writing those down for us?"

"Sure. No problem."

Later, in their suite, Janet said, "Tony I wish we could go to Paris right now, don't you?"

"Yes, but we can't."

"I know. I know. We have to be patient, but we're so close."

"You're assuming they're still in Paris. They could have been there and gone by now."

"Then let's not waste time. Let's find some phones and call the numbers we have. We might get lucky."

"No. We have to waste time. That's why we're here."

"I don't see how calling is going to hurt."

"You can't call from this room and leave evidence for the police. And you can't call from the lobby because if the desk clerk sees you, he'll wonder why you didn't make whatever calls you had to make from the comfort of your suite. We want to be forgotten by the time his shift ends. He sees you on the phone, the memory would be there and accessible to the police."

"So we just relax and have fun?"

"Yes. We get changed and go to one of the restaurants we saw on the way in. There were lots of phones. We have a bite to eat and on the way back, you make the calls to Paris. I don't speak the language, remember? By that time, the lobbies won't be full and they'll have time to answer questions. You'll have to be very apologetic for taking up their time because you don't know the room number, when they checked in, or if they were even at a particular hotel. So you have to charm them and make them want to help you. Don't give them orders like they work for you. Humility is the key."

"Oh, Tony, I don't know what I'd do if it weren't for you. You think of everything."

"Not everything. But hopefully enough."

"It'll be enough. I'm sure of it."

"That makes one of us. We can't afford to be too relaxed. The cops can be buffoons and make a ton of mistakes. We make one mistake and we're finished. So you see the odds are decidedly in their favor."

She walked up to Hatcher, embraced him, and with her head resting on his chest, said, "I want us to get married tomorrow, Tony."

He extended his arms, creating space between them, and said, "Why now?"

She looked into his eyes and said, "Given what we're doing, how long do you think it'll be before I'm with child? I don't want to be pregnant and have a bastard child growing inside me and then have to rush to the altar with a belly sticking out two feet in front of me. That's what whores do, Tony. Please don't turn me into a whore."

"I won't."

"Swear to me, Tony. Please swear to me."

He locked eyes with her and said, "I swear I won't turn you into a whore. We'll get married tomorrow." A few minutes later they were in bed, making love vigorously.

Chapter 42

"Yes, my love. He did."

Later, after stuffing themselves with a scrumptious dinner, Hatcher and Janet walked along Promenade des Anglais looking for a phone booth. Having found one, Janet called the Le Meurice hotel in Paris, hoping lady luck would be on their side, but it wasn't. Next, Janet called the Hotel Pont Royal only to be disappointed again. But upon making the third call, they discovered that the Mastersons had stayed at the Hotel de Crillon, but had checked out—a consolation prize, sure, but they were happy to know they were on the right track. They told themselves that it was only a matter of time before they caught them.

The next day they were married just as Hatcher had promised. They enjoyed the amenities of the Negresco until it was time to leave four days later. They then went to Monaco to gamble, but to also pursue the Mastersons, calling hotel after hotel until they nearly ran out of numbers to call. They had called all over France, Madrid, Lisbon, Brussels, Luxembourg, Frankfurt, Amsterdam, and Budapest, before learning that the Excelsior Hotel in Rome had been their home, but they were on the move again. In the meantime, Hatcher and Janet traveled together as man and wife and enjoyed life, but remained constantly vigilant, waiting for the Mastersons to make a crucial mistake.

After a couple of months of traveling, Janet stopped menstruating. She instantly knew that she was pregnant. The Hatchers flew back to New Orleans and told Janet's sisters and they planned a big celebration. Many of Janet's high school girlfriends were married and pregnant too. They had a marvelous time talking and making plans for the future. Another month passed and Phil Seymour still hadn't been able to get the flight manifests. During that three month period, Janet and Hatcher went to the airport with two bank bags full of coins and assiduously called hotel after hotel, pretending to be Paul or Johnnie Masterson, calling to confirm their reservations. Janet sat in one booth and Hatcher sat in another booth adjacent to it.

Janet gently placed the receiver on the phone, turned her body toward Hatcher, smiled and mouthed, "I've got them." She pulled the folding doors in, stepped outside the booth, and waited for Hatcher.

Hatcher hung up his phone, stepped out, and said, "Where'd you find them?"

"Cairo. They'll be staying at the Mena House. And get this. They've reserved the Sir Winston Churchill suite. If we leave now, we'll be there six whole days ahead of them. That should give us sufficient time to plan the *accident*."

Hatcher matter-of-factly said, "So, they're still on a sightseeing tour of the world. Everywhere they've been there's always some famous sight to see. The Eiffel Tower in Paris. Multiple sights in Rome. I'll give you one guess at what they saw in India."

"The Taj Mahal."

"Uh-huh. If we can't get them in Cairo, I bet we could fly to Athens, get a comfortable hotel, and sooner or later they'll arrive to view the Acropolis."

"Why wait around for them? We know they're going to Cairo to see the Sphinx and the Pyramids," Janet said, full of satisfied excitement. "Seeing what her people accomplished thousands of years ago will be an awakening for Johnnie, I'm sure. But it will also be a time for sleeping. And from this sleep, she will never awaken."

"Call the pilots and let them know," Hatcher said. "We've got them now. Let's get this over with and move on with our lives."

Three days later they were in Cairo. They rented a car, checked into a nondescript hotel under assumed names, and then drove over to the Mena House Hotel. The sun was on the verge of disappearing and the lights of the hotel turned the desert into a beautiful oasis. Surprisingly the hotel grounds were full of lush green grass against the backdrop of the towering Pyramids of Giza. The road that led to the hotel was lined with tall palm trees and the property itself sat on forty acres of scented jasmine gardens. The Mena House Hotel had been receiving guests since 1869. It was the place where political figures and Hollywood royalty lodged. Besides Winston Churchill, some of its distinguished guests were mystery writer Agatha Christie and Charlie Chaplin. Soon, Cecil B. DeMille and Charlton Heston would be numbered among its storied guests when they filmed The Ten Commandments. Now, though, Janet and Tony Hatcher were in its famous lobby and walking up to the front desk.

"May I help you, sir," the clerk said clearly, like he had been speaking English for years.

"Yes. We were told by people in Cairo that this is the best hotel around and that many famous Americans have been guests here. Is that true?"

"It is sir," the clerk said, smiling. "Would you like to make a reservation?"

"Yes we would, but we can't afford an extravagant palace like this."

"I understand, sir. Perhaps you'd like to have a look around then?"

"Could we? We were hoping you'd let us," Janet said.

"It's no problem, ma'am. Americans come here all the time. We let them walk the grounds and look at the pyramids. When they go back home, they tell others about the Mena House and the legend grows. If you go through those doors, you'll be able to see the vastness of the pyramids as the night approaches. The lights of the Mena House against the blackness of night are an awesome sight."

"Tell me," Hatcher began, "I bet you have suites where your guests could look right out their windows and see the pyramids."

"Yes sir. We have lots of suites like that. Would you like to see where Winston Churchill and Field Marshal Montgomery planned Operation Overlord? It has a private terrace."

"Could we?" Janet said.

"Sure, but, please," he grabbed the key and handed it to Hatcher, "limit your visit to no more than fifteen minutes, okay? I'm expecting the guest occupying that room soon."

"I'll make sure we're out in ten minutes."

A few minutes later, they were in the Churchill suite looking around. They made their way to the terrace and looked down at the lighted sparkling blue pool. But when Hatcher saw all the palm trees and grass, he said, "You know, I didn't expect so much greenery in the desert. I thought we'd see nothing but sand for miles."

"It is amazing, isn't it?" Janet said.

"I know I told you we've gotta be patient, but I think we found the perfect place."

Janet closed the door to the terrace and said, "You mean we can take care of her here? Is that what you're saying?"

"That's exactly what I'm saying. But it might prove to be a difficult shot." He pointed out to the thickness of the trees and said, "If they ever had dinner out here or even came out on the terrace, we might have a clean shot. There's no security, so it's possible to get away."

"I thought you said she should have an accident so that no one suspects us."

"No one will if we get Masterson too. He's the only one who knows what happened at the Clementine Hotel. If we're patient enough, they'll come out on their balcony and enjoy the breeze and the scent of jasmine. In three days, they'll be here and we'll be out there somewhere, waiting, watching for an opportunity. Come on. Let's go get a bite to eat and get back to our hotel."

"Oh, Tony, I love you."

"I love you too." He kissed her. "We're gonna need a couple of rifles."

"I already got one on the plane."

"What? I told you it was supposed to be an accident."

"I thought I could change your mind. She's gotta die a violent death."

"You're just bent on having your way, aren't you?"

"I'm only doing what's necessary."

"Fine. You take Johnnie and I'll do Masterson. We gotta do 'em at the same time because if Masterson gets away, we're both finished. The question is where do we get a rifle around here without drawing attention to ourselves?"

"We don't."

"So what are you saying? One gun, one shooter?"

"Yes. When Masterson sees that Johnnie's dead, he'll freeze, if only for a second or two. That's more than enough time to kill him too. And that's how they'll be found—dead in Giza on the terrace of the famous Mena House Hotel at the foot of the pyramids." She smiled and said, "If we're lucky, Agatha Christie will write about it someday."

They went back to the front desk and dropped the key off. They asked the desk clerk if Cairo had any restaurants where they could get something to eat. He told them the Mena House was the best place in town, which was to be expected. But when they told him they were hoping to find someplace in town, he recommended Restaurant 44, which served foods from around the world, and gave them directions. Restaurant 44 was about thirty miles away, but because of the traffic, it could take more than an hour to get there.

"If it could take that long," Janet began. "I would hate to be stuck in traffic and have to go to the ladies room. I'm gonna go now."

"Okay, I'll wait for you on the patio. I wanna get a closer look at the pool."

"I'll be right out," Janet said.

Hatcher went out on the patio and walked around. He wanted to see the pool, yes, but he also wanted to get a closer look at the balconies and the denseness of the trees without being conspicuous to the many guests that were sitting in recliners, drinking beverages with straw hats in them. He walked around the pool, smiling at the guests who saw him, letting them know he was friendly, but also looking toward the pyramids, and focusing on the trees and balconies. He wished Janet had brought two rifles. It would be so much easier. He didn't want to fly somewhere and buy one and then fly right back and run the risk of leaving a trail of travel. He saw a spot that would be perfect. He thought it would cover every balcony on the pyramid side of the hotel. He was certain they could get the room number. With all the phone calls they had made, they were pros now.

"You ready?" Janet called out from the door he'd come out of.

"Come over here for a second," he said. When she arrived, he took her into his arms and kissed her. "Is this a beautiful spot?"

"Yes. Maybe one day when this is all over, we can spend a few days here. Would you like that?"

"I sure would. Perhaps we can do it after the baby's born. We've got our own plane. We could hire a nanny and everything. The plane has plenty of room."

"That's a good idea. Let's do it."

"Are you sure? I didn't know if you'd be interested."

"I'm so in love with you Tony Hatcher that I'd follow you anywhere."

"And this from the woman who once told me not to fall in love with her," he said and kissed her again. "I'm so happy, Janet. I didn't believe I could know this kind of happiness again."

"Me too," Janet said. "How 'bout we go back to the hotel first and then get something to eat?"

"You are insatiable, you know that?"

She kissed him again and said, "You made me this way."

They walked back into the hotel, through the lobby, out the front door, and got into their car. Then they went back to their hotel and made love voraciously. Hatcher was so relaxed that he was at the cutting edge of sleep. When Janet heard him drift off, she shook him.

Hatcher's eyes shot open. "Yeah, sweetie, what is it?"

"Are you kidding me?" Janet said, "I'm hungry. You promised me dinner. I don't mind being treated like an expensive whore, but the least you could do is feed me."

"Okay, let's go. I suppose you wanna go over to Restaurant 44?"

"Where else? We don't know if any of the restaurants we passed will have people that speak English or serve the kind of food we won't throw up."

"Okay, let's get dressed," he said.

"Not before you get back on top of me."

After another round of fever-pitched lovemaking, they finally left. They had driven past Restaurant 44 on the way to their hotel so they knew it was only about a mile away, nestled in amongst a cluster of restaurants and hotels, and decided to walk rather than deal with the traffic.

"Hopefully the restaurant won't be crowded," Janet said. "That way we can hurry back to our room to continue what we started."

Hatcher laughed and said, "Don't you ever get enough?"

"In spurts, but they don't last very long," Janet said. She saw a crowd across the street standing in a line in front of a restaurant. "Tony, didn't you tell me you had a thing for Lana Turner when we were at the Beverly Hills Hotel?"

"Yeah. She's a beautiful dame. I'd love to meet her some day."

"Looks like you're about to get your chance," Janet said, still looking across the street. "I think that's her over there in front of the restaurant."

"Where," Hatcher said and looked too. "Hey, that is her. Let's go meet her." Tony Hatcher stepped into the street without looking and was run over by a hit and run driver.

Janet screamed, "Tony!" as she watched his mangled body fly up in the air, spin, and land hard on the pavement. Cars screeched to a halt. Janet and a crowd of Egyptians ran to Hatcher to get an up close look at the foreigner who didn't bother looking both ways before he stepped into a busy street. Janet fought her way through the crowd of onlookers and saw blood oozing out of his head as well as his mouth and nose. Both legs were broken in several places, his arms too. Strangely though, Hatcher was still conscious. When she stooped down and looked into his eyes, Hatcher was trying to talk, but Janet couldn't understand what he was saying. She put her ear to his mouth.

In a raspy voice riddled with pain, Hatcher said, "I saw him, Janet."

Janet looked into his eyes and said, "Who, Tony? Who was in the car?" She returned her ear to his mouth and heard, "It was Walter Patterson." Janet pulled away and did her best to hold in the glee that was about to bubble over. She then put her lips to his ear and said, "You did it to my mother, Tony, and took her money. You took my father's money and led him to his death. Then you did it to me over and over again. Now I've got your baby inside me. People will feel so sorry for me that they'll never suspect that Patterson and I set this up to get you." She looked into his eyes to see what was going through his mind. She wanted to savor what she saw in them. He was talking again. She put her ear back to his lips.

"What about Johnnie and Masterson?"

"That's still on too. Both of them. Just so you know they stayed at the Mena House a week ago. Right now, the Mastersons are in China visiting the Great Wall, I suspect." When she saw his eyes rolling back into his head, she whispered, "Don't die yet. I've taken out an insurance policy and your ex-wife is the beneficiary."

"What? Why?"

"Why? Are you serious, Tony? Have you bedded so many women that you have forgotten that we stick together? I'll be the one delivering her check and if the cops ever come looking, she'll be a principle witness for my defense. Think about all the women you've screwed, Tony. Now one just screwed you. As for Johnnie Wise, I'll catch up to her in Athens. They should arrive in two weeks time. They'll be staying at the Hotel Grande Bretagne. That should give me plenty of time to fly your corpse home, put you in an expensive mausoleum, play the dutiful mourning wife, and still get to Athens before them. Thanks to all you've taught me, I even know they'll be in suites 701 and 702. I'll have a decidedly smaller suite adjacent to theirs. But that's okay since I'll be the only one in it. Wish me luck!"

He whispered, "I never told you about Lana Turner in Beverly Hills. Patterson told you, didn't he?"

"Yes, my love. He did."

She looked into his eyes and watched him slowly fade away.

Chapter 43

"And I bet the woman had an American accent, right?"

Janet Hatcher had been completely immersed in the role of the grieving widow, having donned the customary all black attire which included a black wide-brimmed hat, black pearls, and black sunglasses to hide her satisfied eyes. Three days had passed since she laid Tony Hatcher in his final resting place. It was interesting watching the faces of his secretary, his second in command, Hawkins, and the rest of his detective team as they wept over their fallen comrade, wondering if any of them suspected that she was the maestro in front of the orchestra, directing the music they listened to. From what she could tell, they were completely in the dark. She smiled within as she hid behind her sunglasses, thinking, "And you call yourselves detectives? Ha! That's a laugh. I'm only eighteen years old and not only did I outsmart Tony, but I outsmarted you all. Why, I have half a mind to withdraw my favor and watch you sink back into the hole I pulled you out of. But I won't do it—at least not now anyway. I need you to remain grateful for *my* generosity a little longer."

When Janet saw Hatcher's children clinging to each other and weeping, she felt sorry for them because she understood the anguish they were experiencing. She watched his ex-wife, looking for signs of love bubbling to the surface now that the man she had hated was dead. She too was weeping and that saddened Janet. She thought she would be glad he was gone. That's when she realized that the ex was still in love with Tony and that her love was her justification for never marrying again. Hatcher's ex-wife lived for punishing him and now that he was dead, she probably realized for the first time in years that she still had much affection for him.

When the ceremony was over, Janet went up to the former Mrs. Hatcher and said, "I'm Janet Hatcher, Tony's widow. I know this is a bad time, but may I speak to you for a few moments in private?" The former Mrs. Hatcher nodded. They walked a few yards away from the crowd. Janet continued, "We were married just a few days before Tony died. I found a number of insurance policies at his house."

"Insurance policies?"

"Yes. They're with Buchanan Mutual, my company. I had no idea that he had taken out a policy for each of you." Janet watched her carefully, looking for any signs of suspicion. There was no insurance policy other than the one she drew up and signed Hatcher's name to. She had learned very quickly that money was the glue that kept lips sealed tight. Satisfied that the ex had no suspicions, Janet handed her an envelope. "I had hoped to see you here. I've taken the liberty of delivering the money to you personally. There's enough in there to take care of you for the rest of your life. There's also enough to cover college tuition for each of your children. Tony apparently loved you all very much. Do think well of him when you think of him."

The former Mrs. Hatcher smiled through her tears, hugged Janet warmly, and said, "Thank you, Mrs. Hatcher. And I'm sorry for your loss. You obviously loved Tony very much to deliver this personally."

The two women exchanged a few more pleasantries, and then Janet watched the former Mrs. Hatcher and her children get into a limousine and head out of the gate. As far as Janet was concerned, the mourning period was over and it was time to get back to business. Three days of pseudo mourning was more than enough for Tony Hatcher. The magical city of Athens harkened—it was Johnnie Wise's turn to meet her maker. Contrary to the way she behaved on the busy streets of Cairo the night Walter Patterson got his revenge, and the handsome booty she paid him for the privilege of slamming a stolen car into the body of his unsuspecting rival, Janet did have a measure of affection for her deceased husband. She would miss the wonderful sex they had which was one of two reasons she craved him so much, knowing she was about to see him die. The other reason she had sex with him so often toward the end was because she needed him completely relaxed. She didn't want him suspecting anything. As much as she would miss their regular joining, she reminded herself that he had to pay for leading her father to his death. That bit of knowledge not only made it easier to watch him die a violent death, but it also quieted a conscience that was constantly trying to reassert itself into her conscious thinking.

Janet had been planning Hatcher's demise since the day she went to his house and let him think he was savvy enough to trick a young maiden into being his plaything. She had played the part of an ingénue while he played the powerful wannabe wise man during what could be best described as psychological ineptitude rather than a well-planned, well-executed seduction. Nevertheless, for her plan to work, she had let him think he had won her over. She even made him think that she loved him, which in a way she did, but not nearly enough to call off his brutal execution. She had no such feeling for Johnnie.

On the contrary, Janet had nothing but contempt for Johnnie and women like her; women who wreck other women's homes and destroy their families. When she was through with Johnnie, she would seek out other whorish women and bring their miserable lives to an end too—it was the justice they brought on themselves, she believed. They knew what they were doing and they didn't care. She was only hastening their entrance into the fiery flames of hell. The way she saw it, Johnnie and Marguerite were only the tip of an enormous iceberg, reminiscent of the one that sank the unsinkable Titanic, and they would all be sadistically removed from the lives of wonderful wives who put their hearts and souls into the men they marry and the children they bore. She had considered killing the men too; after all, the women couldn't be whorish unless the men were whorish too. But she realized that if she killed the husbands, she would then become the object of her own hatred. She realized she would become a homewrecker in her vain attempt to rescue wives and make their homes whole again. In a twisted way, she thought that by ending the lives of homewreckers, she would be saving the country from itself.

The picture of decadence was all too clear for young Janet Hatcher who realized that the United States was teetering on the precipice of oblivion due in large part to its incessant moral decay. Never mind that she had used that same moral decay to further her own ends. But of course she could duly justify her part in it because moral decay had been condoned for so long that her parents were lured by its addicting elixir, and were now dead because of it. Never mind that their own decisions had hastened their deaths. Janet wondered how she, being so young, had figured out what adults bringing children into the world hadn't—that a life of sexual crime came down to one inescapable conclusion—swift judgment and sentencing would invariably send a strong message to weak, wayward husbands who never learned the meaning of sexual restraint, but from their youth learned or believed that sexual frivolity was a virtue to be embraced and worn on one's chest as if it was a badge of honor. It would also be an awesome manifestation of wrath for unsophisticated women who were drawn by the inferno of wicked pleasure, knowing it would one day swallow them whole, who nevertheless refused to respect themselves, exercise discipline, and find a man of their own.

For women who already had a good man and had forgotten it, it would be a shocking awakening from which they would never recover. She had decided that in some cases, she would kill the men too—just to make a point. She was going to put her shotgun against their skulls and blow both their heads off when they were naked and in bed together. Then the world would know what they were doing. By ending their lives without warning, sex criminals would have no time to offer the tired lamentation of being in love as if that justified breaking up families. She even knew who her first victims would be—Anita Jacobson and Everett James. But their deaths wouldn't become a reality until after she took care of her mother's nemesis first.

After packing her bag, Janet went to her parents' bathroom and grabbed a bottle of medicine her mother always gave them when they were sick. While she didn't know what was in the bottle, she did know that within a half an hour, she or her sisters would be fast asleep. She then had her chauffeur drive her to Moisant Field where she boarded her plane and flew to Athens. When she told her pilots she would be in Athens for at least two weeks, they asked her if it was okay to use their expense accounts to spend that time in Istanbul. She granted their request and told them she was staying at the Hotel Grande Bretagne if they needed anything.

Janet had reserved the royal suite and the adjoining suite for two reasons. First, she knew the Mastersons had it reserved and she wanted to know the suite so well that she could navigate in it with her eyes closed. Second, she wanted to have access to their suite after they had moved into it. Her plan was to have a copy made of the key so she'd have unlimited access. She was more than willing to pay him extra or even remove him from the equation if he figured out that it was a hotel key, but she wasn't worried about the latter because foreigners loved American money due to its high exchange rate. A cabbie dropped her off at the hotel and she checked in.

When she walked into the royal suite, it gave her the sense of being in a small palace. Fresh fruit was beautifully arranged in a large golden bowl sitting on the coffee table near the fireplace. The dining table was long, had three golden candle holders on it, and was set for twenty people of distinction. She went into the bathroom and was mesmerized by the royal blue and white marble throughout. A huge tub encased in royal blue and white marble with golden faucets and golden soap trays sat at both ends. When she walked into the bedroom and saw the Acropolis through the picture window sitting high up on a hill, she gasped, and then hurried across the room, sat down in a lounge chair on the terrace, and took it all in.

She closed her eyes, placed her right hand on her belly, and thought about the child she was carrying. She figured she must be a month or two along. The question for her now was whether or not to keep it. Tony was dead and deservedly so, she thought, but the child he left her was innocent. But still, she didn't know if she wanted Tony's child in her. What if it was a boy? Would he look like Tony and be a constant reminder of him and what she felt was her familial obligation? Or would it be a girl? If so, who would she remind her of? Her mother? Unable to answer her own questions, she shifted her focus to murdering Johnnie Wise.

She opened her eyes and looked at the Acropolis again. A smile came forth when she realized how apropos it was to be in Athens, the place of the gods and goddesses. Her father had worshipped Johnnie Wise, his living breathing Aphrodite. Johnnie would therefore die while the famous Greek gods watched from Mount Olympus and perhaps they would think her worthy to take a place among them. She went back into the living room where her luggage was and grabbed a case that contained her disassembled rifle, a pair of binoculars, and took it back out to the terrace. She opened the case and looked at the weapon. Then she ran her fingers across it, caressing the butt, the barrel, and the scope like they were her lovers.

She picked up the binoculars, put them to her eyes, and looked down at the smallish town that sat at the foot of the Acropolis. It occurred to her that a bullet fired from her rifle wouldn't travel the distance necessary to kill that far away; and even if it did, she wasn't sure she could make the shot. Doubt began to creep in from someplace deep within, confirming her thoughts, agreeing that she didn't have the experience it would take to make the shot. She realized that she'd only have one chance. One shot. If she missed, and took another shot, she'd give away her position, which meant she'd have an extremely difficult time trying to escape.

She looked down and saw a lush green forest and decided that the shot, if she took it, could possibly be made from there. She decided to take a few tours and do some reconnaissance. Over the next few days, she toured the Acropolis, the island of Aegina, where she visited Mother Mary's church and bought gifts for her sisters. She also visited the island of Sifnos, where she had a copy of the key to the royal suite made. After that, she visited the ruined Temple of Apollo in Corinth, Hydra where shipping was so prosperous some of the inhabitants were able to build stone mansions. Finally, she walked the streets of Santorini, where white homes with blue domes were quite the sight. Now she was sitting in the hotel restaurant with an incredible view of the Acropolis as the sun set, enjoying a plate of lobster linguini with a chardonnay, and thinking about the Mastersons who should be arriving the next afternoon. She had it all worked out. She was moving out of the royal suite after dinner and into the suite next to it. She had her keys and everything was all set.

She had never killed before, but she thought she'd be able to do it. What would be difficult for her was waiting. She knew she had to wait a day or two so that it wouldn't look like someone was waiting for the Mastersons to arrive.

The next afternoon came quickly. Before she knew it, she was having smoked salmon with potatoes and a garden salad for lunch on her terrace, enjoying the gentle caress of the sun and the accompanying breeze when she heard voices coming from the adjacent terrace. Her heart was pounding as she leaned toward the direction of the voices, listening closely, hoping it was the maid, cleaning up the room for its next guests. She wanted to be in the lobby reading a book when the Mastersons came into the hotel. She wanted to see their faces from a distance to determine how happy they were before she put her plan into motion. Now all of that would be taken from her because she had gotten lazy.

Check-in time was two, but she wanted to be there just in case they came in early. She looked at her watch. It was nearly 1:30. She heard more muffled talking, and focused her ear toward the cement partition that separated the suites. She breathed a sigh of relief when she recognized that whoever was there was speaking Greek. Nevertheless, she grabbed her disguise, which consisted of a white hat that matched her white dress and sunglasses perfectly, put them on, and fast-walked through her suite, out the door and to the elevator. She was about to push the button when the doors opened and she saw the Mastersons with a bellhop. She gasped.

"Sorry to startle you ma'am," the bellhop said with a Greek accent.

"Oh, it's okay," Janet said without thinking, inadvertently letting the Mastersons know she was an American. She was supposed to be a French heiress from Monaco if something unexpected happened and thrust them together. Now that they knew she was American, they would soon ask lots of questions that she wasn't prepared for. They would want to know her name, where she was from, what was she doing in Athens, was she married, did she have any children? And the questions would continue on into the night. But instead of bombarding her with questions, they spoke politely and followed the bellhop to their suite.

She watched them enter and then hurried back to hers. Immediately, she grabbed a glass, put it to the wall like she and her sisters had done many times when they thought their parents were discussing their punishment or making love, and she listened. It was quiet for a while and then she heard them grunting and groaning. Her face twisted into an ugly scowl as she realized they were making love. Then she remembered the look on Seymour Collins's face when he and the coroner were in the morgue office talking about the semen found in her father's penis and on his leg. She couldn't help thinking that whatever Johnnie was doing to Paul Masterson, she had done it to her father hundreds, perhaps thousands of times, and her anger began to boil. She was planning to wait at least a day to put phase one into action, but now she wasn't going to wait. She figured they'd fall asleep when they finished and when they woke up, they'd be hungry. Instead of waiting until they ordered, she would order for them, dress up like a waitress, and deliver their meal with wine and the potion she'd brought with her. It was approaching six-thirty when she thought she heard someone moving in the suite. She picked up the phone and had the front desk connect her.

"Hello," she heard Johnnie say.

"Room service," Janet said, doing her best to imitate a Greek accent. "What would you like?"

"We didn't call, ma'am," Johnnie said. "The phone rang and I answered."

"Oh. That's what happened here too," Janet said. "Sorry to have bothered you."

"Wait," Johnnie said quickly and then covered the phone.

Janet strained as she listened. Johnnie was asking Paul if he was ready to order.

"We'll order now," Johnnie said.

Janet took both of their orders and then called room service. They delivered both meals to her suite. She signed for it and then quickly put on a black and white outfit that could easily pass for a waitress's uniform. She poured the potion into each glass before pouring in the wine. But she poured twice as much into the glass next to Johnnie's meal. She wanted her to sleep longer than Paul. Then she opened her door and pushed the cart into the hall. Her heart raced as she neared the royal suite. She was hoping they wouldn't recognize her. Then she told herself they barely looked at her when they passed her going to their room. She told herself to keep the conversation short and get out of there. She looked to the left and to the right, praying that a real waiter wouldn't come up to deliver room service to another guest. She knocked on the door and said, "Room service."

Paul Masterson opened the door. He was wearing pajamas and a robe. "We're going to have dinner on the terrace."

"Very good, sir," Janet said, working hard to disguise her American accent and looking at the floor in an attempt to hide in plain sight. "Please push the cart into the hall when finished, sir."

"No, problem," Masterson said. "What's the total?"

"I forgot to bring the check," Janet said. "If it's okay, I'll tell them to charge it to your room."

"Do you mind pushing our dinner out to the terrace?"

"Very good, sir," Janet said.

"And please tell my wife I'll be right out and to feel free to start without me."

Janet pushed the cart onto the terrace where Johnnie was waiting. She was wearing matching pajamas and a matching robe. Janet knew she should just leave, but she couldn't help herself. She had to see Johnnie. She had to look into her face and try to see what her father saw. She had to see what this Negress had that the woman who brought her into this world didn't, if anything at all. She was beautiful, Janet acknowledged within, but being beautiful only made her want to shoot her right in the nose. *How beautiful would she be then?* It was going to be a closed casket funeral when she got Johnnie in her sights. But first, she was going to even the score. She watched Johnnie pick up the glass she had carefully positioned near her and drink the wine she had poured. She wanted to roar with laughter. In thirty minutes, the fun would begin.

"Is the wine okay, ma'am?" Janet said.

"It's perfect," Johnnie said, smiling. "Thanks for asking."

Janet hustled back to her suite and out to the terrace. She wanted to listen to them talk. As the night fell forty minutes later, the Acropolis lights were turned on.

"Oh, look at that, Paul," Johnnie said, yawning. "That's where we're going tomorrow, right?"

"Yes, we are," Masterson said, "first thing in the morning."

"I'm tired," Johnnie said. "Are you?"

"Yeah," Masterson said. "It's all the traveling we've been doing, zigzagging all over the globe. At some point we might have to sleep for a week just to catch up to whatever time zone we're in."

"Do you miss the United States?"

"Not really. You?"

"Nah. I'm having a wonderful time. I want this to go on forever. Don't you?"

"Yes. I do."

Janet heard them kissing and grew even more angry.

"Come on, sweetie," Masterson said. "Let's get to bed. Tomorrow we see the Acropolis."

"Okay," Johnnie said. "Don't forget to push the cart into the hall."

"I won't."

Thirty minutes later, Janet was back in their room, heading straight for the bedroom, easily negotiating her way through the dark suite. Standing over the bed now, she looked down at them as she disrobed. It was time to exact a little revenge for her mother. Johnnie had slept with her mother's husband and now Janet was going to sleep with Paul Masterson. Nude now and incredibly stimulated by the idea of what was about to happen, she pulled the covers back. It was going to be so sweet. Not only was she going to have Masterson, but she was going to have him while Johnnie was in the same bed, in a deep sleep. She reached out and found Masterson's tool. It was stiff already as he slept. Then she pulled it through the pajama slit. She stopped when she heard Masterson clear his throat. She waited awhile and when she thought he was in a deep sleep again, she carefully climbed on top of him, positioned him to enter her, and eased down until she had all of him.

"Can't get enough, huh?" Masterson said, joining the romp, thinking it was his wife.

When Janet felt his hands searching for her breasts, she pushed them down until his knuckles were flat on the sheets. And then she rode him, trying to make him finish before he figured out what was going on, but she didn't realize that getting this kind of revenge was going to be so fulfilling and she too moaned.

"Johnnie?" Masterson questioned, but didn't stop his rhythm.

"No. Not Johnnie," Janet said.

But by then it was too late. Even though he knew it wasn't his wife, the stimulation and the drug made him finish the romp. He reached out for her and grabbed her arm, but she snatched away from him, picked up her clothes, and walked out of the room. He fell right back to sleep and when he woke up, it was morning and Johnnie was on top of him, riding him hard and fast. He thought about what happened the night before and tried to pass it off as a dream, but he couldn't shake the feeling that he'd had sex with another woman. If he had to guess, he would have said it was their waitress. He got up and showered.

Johnnie rolled out of bed and was about to join Paul in the shower when the phone rang. "Hello?"

"I had sex with your husband in your bed last night," Janet said, "right next to you. How does it feel?"

"Who is this?" Johnnie screamed.

"You know who this is, you whore!"

"You've got the wrong number."

"No, Mrs. Masterson, I don't. He asked me if it was you. I told him, 'No it wasn't.' And he kept right on doing it. He didn't even slow down. How does it feel?"

"You're lying! Paul would never do anything like that."

"No. I'm not. And you know it! Ask him." Then she hung up the phone.

Johnnie walked into the bathroom and got into the shower with Masterson. She had a puzzled look on her face.

"What's wrong, Johnnie?"

"I just got a call from a woman saying she had sex with you last night in our bed with me still in it."

Masterson's face drained of blood when he realized it wasn't a dream, but he played it off by saying, "It was probably some prankster upset that we're together. That's all."

"But she knew my name, Paul?"

"Then that means it's either a hotel guest or someone who works here. I'll speak to the manager before we leave, okay?"

"But it seemed so real, Paul."

"I'm sure that's how she wanted it to sound. That's how racists are. They're cowards. I know you know that. You've had a lot more experience with it than I have. I told you that there would be some people in Europe who wouldn't like it, didn't I?"

"Yes."

"And I bet the woman had an American accent, right?"

"Right."

"Then there you go. Don't worry about it. I'll handle it, okay?"

Chapter 44

"Live or Die?"

Janet Hatcher had been awake for several hours. Having accomplished phase one of her mission, she was about to accomplish phase two. She cracked open her door so she would hear the elevator bell. That way she could see who was leaving and know when the Mastersons left their suite. She had enjoyed toying with Johnnie and she wished she could have seen Masterson's face when Johnnie told him about the phone conversation. She had listened with a glass to the wall and hadn't heard any screaming. She figured he must have gotten out of it somehow. She then wondered if he would ever figure out that it was her. It was possible that he would. It was simple enough. All Masterson had to do was check with the desk clerk and find out how many Americans were staying at the hotel and narrow it down to women staying alone and he'd have her, which was why Johnnie was going to die that very day. During all the commotion, she would disassemble the rife and mail it back to her home in New Orleans.

She ran to the door when she heard a door close. She looked out and saw Johnnie and Masterson standing in front of the elevator. Johnnie was wearing a blue dress with the back out, a white pearl necklace with matching pearl earrings and wrist bracelet, and high heels. They were talking about taking a trolley to a restaurant a few miles from the hotel. The elevator bell rang out and the doors parted. Janet hustled out to the patio, put her rifle together and watched for them to emerge on the street through the scope. When she spotted them, she chambered a bullet and took aim again. And then, as if someone had called her name, she watched Johnnie look over her shoulder. A half a second later, Janet heard a gun cock near her right ear.

"Sir, we've got the target in sight," an agency operative said into a telephone, while looking through binoculars. "She's about to shoot Mrs. Masterson."

"It's your call," Yarborough said. "If you think she's going to shoot, take her out. We'll deal with the fallout later."

Still looking through the binoculars, the operative said, "Sir, we have a wild card in the game. He has the drop on the subject. What are your orders?"

"Let it play out," Yarborough said. "If the wild card kills her, let him walk. But under no circumstances do you let Mrs. Masterson die. Have I made myself clear?"

"Yes, sir."

"Live or die," Janet heard a man say.

"Live," Janet said, quickly, and dropped the rifle.

"Now turn around."

She turned around and saw Hawkins, the man she'd seen with the other detectives at the graveyard. He was holding a .45 with a sound suppressor attached. That's when she knew that Tony Hatcher never trusted her. He had a backup plan all along.

Hawkins sat in one of the chairs, pulled out a cigarette, and offered her one.

She folded her arms and leaned against the balustrade wall. "No, thank you."

Hawkins lit his cigarette, took a long drag, exhaled and then blew out the smoke. "Hatcher told me to give you the choice."

"What choice?" Janet asked.

"He told me he told you a long time ago to give up this notion of killing Johnnie Wise. He said he told you that people who try to kill her always end up dead themselves. Is that true, Mrs. Hatcher?"

"Yes."

"So was it your plan to kill Hatcher all along or what?"

"He had sex with my mother, Mr. Hawkins," Janet said.

Hawkins smiled before saying, "Did he rape your mother or was it consensual?"

Janet cut her eyes to the left for a brief second and then said, "He took my father's money and he had sex with me. He was unethical."

"That he was. I can't argue with you on that one, Mrs. Hatcher. But all three of you made an agreement with him, didn't you? Your mother was unethical when she slept with him. Your father was unethical when he slept with Johnnie. You were unethical when you slept with Hatcher, got him to marry you, and then had Walter Patterson run him down. The way I see it, Mrs. Hatcher, everybody involved in this thing is unethical."

"Then you're going to let me go?" she said, relaxing a little.

"Depends."

"On what?"

"On what you're willing to do to live, of course."

"What do you want, Mr. Hawkins?"

"What's it worth to you?"

"I'll do anything you want. Anything. Right now. Here. Out in the open."

"I believe you would. But what I want is this. Can you leave Johnnie Wise alone? If you can, you get to live."

"That's it?"

"That's it."

Janet unfolded her arms, smiled and said, "Whew, for a second I thought—"

Hiss! A single bullet entered Janet Hatcher's forehead. The force of the bullet took her right over the edge and she plummeted down onto the sidewalk. Hawkins holstered his weapon, walked out of the suite, down the stairs, and out of the front door, past the crowd hovering over Janet Hatcher's mangled body. He flagged a cabbie and went straight to the dock, where he boarded a ship that would eventually return to the United States.

"It's over, sir. The wild card shot Mrs. Hatcher. She went over the side and landed on the sidewalk. She's dead sir."

"What about the wild card?" Yarborough said.

"He's in a cab. I assume he's on the way to the airport."

"Did you get pictures?"

"Yes sir. We've got sound too. We've got the whole thing on tape."

"Good. We'll hold on to it. If we ever need Mr. Hawkins in the future, he's ours. Come on home."

"Yes sir."

When Johnnie and Paul Masterson returned to the hotel, the cops were all over the place. Masterson could tell Johnnie was afraid, thinking they might question her and find out who she was and that she was on the run, so he told her to wait in the lobby while he found out what happened. He went over to the front desk. The clerk gave him an envelope and told him who the dead woman was. The clerk went on to explain that Janet Hatcher was registered under a phony name, that a bullet to the brain was the cause of death and not the fall, that the police found a rifle with a scope in her suite, and that she had previously stayed in the suite he and Johnnie now occupied. Masterson realized that none of what happened twelve hours earlier was a dream. He also knew what was inside the envelope he was holding. But at that moment, the memory of Janet Shamus Hatcher coming into his hotel room and having enjoyable sex with him filled his mind, quickly followed by the lie he had told Johnnie when she confronted him about the phone call she'd received.

He hated lying to her, but he didn't see any other way of dealing with the truth. Once he told her the truth, she would have questions and those questions would lead to more uncomfortable questions and more uncomfortable answers. A few moments of truth would lead to a lifetime of distrust and dismantle what they had built over the months. Besides, they were having a marvelous time together and so he convinced himself that there was nothing to gain by revealing an unsavory truth. Instead, he was going to let her think she had jumped to her death, that way she could enjoy their time together without the intrusive interruption of her past. The last thing she needed to know was that Janet Shamus had tracked her down and had every intention of killing her. He then paid to have a member of the hotel staff to pack their bags and send them to another hotel, where they would stay for the next two weeks, enjoying the sights in the land of gods and goddesses.

He headed over to the elevator. There was a woman inside already but he didn't bother looking at her. As the elevator ascended, he opened the envelope and read the note.

Consider the debt paid in full, old friend.
You and I are both free.
I no longer owe you for rescuing junior.
And you no longer owe the "Company".
Sorry for the cloak and dagger.
But it was necessary.
I'm sure you remember how things work.
I wish you well.
If you ever want or need my services again, the door is open.

Marcus

With that, Masterson believed that Marcus Yarborough had killed Janet Shamus. Whether he had or not was immaterial. It was time to collect his wife and go to another hotel where she would feel safe, and eventually to another country. To make up for what he had done with Janet and the lies he had told to cover it up, he was planning to spoil Johnnie by buying her anything she wanted. When they had traveled for a few more years, they would return to the United States; specifically, Providence, Rhode, Island where he had purchased a home. It was finally over and he smiled.

"Must be a letter full of promise," the woman said.

Masterson looked at her for the first time since stepping into the elevator. She was stunning and she had a thousand watt smile. At first glance she looked like Anita Wilde. He stiffened and knew that the demons that plagued him years ago when he was with the CIA were back and he knew he was in trouble. A few beads of sweat formed on his forehead.

"Just a note from an old friend," Masterson said.

"Are you here alone? I could use some company tonight. No strings attached."

The doors opened and Masterson ran to the suite.

Coming Soon

Little Girl Lost
Introducing Antoinette Jacqueline Gabrielle Baptiste January 2011

Coming soon

Little Girl Lost

Domestic Violence March 2011

The Men of Little Girl Lost
Jericho Wise

·

LaVergne, TN USA
03 February 2011
215082LV00004B/24/P

9 781935 825012